THREE FRENCH WRITERS
AND THE GREAT WAR

THREE FRENCH WRITERS
AND THE GREAT WAR

STUDIES IN THE RISE OF
COMMUNISM AND FASCISM

FRANK FIELD

Senior Lecturer in History, University of Keele

CAMBRIDGE UNIVERSITY PRESS

CAMBRIDGE

LONDON · NEW YORK · MELBOURNE

Published by the Syndics of the Cambridge University Press
The Pitt Building, Trumpington Street, Cambridge CB2 1RP
Bentley House, 200 Euston Road, London NW1 2DB
32 East 57th Street, New York, NY 10022, USA
296 Beaconsfield Parade, Middle Park, Melbourne 3206, Australia

Library of Congress catalogue card number: 75–22982

hard covers ISBN: 0 521 20916 1

First published 1975

Printed in Great Britain by
Western Printing Services Ltd
Bristol

For
D.M.H and R.S.H

CONTENTS

ACKNOWLEDGEMENTS

I would like to thank the many people who have helped me in the preparation of this book. To Dr John Eros, Mr Crispin Geoghegan, the Rev. R. S. Hawkins, and Professor Donald Nicholl, I am grateful for many helpful comments and suggestions. To Mrs Patricia Williams, Mr Iain White, Mr John Trevitt, and their colleagues at Cambridge University Press I am greatly indebted for much valuable advice. To Mrs Carolyn Busfield I am extremely grateful for the patience with which she deciphered and typed a series of illegible manuscripts. To my wife and family, and to my parents, my indebtedness is, as before, beyond acknowledgement.

I am indebted to the following for permission to quote from works of which they hold the Copyright:

Bodley Head and Librairie Plon: *Star of Satan, Diary of a Country Priest, Les grands cimetières sous la lune*, by Georges Bernanos.

Mrs Margarete Buber-Neumann: *Von Potsdam nach Moskau*.

J. M. Dent & Sons: *Under Fire*, by Henri Barbusse (Everyman series).

André Deutsch: *Communism and the French Intellectuals*, by David Caute.

Éditions Flammarion: *Lettres d'Henri Barbusse à sa femme, Paroles d'un combattant, Clarté, Staline*, by Henri Barbusse.

Éditions Gallimard: *La Comédie de Charleroi, Écrits de jeunesse, Récit Secret, Socialisme Fasciste*, by Drieu la Rochelle; *Drieu la Rochelle*, by Frédéric Grover; *Les Enfants Humiliés, La France contre les robots, Nous autres Français, Scandale de la Vérité, Le Chemin de la croix-des-âmes, Oeuvres Romanesques*, by Georges Bernanos.

Éditions Grasset: *La Grande Peur des Bien-pensants*, by Georges Bernanos; *Mesure de la France*, by Drieu la Rochelle; *Drieu, témoin et visionnaire*, by Pierre Andreu.

Oxford University Press: *Memoirs of a Revolutionary*, by Victor Serge.

INTRODUCTION
THE FIRST WORLD WAR AND
LIBERAL VALUES

When the Peace Conference that ended the First World War opened in Paris on 18 January 1919, a stranger to the European scene might have been forgiven for thinking that the principles of nineteenth-century liberalism had now reached their apotheosis. 'The new things in the world', President Wilson had proclaimed to the naval cadets at Annapolis on 5 June 1914, 'are the things that are divorced from force. The things that show the moral compulsions of the human conscience, those are the things by which we have been building up civilisation, not by force.'[1] Now, with the victory of the Western Allies at the end of the First World War, it seemed that Wilson's confidence in the stability of Western civilisation had been justified. The Central Powers had been defeated. The Hohenzollerns and the Habsburgs had followed the Romanovs into oblivion. At last it seemed that mankind was within reach of a world order based on freedom and justice.

Twenty years later, the situation looked very different. Never had the future for liberal ideals seemed so bleak. It was not merely that the provisions of the treaty of Versailles had been progressively repudiated by the Nazis in the course of the 1930s, and that by 1939 Europe was facing the prospect of a second major war within the space of a generation. What was even more alarming was that most of the continent had fallen under the control of totalitarian régimes – whether Fascist or Communist – which openly despised the principles that had inspired Woodrow Wilson. Even in England and France where the democratic, parliamentary tradition was most deeply rooted, liberal ideas were coming under increasing attack. In 1919 the poet Paul Valéry, an artist whose work is usually thought of in terms of an intense and hermetic aestheticism, warned his countrymen of the magnitude of the dangers that confronted them when he wrote that 'we later civilisations. . .we too now know that we are mortal'.[2] This statement may have seemed unduly pessimistic in 1919. By 1939 it could only be interpreted as stark realism. By 1939 it was evident that the victory of France and her allies in 1918 had been a Pyrrhic one, and that the First World War, far from ensuring the final triumph of liberal values in Europe, had marked a crucial stage in their decline.

Of course, it cannot be claimed that it was the First World War *alone* that was responsible for this development. In one sense the turning point came some time after the war, for the prospects for democracy in Western and Central Europe seemed reasonably assured in the boom period of the middle of the 1920s, and it was the economic depression of the 1930s that was the precipitating factor in bringing the Nazis to power in Germany. In another, deeper, sense the decline of liberalism must be dated earlier than the outbreak of the First World War, for, although libertarian ideas were triumphant in the France of the Dreyfus Affair, the liberalism practised by Cavour's successors in Italy was extremely corrupt, while in Germany and Russia − where liberal ideas had in any case never been dominant − they were under an increasingly fierce attack; by 1914 it was clear that the Second Reich in Germany rested far more on Bismarck's blood and iron than on the ideas of Kant, and that in Tsarist Russia, particularly after the crushing of the 1905 revolution and the progressive reduction in the powers of the Duma, the future lay in violent, rather than peaceful, change.

In the years before the First World War, then, the prospects facing liberalism were far from reassuring, and Charles Péguy was only stating the realities of the situation when, at the time of the first Moroccan crisis in 1905, he pointed out the restricted nature, the narrow geographical boundaries, of freedom in the modern world:

> The free and cultured peoples, the liberal and liberty-loving nations, that is, the people who have some culture. . .how little culture, how little liberty I know as well as anyone else, but who have at least a little culture, a little freedom. . .France, England, Italy (the North), some parts of America, some parts of Belgium and Switzerland. . .they occupy a small space on the map of the world, a few patches, they are miserably precarious, narrow in width and lacking in depth, a thin fragile skin. . .[3]

But Péguy was if anything underestimating the gravity of the situation, for, at the time he wrote this passage, a general revolt was taking place in Europe against the limitations of nineteenth-century liberalism, a revolt in which Péguy himself played a prominent rôle.

This revolt manifested itself in many countries, and in many different ways. In France it showed itself in the Nationalist and Catholic revivals, and in the sympathy that many writers were prepared to extend to the ideas of revolutionary syndicalism. In Italy it showed itself in the Nationalist movement and in Futurism. In Germany there was the Jugendbewegung, Expressionism, and the pervasive influence of Nietzsche. But, however important were the differences that divided these many movements and tendencies, equally important were the features that united them – a hatred of the dehumanising effects of industrialisation, a belief in the supremacy of the will over the intellect, a burning desire for heroism, brotherhood and self-sacrifice.

This can quite clearly be seen in France, where many of the movements hostile to the ideas of nineteenth-century liberalism drew much of their inspiration from the same source, the philosophy of Henri Bergson.[4] Admittedly Bergson, like Nietzsche, cannot be held responsible for many of the ideas that were attributed to him by his followers, and it is important to remember that he was not regarded with universal sympathy by those whose causes gained in favour because of his influence; by both the leader of the militantly royalist and nationalist Action Française, Charles Maurras, and the hierarchy of the Catholic Church, for example, the author of *Matter and Memory* and *Creative Evolution* was regarded as a dangerously anarchical force. Nevertheless, the stridency of Maurras's onslaught on Bergson was damaging evidence of the extent to which Maurras's own much-vaunted attachment to rationalist and anti-romantic principles was more apparent than real, and it would be impossible to deny that, in the attack that he launched on the limitations of rationalism and positivism, and in the importance that he attached to the intuitive and instinctive elements in the human personality, Bergson was expressing the spirit of the age as a whole. Not only aesthetes like Proust, but also Nationalists and Catholics like Péguy, and self-appointed theoreticians of revolutionary syndicalism like Georges Sorel, were greatly in his debt; and this shows the profound influence, both direct and indirect, that Bergson exercised on French intellectual life in the years before 1914. There hardly seemed any way that one could escape from this philosophy. In the period immediately before the outbreak of the First World War, for example, a number of Maurras's disciples were instrumental in creating the Cercle Proudhon, a remarkable organisation that attempted to unite the principles of integral nationalism with Sorelian syndicalism. It seemed that having repulsed Bergson himself from its front door the Action Française was being steadily infiltrated by other varieties of Bergsonism at its back.

As matters turned out, the differences between Maurras's ideas and those of Sorel were so great that this particular initiative was doomed to failure, and Sorel had to wait until the closing years of his life before he was able to hail first Lenin and then Mussolini as those heroic saviours of mankind from bourgeois decadence whose advent he had been anxiously awaiting for the previous thirty years. Still, the attempt of the Cercle Proudhon to combine the extremes of socialism and nationalism has some significance for the student interested in the pre-history of Fascism, and already in the very title of the book, Reflections on Violence, that he published in 1908, Sorel had identified one of the most important elements in the revolt against liberalism that was taking place amongst European intellectuals in the years before the outbreak of the First World War.

For, although neither Sorel nor his contemporaries were in favour of indiscriminate violence, violence was certainly in the air. To take only a few examples at random, a fascination with violence could quite clearly be seen in the ideas of the Vorticist movement in England, in the glorification of blood sacrifice by the Irish nationalist Pádraig Pearse, in the prophecies of war to be found in the work of many Expressionist writers and painters in Germany, and in the hysterical demands by the Futurists that all the relics of the Italian past should be destroyed. The savage attacks launched by the French Catholic Léon Bloy on a generation that ignored his warnings that the Apocalypse was near, can also, quite legitimately, be seen as part of this general pattern.

In one sense, of course, these calls to violence were prompted by the growing possibility that a major European war would break out in the near future: the murderous threats uttered by

Maurras and Péguy against the Socialist leader Jaurès must be seen against this background; and it is worth remembering that Spengler conceived the idea of *The Decline of the West* not as a result of the First World War, but of the second Moroccan crisis in 1911. But the expressions of violence were so widespread that they must be seen as part of a general rebellion against nineteenth-century rationalism and materialism and not merely as the product of increasing diplomatic tension. Gone forever was the aestheticism of the 1890s. Writers and artists were descending from their ivory towers and were engaging in a militant on-slaught on the values of the society in which they lived:

> There was Nietzsche, Darwin, Spencer. There was Kipling, d'Annunzio, Futurism, Pragmatism, revolutionary syndicalism, Georges Sorel. There was the Barrès of the *Roman de l'Énergie Nationale*. Charles Péguy and Charles Maurras taught virility . . .Even in Claudel and Rimbaud I found inspiration for violence, Violence sounded all round me.[5]

It was in these terms that the Fascist intellectual Drieu la Rochelle was to describe the formative influences of his youth. Clearly a sense that European liberalism was in the throes of a profound crisis was widespread already in the period before 1914.

Nevertheless, in spite of all this, the central importance of the First World War itself for the decline of liberal values must not be minimised. In the years before the war it may have been fashionable for many intellectuals to mock the illusions and the limitations involved in their elders' veneration of the ideas of Science and Progress, and yet the fact that it was deemed neces-sary to attack these ideals showed that they still possessed considerable vitality. It is true that their survival was partly the result of a situation in which, despite many alarms and excur-sions, the great powers of Europe were still at peace with one another; and the growing material prosperity enjoyed by most European countries was a further factor that enabled many to shut their eyes to the dangers that confronted them. Still, there were positive as well as negative reasons for believing that the heyday of nineteenth-century values was not yet over.

Take the literary and artistic world, for example. Whilst expressing their concern over the problems inherent in the emergence of a mass industrialised society by no means all the writers and intellectuals of Europe succumbed to the violence that was preached by some of their number in the years before 1914. In England there was H. G. Wells attempting to demonstrate that by the proper use of science mankind could be led to a better future. In France there was Romain Rolland warning his countrymen of the dangers of a European war in his *Jean Christophe*. Above all, there was the enormous influence of Tolstoy's pacifist and humanitarian ideas throughout Europe in the years that preceded the outbreak of the First World War.

Even in the political front it would be foolish to exaggerate the decline of liberal ideals in the period before 1914, for, as the power of the middle class waned and that of the masses grew, so the task of championing liberal principles was not abandoned, but was increasingly taken up by the dominating group within the Western Socialist movement. These Socialists may have been hostile to the selfishness and greed that were encouraged by the economic teachings of liberalism, and Ramsay MacDonald may have been thinking in narrowly British terms when he claimed that 'Socialism. . .retains everything that was of permanent value that was in Liberalism by virtue of its being the hereditary heir [sic] of Liberalism.'[6] And yet, in their faith in the power of reason, in their hatred of violence and in the optimism with which they professed to view the future, the Socialists were true sons of the nineteenth century. Indeed, it could be argued that, in Western Europe, and even to a certain extent in Central Europe, it was the socialist movement that was the most effective protagonist of certain liberal beliefs and values by 1914. On the burning issue of peace or war, for example, it was the socialist movement, alone amongst the major political groupings, which attempted to concert some kind of international action to avert a major European conflict in the period before the outbreak of the First World War.

These efforts to preserve peace ended in failure, however, and Jaurès, the incarnation of the noblest humanitarian ideals of the nineteenth century, was assassinated by a nationalist fanatic in July 1914. No event could illustrate more dramatically the defeat that was inflicted on the democratic cause by the outbreak of the First World War. But worse was to follow. From 1914 onwards it seemed clear that the premises on which Jaurès had acted throughout his career were sentimental and utopian. Faced with the mass slaughter that occurred between 1914 and 1918 it became increasingly difficult to believe that men could be ruled by reason alone. What the First World War seemed to show was that the prophets of violence had been correct, and that it was only by means of ruthlessness and force and in the shared experience of suffering that the ideal of human brotherhood could be achieved.

These lessons seemed to be further borne out by Lenin's seizure of power in Russia in 1917, for, whatever else may be said of Lenin's activities during the war, at least they had the virtues of a brutal realism: while the majority of European socialists tamely supported their national governments in 1914 and got themselves hopelessly involved in arguments as to which of the two contending alliance systems represented the forces of progress and democracy, Lenin denounced both the Triple Entente and the Central Powers as representatives of a capitalist system in its final stage of decline; and while the majority of Socialists continued to talk, as they had talked for the previous fifty years, about the circumstances in which they would eventually come to power, Lenin and the Bolsheviks simply went ahead and took it.

With the benefit of hindsight it is easy to see that Lenin's seizure of power in Russia was the most important single event of the war, and that the implications of the Bolshevik revolution were to be catastrophic for the future prospects of liberalism in Europe. And yet a number of years had to pass before this became fully apparent. With the entry of the United States into the war in 1917 it seemed that the First World War really was 'a war to end war', a conflict in which the forces of democracy were fighting a crusade against tyranny and autocracy. And with the victory of the Western Powers in November 1918 the triumph of liberal principles seemed assured. Everywhere there was talk of democracy and self-determination. Everywhere it was assumed that the peace settlement would be governed by principles of justice and equity. Nor were these sentiments confined to the victors: for a short period at the end of the war President Wilson and his Fourteen Points were regarded with even greater admiration and expectation by the defeated nations than by his allies.

The terms of the Treaty of Versailles changed all this, however. It was, perhaps, understandable that, in the course of the war, the Western Allies should have used all the rhetoric of liberal democracy in order to galvanise their peoples into making the enormous sacrifices that were needed if their cause was to prevail. As a result of the devastation caused by the war, it was, perhaps, inevitable that the overriding concern of Britain and France (and particularly the latter) at the Peace Conference should have been to ensure that Germany would never again be allowed to launch a major offensive against them. When British and French statesmen claimed that the terms of the Treaty of Versailles constituted, not an act of retribution against the Central Powers, but a triumph for liberal principles, however, it could not but seem that they were guilty of gross, if not entirely conscious, hypocrisy.

The results of this were extremely serious. In view of the provisions of the Versailles treaty it is hardly surprising that the dominant reaction in Germany and Russia to the peace settlement should have been one of revulsion against the values of the West. What few people could have foreseen in 1919, however, was that the seeming bankruptcy of Western liberalism proclaimed at Versailles would have profound repercussions in Western Europe itself, and that within the space of a few years Communism and Fascism would exert a significant appeal, not merely in the nations that had been defeated in the course of the war, but also in those that had seemed to be the victors. Far from resolving the problems of Europe, therefore, the peace that followed the First World War contained within it the seeds of even greater catastrophes in the future.

The object of these studies is to offer a commentary on the crisis created by the impact of the First World War on European liberalism, and to do this through an analysis of the political careers of three French novelists—Henri Barbusse, Pierre Drieu la Rochelle and Georges Bernanos—who all served in the ranks during the First World War, and never ceased to regard this as the central experience of their lives. Long before 1914 all three felt themselves to be profoundly alienated from the soullessness of the bourgeois society in which they lived, but it was the events that they witnessed in the years between 1914 and 1918 that finally convinced them that something much more positive than liberalism was required if civilisation was to survive. Only a faith that was all-embracing, they proclaimed, only a creed that tried to satisfy mankind's desire for brotherhood and solidarity would measure up to the situation in which Europe now found itself after four years of total war.

For Henri Barbusse, the oldest of these writers, the only solution to the problems created by the war lay in Communism. In some ways this was a surprising departure, for, although he had been a socialist in the period before 1914, his political position in these years had been closer to that of Tolstoy than to that of Lenin; indeed, once the heroic days of the Dreyfus Affair were over, he had felt alienated from the world of politics and was consumed with despair at the cruelty and meaninglessness of life.

The early career of Barbusse, in fact, provides significant evidence of the dangers of any simplistic analysis of the French intellectual scene in the years before 1914. Fifteen years older than Bernanos and twenty years older than Drieu, Barbusse belonged to an epoch and to a milieu in which rationalism was still a powerful force. At the same time he was young enough to be susceptible to the influence of Bergson. Divided in this way by the contradictory elements in his experience Barbusse first sought refuge in the aestheticism of the 1890s. Dissatisfied with this, he then moved to a position which compassion for his fellow-men mingled with despair. Whichever way he turned, however, he seemed condemned to a situation of impasse.

How, then, did Barbusse eventually find some resolution of his difficulties in Communism? Undoubtedly it was the First World War that liberated him. Already in the years before 1914 it was clear that behind Barbusse's despair there was an ardent desire for human brotherhood. In 1914, therefore, he welcomed the Union Sacrée as a portent of that universal fraternity to which he aspired and although these hopes were to be disappointed, his experience both of the horror and the camaraderie of war, experiences that he so vividly described in his famous novel *Le Feu*, together with his bitter disillusionment with the Peace Settlement eventually had their effect. His first reaction to the horror of war had been to see it as a judgement on mankind for rejecting the principles of rationalism and humanitarianism, and it was in an attempt to reassert the importance of these principles, principles that had played an important part in his own early education, that in 1919 he launched the Clarté movement. The terms of the Treaty of Versailles soon convinced him that rationalism and socialism by themselves were insufficient to solve the problems of the world, however, and he quickly came to realise that it was only if the teachings of the Enlightenment were supplemented by a violent revolt of the masses that a just and lasting peace could be established.

Although he did not formally join the French Communist party until 1923, from 1919 onwards Barbusse was to urge the necessity for a revolution to destroy the forces of capitalism and imperialism, the two forces which, he believed, were the principal causes of war, and it was to the task of creating a powerful organisation that would unite both the intellectuals and the common people against militarism that he was to devote the remaining years of his life. Clarté began to disintegrate as soon as Barbusse indicated his growing sympathy with Communism. Soon afterwards the author of *Le Feu* became involved in a public controversy with Romain Rolland over the rôle of violence in the Bolshevik revolution, a controversy that further weakened the movement. Nevertheless Barbusse persisted in his attempts to identify Communism with the fight for peace and human brotherhood, and in the early 1930s he was able to launch the most famous of the many organisations with which his name is associated – the Amsterdam–Pleyel movement against fascism and war, a movement which enjoyed a considerable degree of success. Barbusse died in 1935, his death undoubtedly having been hastened by his experiences during the First World War and by the strenuous campaigns for peace that he had led in the years that followed it.

Drieu la Rochelle reacted in a quite different way to his experiences in the First World War, for already before the outbreak of the war he had been an ardent nationalist, a supporter of the Cercle Proudhon, and an admirer of Barrès, Sorel and Nietzsche, and such was his nostalgia for the virile and ascetic discipline that he had encountered in the early battles of 1914 that, twenty years later, he proclaimed his conversion to Fascism. This did not mean that he was in favour of *all* aspects of modern warfare. Indeed, like Ernst Jünger, Ernst von Salomon, and so many other intellectuals who could loosely be described as being sympathetic to Fascism in the interwar years, Drieu was an aesthete at heart, and he deplored the dehumanising tendencies of twentieth-century science and technology, tendencies that had certainly made themselves manifest in the course of the First World War. But the joy that he had experienced in the initial stages of the war, and the horror with which he reacted against the materialism and escapism of French society after 1918, eventually had their effect. He became convinced that the only way in which Western civilisation could be saved from the decadence that threatened it was for men to embrace the heroic virtues inherent in Fascism. So certain was he that Fascism was the last hope for Europe and that the decline of Europe could only be halted by some kind of Fascist internationalism, that he supported a policy of collaboration with Hitler after the French defeat in 1940.

In the course of the 1930s Drieu had established himself as one of the most intelligent and sophisticated, if one of the most way-ward and subjective, interpreters of the ideology of Fascism. His intelligence did not save him from the consequences of his actions, however, and, like many of the characters in his novels, he was possessed of an irresistible urge towards self-destruction. After the failure of Germany to fulfil the rôle that he had assigned to her as the founder of a regenerated Europe, he committed suicide in 1945.

Georges Bernanos is better known to the outside world for novels like the *Journal d'un curé de campagne* and a dramatic work like *Dialogues des Carmélites* (later used as the libretto of the opera by Poulenc) than for his political writings. But, like Drieu la Rochelle, he was passionately involved in the politics of the Right in France: already before 1914 he had been a member of the Action Française and a supporter of the Cercle Proudhon; his experiences in the war made him even more convinced of the emptiness of the principles of liberalism and democracy; and, for some years in the late 1920s and early 1930s, he seemed to be moving close to Fascism. Unlike Drieu la Rochelle, however, Bernanos was a man of deep religious convictions, and his hopes that some kind of synthesis between Catholicism and Fascism might lead to a rebirth of the Christian values of the Middle Ages were inevitably doomed to disappointment. In any case, despite all the extravagances that he displayed in his polemical writings, Bernanos, like Péguy, was far too anarchic in temperament and far too libertarian in his sympathies to support any form of authoritarianism for very long.

In view of all this it is not surprising that, after settling in Majorca in 1934, Bernanos should soon have been appalled by what he saw of the behaviour of the Nationalists during the Spanish Civil War, or that he should eventually have written that massive indictment of the alliance between the Spanish Church and Franco, *Les grands cimetières sous la lune*. As a result of what he had experienced in Spain, and as a result, too, of the long-term effects of the First World War on his religious development, he was to devote the remaining years of his life to attacking all the tyrannies to which the modern world is subject. In despair at the state of France and of Europe by the late 1930s Bernanos moved to South America in 1938, and from there he produced a stream of books and pamphlets attacking the moral degradation of the French Right during the German occupation. He returned to Europe at the end of the Second World War and died in 1948.

Even from this very brief résumé of their careers it should be obvious that, despite their common repudiation of liberalism, these three writers were representatives of very different French political traditions. Whatever doubts and anxieties continued to haunt him in private, from the outbreak of the war in 1914 Barbusse's public persona was very much that of a Jacobin: a devoted adherent of the humanitarian principles of 1789, but a determined opponent of those who would try to destroy them; a child of the Enlightenment, who believed that reason should be applied to the conduct of human affairs, but also a stern and inflexible moralist who would not shrink from supporting extreme measures if this was the only method by which reason could prevail.

Drieu la Rochelle, by contrast, as befitted a disciple of Barrès, was clearly a product of the Bonapartist tradition, a tradition which accepted many of the social and economic achievements of the French Revolution but attached particular importance to the need for France to combine a strong centralised government at home with a vigorously nationalist policy abroad. Whereas Barbusse, the Jacobin-turned-Communist, was prepared to support the dictatorial régime of the Bolsheviks because he saw in this dictatorship the only effective guarantee of the principle of equality, Drieu, the Bonapartist-turned-Fascist, was fascinated by the Napoleonic idea as an end in itself – its authoritarianism a symbol of mankind's need for order, its nationalism the expression of an essential human desire for fraternity, a desire that was particularly understandable in an epoch in which orthodox religion was in rapid decline.

Drieu's political ideas, in fact, were always intensely 'modern'. Those of Bernanos, on the other hand, were based on much older traditions of the French Right, traditions of Royalism and Catholicism that eventually led him to repudiate many of the newer forces at work within the Right in France. At first sight, for example, Bernanos's Legitimism owed a great deal to the influence of Maurras and the Action Française, but, whereas Bernanos had a genuine attachment to his vision of a Christian and monarchical France, Maurras was a positivist and an atheist whose support for the monarchy and the Catholic Church was largely a device for demonstrating his opposition to the values of the hated Third Republic. Sooner or later a rupture of relations between the two men was inevitable, and although for a time in the 1930s Bernanos seemed to be moving away from the values of St Louis and Joan of Arc towards some kind of flirtation with Fascism, the events that he witnessed in Spain during the civil war were to confirm him in his belief that it was only by returning to the ideas that had governed medieval Christendom that mankind could be saved.

The differences between these three writers were, therefore, real and extremely important. Barbusse regarded the principles that inspired Drieu and Bernanos as reactionary and obscurantist. They, in turn, could understand the appeal of Communism to the war generation, but regarded Barbusse's uneasy amalgam of rationalism, anti-militarism and Communism as facile and inherently unconvincing.[7] While Barbusse and Drieu made a tremendous effort to come to terms with the modern world, and, as a consequence of this, felt that they had no other alternative but to cling desperately to the totalitarian ideologies they had embraced in the years that followed the outbreak of the First World War, Bernanos was able – perhaps because of the very 'archaic' nature of his religious and political beliefs – to defy both Communism and Fascism, and to defend the idea of liberty.

Still, it would be wrong to conclude from this that it is the differences alone that are important and that there were not many similarities that united these three men. In the first place they were all romantics, ardently searching for some all-embracing explanation of the world, for some form of brotherhood that would enable them to transcend the loneliness of the human condition. As a corollary of this, all three were prone to the temptation of despair when they realised the difficulty, if not the impossibility, of the task they had set themselves. Each of these three writers experienced prolonged periods of despair in his youth. After initially welcoming the outbreak of the First World War as the fulfilment of his hopes each of them came out of the war with his basic pessimism greatly accentuated.

To the end of their lives, all three remained divided personalities. For all of them the lessons they had learnt in the First World War were profoundly contradictory: on the one hand they saw the need for a total reordering of society; on the other hand they all shrank from the means that were necessary to fulfil their ideals. Barbusse was torn between the violence inherent in Bolshevism and the sympathy that he felt for pacifist and humanitarian principles. As a Fascist Drieu exalted the forces of nationalism and war, but as a human being he detested them. Throughout his life Bernanos was attracted by right-wing movements which claimed to be inspired by the spirit of medieval Christianity, but throughout his life he was to be repelled by the hypocrisy and blasphemy inherent in any attempt to secure a religious end by political means.

The tensions that afflicted these men were spiritual as well as political. Despite his conversion to Communism and his militant commitment to rationalism, Barbusse never emancipated himself from the despair and the frustrated romanticism that had dominated his youth. Drieu committed suicide in 1945, not only because Fascism had been defeated but also because he could not come to terms with the meaninglessness of life. As for Bernanos, the spiritual despair that haunted him is apparent in every page that he wrote.

But simply to give oneself up to despair is an admission of failure, and what all three writers had experienced in the war was that, in circumstances of hardship and danger and in the constant presence of death, it is possible for men to achieve a sense of solidarity in the face of despair. Perhaps it is this that constitutes the most important link between Barbusse's Communism, Drieu's Fascism and Bernanos's Catholicism, for all three writers came out of the First World War convinced that mankind must strive for unity or perish, and all three looked back to the comradeship they had experienced during the war as a source of inspiration and hope.

Barbusse expressed this nostalgia for the camaraderie of the trenches on many occasions in the years after 1918, while Drieu once remarked that during the war he had found the tone adopted by non-combatants like Barrès, Claudel and Rolland equally irritating, and that once one had been a soldier there was a certain attitude of detachment that one could no longer adopt towards the problems of the world.[8] But perhaps it was Bernanos who best conveyed the sense of brotherhood that many had experienced in the course of the war and the life-long consequences that flowed from this experience. In an article that he wrote at the beginning of the Second World War, in which he contrasted the war experiences of his contemporaries with those that his children's generation were likely to encounter, he pointed out that, since warfare had now become fully mechanised and motorised, his sons would never appreciate what the reality of the trenches had been:

> They will never know our muddy cloisters, they will never
> belong to our contemplative orders, they will never know to
> what point, to what depth, to what depth of the soul our
> patience extended. . .It is one thing to see a friend die, it is
> another thing to see his body rotting in a place that one cannot
> really reach beyond the barbed wire, to see this familiar bundle
> every morning at dawn when one is filling one's pipe, this
> bundle that has been ravaged by gas and the rats, this carcass.
> Our sons will be more heroic than us, but they will not be
> heroic in the same way, at least I hope not. They will go
> through their war and then leave it in a friendly fashion,
> without gratitude or rancour. Whereas our war has become
> part of our being. It did this while our boots were rooted in the
> mire. It still clings to our bones.[9]

According to Bernanos, therefore, the significance of the First World War was that it had been a war of expiation and redemption. Living together in the battle zone the soldiers on both sides had come to realise that they were members of the same suffering body, that they shared in the merits of the same church, the universal church of soldiers living and dead. With the conclusion of the war this 'church' had been destroyed in the course of six months, but the sacrament that had bound these men together had been a lasting one, for one might be 'a demobilised soldier for only a few days, but one is defrocked for the rest of one's life'.[10]

The terms employed in this passage were clearly influenced by Bernanos's own religious preoccupations, but the experience they described was one that would have been acknowledged, not only by Barbusse and Drieu, but by most of those who had served in the First World War.

It is obvious, of course, that a study which confines itself to an examination of the careers of three writers, and three *French* writers at that, can only offer an extremely limited account of the influence of the First World War on a whole generation of European intellectuals and men of action. After all, it was in areas of Europe *East* of the Rhine – in the Russia of the Bolsheviks and the Germany of the Nazis – that the war had its most spectacular results, whereas in France the effects of the war were quite different. The truth of the situation is that although France suffered terrible losses in men and resources during the First World War, being one of the victors helped to engender in her a false sense of security in the period after 1918. The exhaustion that she suffered as a result of the war tended to reinforce the social and political conservatism that she exhibited in the years between 1918 and 1939. While it is true that in the 1930s – and particularly after the riots that followed the Stavisky affair in February 1934 – French politics followed the general European trend in becoming increasingly polarised between Left and Right, the French social structure was too stable and the French nation too lacking in vitality for this conflict to result in a real revolutionary situation as it did in Germany or in Spain. The Maginot line was symbolic not only of certain features of French foreign and defence policy in the 1930s, but also of the general nature of French internal politics in that decade, and the defensive mentality of both the extreme Left and the extreme Right as they developed in the years before the outbreak of the Second World War meant that both French Communism and French Fascism

were only pale imitations of forces that achieved their most ruthless and dynamic expression elsewhere on the continent.

Yet another defect inherent in the approach adopted in this
study arises from the strength and resilience of the rationalist
tradition in France, a tradition which continued to influence many
of those who had ostensibly rejected it, and a tradition that made
it extremely difficult for many French intellectuals to penetrate
beneath the surface of phenomena such as Bolshevism and
Nazism. Admittedly, Bernanos must largely be exempted from
this criticism, but neither Barbusse nor Drieu la Rochelle were
ever really capable of understanding the essentially irrational
nature of the political systems that had been established in Russia
and Germany. Even if the extent to which Barbusse really
believed in rationalism is open to debate, there is no doubt that
he was so imbued with rationalist principles that he was incapable
of understanding Marxism, still less Stalinism; while Drieu la
Rochelle clung to an idealised interpretation of Fascism long
after he had come to realise that it bore no relation to the actual
policies pursued by Hitler and Mussolini.

Despite these qualifications, it is still to be hoped that these
studies will throw a certain amount of light on the situation
created by the First World War and its aftermath. The political
positions that Bernanos adopted in the course of his life may
appear to be so subjective that they border on the eccentric, and
yet his writings on politics are full of illuminating insights. And
while Barbusse and Drieu la Rochelle may be open to the charge
of superficiality, they made a strenuous attempt to escape from
that kind of parochialism masquerading as universality that was
the besetting temptation of so many other French artists and
intellectuals between the wars.

Whatever their idiosyncrasies, the writers dealt with in this
study have some claim to be representative figures of their epoch.
In his denunciation of the First World War and his involvement
in left-wing politics after the war, Barbusse had some affinities
with a number of other European writers such as Arnold Zweig,
Ludwig Renn and Ernst Toller; while the similarities between
Drieu's attitude towards Fascism and that of other men like Ernst
Jünger in Germany and Malaparte in Italy are immediate and
striking. Bernanos, too, is not quite so isolated as he might at first
sight appear: in his repudiation of totalitarian ideologies and in

his fierce insistence on the rights and liberties of the individual his political position was in a number of ways analogous with that of Orwell and Simone Weil.[11]

In any case, despite all the deficiencies and limitations in these essays, there is a sense in which a study of Communism and Fascism written from the vantage point of France has a particular value of its own, since, of all the major powers of the continent of Europe, it is France which possesses the longest and the most deeply-rooted libertarian tradition. That Russia and Germany should repudiate the idea of liberal democracy in the years after 1914 is hardly surprising, for liberalism was never a particularly sturdy growth in these countries. But, if Péguy was right in asserting that the rôle that France must play in the world is to defend the principles of 1789, then the political and spiritual decline that France experienced in the years after 1918, and the attraction that was felt by so many of her writers and intellectuals towards political movements that were hostile to the idea of freedom – both these were developments that could not but bode ill for the future. For a time, indeed, it seemed as if Spengler had been correct in his predictions. For a time it seemed that, with the decline of France, the West as a whole was doomed.

PART I

HENRI BARBUSSE AND COMMUNISM

You say that I am the champion of equality while you, rather, are the champion of liberty. Perhaps this phrase illuminates the essential point of our debate, a debate that has its origins in two different ways of thinking. Alas, liberty is essentially utopian in character: it is a piece of poetic licence. . .like violence liberty is a word which one can use only too easily to suit every circumstance. It does not require great ingenuity on my part to prove that imperialistic capitalism, which foments misery and war, is founded on the excessive liberty which is allowed to certain individuals to acquire and to utilise what has been produced by humanity as a whole. . .However generous and noble the harbingers of liberty may be, it is a dangerous force to control because it is disordered, without limit and, to be frank, without substance. Equality, which is restrained and positive, is a better material to use in building a social structure.

'À propos du Rollandisme', *Clarté*, 1 April 1922.

1

UNDER FIRE

It was only to be expected that nationalist circles in every country should have welcomed the outbreak of the First World War, for long before 1914 French and Russian patriots had come to believe that it was only by standing firm in any crisis that confronted them that they could hope to hold in check the restless urge to expansion which characterised Wilhelminian Germany, while Germany for her part had for some time been haunted by the fear that she was in danger of attack from the encircling power of the Triple Entente. Ever since the 1890s, the nationalists could argue, two great alliance systems had been struggling for hegemony in Europe, and ever since the First Moroccan crisis in 1905 it had been clear that this struggle would lead to war. Now, at last, there was a chance that this deadlock could be broken.

If the attitude adopted by the Right to the events that were taking place in Europe in the summer of 1914 was predictable, however, the same could not be said of the reaction of the Left. It was not that the Left had ignored the possibility of a European war. Within the ranks of the Socialists continual efforts had been made to prevent the drift towards war in the years after 1905, and, at its congresses in Stuttgart in 1907, Copenhagen in 1910, and Basle in 1912, the Second International had shown that it was greatly concerned by the prospect of a major conflict breaking out in Europe, a conflict in which workers would be called upon to fight on opposing sides. Indeed, it was in order to prevent this situation from developing that Socialist leaders such as Jaurès had consistently urged that the working class should refuse to support their governments and should call a general strike if a serious threat of war materialised.

And yet, in spite of this, all the resolutions of the International came to nothing when they were put to the test in the weeks which followed the assassination of the Archduke Franz Ferdinand at Sarajevo. When the diplomatic crisis finally erupted into a trial of military strength, the Austrian and German Social

Democrats supported the Habsburgs and the Hohenzollerns in a war which they held to be primarily a struggle against the reactionary force of Tsarist Russia – the power which had crushed the Poles and the Hungarians in the course of the nineteenth century, the power which, both Marx and Engels had proclaimed, must be destroyed if revolution was to succeed in Central Europe – while the majority of the English and French Socialists supported their governments in a war which they held to be primarily a struggle to safeguard the freedom of Europe against the militaristic and autocratic nature of Imperial Germany.

These two different interpretations of the war could not be correct at the same time, of course, and from the start there were some Socialists who entertained grave misgivings over the moral problems that now confronted them: in England and France there were those who were worried by the inclusion of Tsarist Russia in any alliance that was intended to liberate Europe from the threat of tyranny; and in Germany and Austria there were many who were distressed by the fact that they were now committed to a battle against the democratic forces of the West. But at first many consciences were salved by the thought that the struggle would be a short one. In any case, it was widely believed that the war would lead to far-reaching changes in the domestic and social policies of the European powers, changes that would at last enable the socialist parties to play an accepted rôle within their national communities.

This desire for national unity was, in fact, the strongest emotion that was felt by *all* classes and nearly *all* sections of public opinion in the summer of 1914. Once and for all, it was hoped, the social and political divisions that had been apparent in every European country in the years before the outbreak of the First World War could now be overcome in a concerted struggle against the enemy. 'I do not see parties any more. I see only Germans',[1] Wilhelm II proclaimed when he greeted the Burgfrieden, the political truce that was declared by the leaders of the country at the beginning of the war. In France, too, the bitter divisions between Left and Right were momentarily forgotten in the euphoria created by the Union Sacrée: Jules Guesde, one of the most prominent personalities in the Socialist Party, a man who, several years earlier, had refused to give his full support to the Dreyfusard cause on the grounds that the Dreyfus Affair was a dispute confined to the bourgeoisie, a dispute which did not concern the working class, now became a minister in the French government; and Gustave Hervé, who had led a series of violent campaigns against militarism in the years before 1913, but who had modified his views when he discovered that German militarism was even more dangerous than that of the French, now went further and became a fire-eating patriot. It was no accident, therefore, that this rallying of the majority of the French Socialists to support the French war-effort was greeted with enthusiasm by a nationalist writer like Maurice Barrès. Now at last, it seemed, the different spiritual families of France – Republicans and Monarchists, Socialists and Nationalists, Protestants, Catholics and Jews – could unite in a common cause.[2]

This sense of unity did not last for very long, however, for after the initial excitement in the summer of 1914 the war soon changed in character. At least on the Eastern Front there continued to be some kind of war of movement that enabled the generals to claim sweeping successes at the expense of their opponents. In the West, by contrast, after the French armies under Joffre had checked the German advance on Paris at the Marne in September 1914, the situation became one of stalemate and France became the scene of endless trench warfare. Efforts to break through the deadlock were continually made. The English opened an offensive in 1915 in Artois, and the French did the same in Champagne. The next year, 1916, was the year of the German attack on Verdun, an epic struggle in which the Germans lost 330,000 men and the French 30,000 more. But it was all to no avail. By the end of the year both the forts that the Germans had captured at the beginning of the campaign at Verdun had been retaken and the overall situation remained unaltered.

By 1917, then, it was evident even to the most phlegmatic amongst the politicians and the generals that the status quo could not continue and that the war must either be prosecuted more vigorously or brought to an end by some kind of compromise peace. Not surprisingly, both sides in the war experienced in varying degrees the stresses and strains that were inherent in the situation. On the one hand the accession to power of Lloyd George as prime minister in December 1916 and the entry of the United States into the war in April 1917 intensified the determination of the Entente to fight on to a final victory: and within the camp of the Central Powers the same will to victory led to the open assumption of political power in Germany by Hindenburg and Ludendorff. On the other hand there was the war-weariness that was making itself increasingly felt amongst all the peoples of Europe, and this was a mood to which the Left was bound to respond. In Germany the Social Democrats urged the government to support the idea of a peace without annexation, a policy which, much to the annoyance of the generals, was eventually enshrined in the Reichstag Peace Resolution of July 1917. In Austria the Socialists supported the efforts that were being made by the new Emperor, Karl, to take the Habsburg Empire out of the war. In Russia the Left was able to secure the most spectacular success of all: not only was Tsarism overthrown in the revolution of March 1917, but Lenin and the Bolsheviks were able to seize power in October because they pledged themselves to the task of securing peace.

In France the clash between the war party and the peace party was particularly protracted because the nation was so extremely confused and divided. Already in December 1916 there had been an ominous significance in the fact that nearly half the delegates at the annual congress of the Socialist Party had shown themselves to be opposed to the continued participation of the Socialists in the war effort and that nearly half had voted in favour of resuming fraternal relations with Socialists in enemy countries. In the course of the next year the widespread mutinies that broke out in the French armies following the disastrous failure of the Nivelle offensive in April, and the enthusiastic welcome that was given by many sections of French public opinion to the overthrow of Tsarism in Russia, provided even more striking indications that the French people were no longer unanimous in their desire to see the war prosecuted without regard to the cost. To the French Socialists the downfall of the Romanovs seemed to remove the last main obstacle that prevented the German and Austrian Social Democrats from coming out openly against the war. To the French Right the great danger of the situation was that, in their desire to re-establish relations with the Socialists in Berlin and Vienna, the French Left might be playing into the hands of the German High Command. Clearly, 1917 was destined to be a year of crisis in French politics.

It was in this critical year that a book became widely known in

France, a book which, since it described in a particularly vivid way the reality of the life that was being endured by the soldiers in the trenches, gave powerful support to the arguments of the peace party. This was *Le Feu* by Henri Barbusse.

Le Feu is the story of a squad of troops on the Western front, and it is with an evocation of the scene at the front that the book opens:

> The great pale sky is alive with thunderclaps. Each detonation reveals both a shaft of red falling fire in what is left of the night, and a column of smoke in what has dawned of the day. Up there – so high and so far that they are heard unseen – a flight of dreadful birds goes circling up with loud and tremulous cries to look down upon the earth.[3]

The earth itself is a water-logged desert that begins to take shape in all its desolation as the dawn slowly breaks:

> There are pools and gullies where the bitter breath of earliest morning nips the water and causes it to shiver; tracks traced by the troops and the convoys of the night in the barren fields. . .masses of mud with broken stakes protruding from them, ruined trestles, and bushes of wire in tangled coils. With its beds of slime and puddles, the plain might be an endless grey street that floats in the sea and has here and there gone under. Though no rain is falling, all is drenched, oozing, washed out and drowned, and even the wan light seems to flow.[4]

Shadows like those of bears move around in this devastated landscape. These are the members of Barbusse's squad, men of different ages and occupations – a miner, a boatman, a chemist, a porter, a factory foreman, a peasant and many others. They grumble about the cold, about the food, about the shirkers and civilians at home. Lamuse, a farm-worker, contributes his own philosophy of life to the discussion:

> 'I've often got up to dodges so as not to go into the trenches, and its come off no end of times. I own up to that. But when my pals are in danger, I'm not a dodger any more. I forget discipline and everything else. I see men and I go. But otherwise, my boy, I look after myself.'[5]

They speculate as to the real character of the enemy:

> 'We talk about the dirty Boche race' says Tirloin, a carter,
> 'but as for the common soldier, I don't know if it's true or
> whether we're fooled about that as well, and if at bottom
> they're not men pretty much like us.'[6]

Two gentlemen of the Press, 'trench tourists', as the soldiers
contemptuously call them, visit the squad. They behave somewhat nervously – just as if they were looking at beasts in a
Zoological Garden. After they have gone, one of the soldiers,
pretending that he has a newspaper in front of him, satirises the
war propagandists:

> 'The Crown Prince is mad, after having been killed at the
> beginning of the campaign, and meanwhile he has all the
> diseases you can name. William will die this evening and again
> tomorrow. The Germans have no munitions and are chewing
> wood. According to the most authoritative calculations they
> cannot hold out, beyond the end of the week. We can have
> them when we like, with their rifles slung. If we can wait a few
> days longer, no one will want to leave the life of the trenches.
> We are so comfortable here, with water and gas laid on, and
> shower-baths at every stop. The only drawback is that it is
> rather too hot in winter. As for the Austrians, they gave in a
> long time ago and are only pretending.'[7]

Bored and aimless for most of the time between spells of duty
at the front, the soldiers observe life that is being lived in the
villages near the front line, villages crowded with soldiers and a
strange assortment of civilians – prostitutes, shopkeepers, children
and old men. One of the squad, Volpatte, returns to the front
after two months sick-leave. He is full of contempt for the huge
military bureaucracy behind the front, a bureaucracy largely
staffed by men who have used every device and excuse in order
that they should not be sent out to fight. Another of Barbusse's
men discovers that his wife, who is living in a part of France
occupied by the Germans, spends her time laughing and smiling
in the company of German soldiers.[8]

The squad return to battle, and some of them are killed. In the
course of the battle they are subjected to a heavy bombardment
by the German artillery, a bombardment which, to their horror,

does not spare those that are already dead. A macabre Dance of Death is set in motion:

> In front of us, a dozen yards away at most, there were motionless forms outstretched side by side – a row of mown-down soldiers – and the countless projectiles that hurtled from all sides were riddling this rank of the dead! The bullets that flayed the soil in straight streaks and raised slender stems of cloud were perforating and ripping the bodies. . .breaking the stiffened limbs, plunging into the wan and vacant eyes, bursting and bespattering the liquefied eyes; under the avalanche the file of corpses stirred and moved.[9]

The wounded huddle together in a refuge where a doctor and his orderlies desperately try to alleviate their pain. The injured and the shell-shocked chant an unending lament as the bombardment continues overhead:

> 'I'm gangrened. I'm smashed. I'm all in bits inside', droned one who sat with his head in his hands and spoke through his fingers, 'yet up to last week I was young and I was clean. They've changed me. Now I've got nothing but a dirty old rotten body to drag along.'
> 'Yesterday', says another, 'I was twenty-six years old. And *now* how old am I?'
> 'It hurts!' humbly says someone who is invisible.
> 'What's the use of worrying?' repeats the other mechanically.[10]

The enemy artillery penetrates the refuge. More of its occupants are killed.

The novel draws to a close with a discussion during the dawn that follows a battle, a discussion in which the survivors of the squad give vent to their anger at the ability of human beings to forget the sufferings which they have endured. 'If we remembered', says one, 'there wouldn't be any more war.'[11] Eventually, however, they come to the conclusion that if all men are equal in the face of death then it is the revolutionary principle of equality that salvation may be attained. Already in the middle of the novel Barbusse had praised one person who had risen above the hatreds and the divisions of war. That person was the German Socialist

Karl Liebknecht who, together with Rosa Luxemburg, had opposed the war from the start and had been imprisoned by the German government for refusing to end his appeals for a European revolution that would bring the war to a finish.[12] Now Barbusse tells his readers that only if the people of France are capable of responding to Liebknecht's call is there any hope left for the world. Mankind must accept the principle of equality or it will perish:

> I tell them that fraternity is a dream, an obscure and uncertain
> sentiment; that while it is unnatural for a man to hate someone
> whom he does not know, it is equally unnatural to love him.
> You can build nothing on fraternity. Nor on liberty either; it is
> too relative a thing in a society where everything is at the
> mercy of force. But equality is always the same. Liberty and
> fraternity are words, while equality is a fact. Equality is the
> great human formula.[13]

The discussion ends with the men, clearly realising that they are standing on the threshold of a revolution that will be greater in its implications than that of 1789, repeating the word 'Equality'.

Henri Barbusse was born in 1873. The fact that his mother (who died when her son was only three years old) was English, and that his father came from a Protestant family which had its origins in the Cévennes, is not, perhaps, without some significance for his subsequent career, for his mother had the independence of mind that is often associated with the inhabitants of Yorkshire, and although his father became an atheist at an early age, Adrien Barbusse – like so many Frenchmen who had been brought up within the Protestant Community of the Midi, a community which had been severely persecuted by the kings of France in the past – seems to have subscribed to the anti-monarchical and anti-clerical ideals of the French Revolution with a fervour that can only be described as being religious in character. Henri Barbusse was brought up in a family with a strong radical tradition, therefore. Long before 1914 the author of *Le Feu* was a convinced socialist, atheist and humanist. It goes without saying that at the time of the Dreyfus Affair he was one of those who believed in the innocence of the accused. He was also an anti-militarist with pacifist leanings and contributed articles to the review *La Paix par le Droit* which advocated international arbitration as a substitute for war.

Despite the concern that he showed for political problems in later years, however, politics were not at the centre of Barbusse's early life. He was soon disillusioned by the way in which the idealism of the Dreyfusards was used to serve party political ends, and the growing tendency of the French Socialists to involve themselves in parliamentary manoeuvring he found infinitely depressing. In any case throughout his career he never fully emancipated himself from his early fears that human existence might be without significance or meaning. With one part of his being, it is true, he was eager to accept the rationalism and positivism that had inspired his father's generation, and, in an interview he gave to a German newspaper some years after he joined the Communist Party, he claimed that it was at an early age that he had realised that there is only a superficial and not an essential difference between scientific and metaphysical truth on the one hand and the reality that is apparent to our senses on the other.[14] But there was a defensive element in remarks such as this, and the truth was that he was far from satisfied that science provides an adequate explanation of human destiny. The fact that Bergson had been one of his teachers during his period at the Collège Rollin is not without some significance for an understanding of the extremely complicated nature of Barbusse's intellectual evolution, and, despite the self-confidence that he exhibited in his later public controversies, he was haunted throughout his life by the fear that rationalism alone could not remedy the miseries of mankind.

In his youth, therefore, he attempted to escape from the contradictory elements in his experiences by seeking refuge in dandyism and aestheticism, and in the 1890s he was more attracted by the combination of aestheticism and elusiveness to be found in the Symbolist poets of the *fin de siècle* than by any kind of political commitment. As he explained in one of the poems that he wrote during this period, it was only in contemplating objects and not human beings that he could discover some kind of peace:

> Vous les dites inanimées,
> Mais elles voient notre tourment,

Elles vivent obscurément
Lorsque nos mains les ont animées.

Elles sont douces avec nous
Caressant nos âmes craintives.
Là-bas, les branches sont plaintives
Tant nous avons pleuré dessous.

Tous nos rêves les plus rapides
Les aiment un peu tour à tour,
Et c'est pourquoi leur vague amour
Nous suit avec ses yeux placides.[15]

And for a time Barbusse seems to have been content in giving
voice to lachrymose sentiments such as these. Certainly there is
no evidence that he was really unhappy during these years.
Already in 1892, while still a university student, he had won a
prize in a poetry competition organised by *L'Écho de Paris*, and
although, after leaving the Sorbonne, he was unable to devote
himself entirely to literature and was forced to take a post in the
press bureau of the Ministry of the Interior, he mixed freely in
literary circles, and was on friendly terms with personalities such
as Proust, Mallarmé, Claudel, Valéry and Oscar Wilde. In 1898
he married the daughter of the poet and critic Catulle Mendès,
a leading figure in the demi-monde, famous alike for his love of
perfumes and duels. In view of all this it would clearly be wrong
to argue that Barbusse was entirely given up to despair in the
1890s.

And yet it would be equally wrong to conclude that he was
either a poseur whose despair was not genuine, or an aesthete
without sympathy for the plight of his fellow-men. On the contrary, he was possessed of an almost feminine sensitivity to the
sufferings of others, and although his poetry observed the forms
of Symbolism it was completely lacking in the spirit of detachment that was characteristic of much of the work that was produced by the Symbolists; as early as 1895, for example, the year
in which he published his collected poetry in a volume entitled
Pleureuses, Barbusse described his vocation in life in Tølstoyan
terms as being that of a lay 'priest', observing and doing what
little he could to alleviate the distress that existed in the world.[16]
When the vogue for aestheticism began to fade at the end of the

1890s, therefore, and when literature began once again to involve itself in a criticism of society, Barbusse was more than ready for a change of direction. In 1902 he left the Ministry of the Interior and joined the publishing house of Lafitte for whom he edited a number of magazines including a popular science journal *Je sais tout*. About the same time he decided to abandon poetry altogether.

This decision to abandon poetry is particularly interesting for, although Barbusse turned instead to the naturalistic novel as it had been developed by Zola, he found it impossible to accept the naïve certitudes that had satisfied Zola's generation, and although his decision to involve himself in scientific journalism indicated that he was ready to make a partial return to the rationalism and positivism of his youth Barbusse clearly felt that the scientific method was of little relevance to the problems of the human condition. His work in the period before 1914, therefore, is nearer in spirit to the tortured existentialism of the German Expressionists than to the harrowing, but ordered, world of the French Naturalists. This can be seen in the novel with which Barbusse made his greatest impact on the French literary scene in the years before the outbreak of the First World War, *L'Enfer*, which appeared in 1908.

L'Enfer tells the story of a young man from the provinces who comes to Paris to work in a bank. In the room in which he lives there is a crack in the wall near the ceiling, and, by standing on his bed, he is able to see as well as hear what is taking place in the next room. He is so bored and lonely that he watches his neighbours continually, and what he sees appals him. The incidents that take place in the next room reveal to him that although men are dominated by sexual desires and by ambitions for money and power, they only behave in the way that they do because they want to forget that they have no lasting communion with one another, because they want to forget that ultimately they must die, and that all their efforts to transcend their sufferings are doomed to futility. Faced with this situation the young man himself has to admit that there is no remedy for the misery that he has witnessed:

What is to be done? Pray? No: the eternal dialogue in which we are always alone is soul-destroying. Find ourselves an

occupation and work? That is useless: work is never completed
but has always to be started again. Have children and bring
them up? That means that we have given up our own lives and
that we are repeating things that are to no purpose. . .What
will save us! And even if we are saved! We die, we are going
to die.[17]

From the evidence of statements such as these, then, it is quite
obvious that, whatever Barbusse's real state of mind when he
wrote his poetry in the 1890s, his pessimism was now genuine
and almost totally unrelieved. Admittedly Barbusse makes it
clear that man's solitude in the universe is the source of his
grandeur as well as of his misery, and there are passages in
L'Enfer in which the author indicates that in a certain sense men
can achieve some kind of fraternity if they experience suffering
or if they are willing to use their powers of reason to recognise
the fundamental absurdity of their existence. There are also
passages which show that Barbusse was not entirely lacking in
views on political questions: at one point in the novel, for
example, two doctors are called to the bedside of a patient dying
of cancer and, in the course of their conversation, one of them
talks not only of the disease that is killing the person who lies
before them but also of the cancer that is destroying society as a
whole, a disease that he identifies as the nationalism and militarism that was being propagated in France at this time by
Barrès and Maurras.[18] Notable as this episode it, however, it is
only a negative statement of position. In the years before 1914
Barbusse subscribed to a vague form of anarchistic socialism and
a vague form of pacifism but he had little confidence that the
rest of mankind could ever emancipate itself from its selfishness
and greed.

It was only with the outbreak of the First World War, in fact,
that he was able, both as a human being and as a writer, to break
out of the isolation to which he felt himself to be condemned. In
the course of the war he was to lose many of the illusions that he
entertained at the beginning of the conflict, but he never forgot
the comradeship that he had experienced at the front and from
now on he was convinced that it would be an unpardonable act
of defeatism and sentimentality to revert to the despair that had
dominated his youth. Paradoxical though it may seem, it was only

in the campaigns of 1914 and 1915 that the one-time contributor to
La Paix par le Droit was to find a meaning and a purpose in his life.

Exempted from military service on the grounds of ill-health,
Barbusse was not obliged to join the army at the beginning of
the war, but he believed passionately in the cause for which he
had enlisted. For once, he believed, the exigencies of patriotism
and the demands of humanitarianism were identical: France was
now fulfilling her duty as the standard-bearer of freedom and
justice in Europe, the rôle which it was incumbent on her to play
as the nation which had enunciated the principles of Liberty,
Equality and Fraternity during the Revolution of 1789. As for
his pacifism, there was no incompatability between his hatred of
war and the Jacobinical enthusiasm that he now displayed for
the fight, for this could be the war to end all wars:

> Far from having renounced the ideas which I have always
> defended to my cost, I think that I can serve them by taking
> up arms [he explained in a letter published by the Socialist
> newspaper *L'Humanité* in August 1914]. This war is a social
> war which will mark the decisive step – perhaps the definitive
> step – in the fulfilment of our cause. The war is directed
> against our old notorious enemies of the past: militarism and
> imperialism, the Sabre, the Jackboot and the Crown. Our
> victory will result in the destruction of the stronghold of
> emperors, crown princes, noblemen and mercenaries, the forces
> that keep one nation in prison and would like to imprison the
> others. The world can only liberate itself from them by fighting
> them.[19]

For the moment he forgot the depression and melancholia from
which he had suffered in the years before 1914. For a time he
overlooked the fact that there had been a powerful nationalist
and revanchist movement in France in the period before the outbreak of the war, a movement against which he had inveighed in
L'Enfer. All that concerned him now was that in the crisis that
confronted Europe France was clearly the victim of the aggressive
ambitions of Germany.

> England has declared war on Germany who now seems to be
> possessed by a kind of madness. She has almost the whole of
> Europe against her. . .It is impossible that she should be

victorious. I believe she will ask for peace before she is
destroyed.[20]

Despite his belief that the war would be limited in its duration
and that Germany would inevitably be forced to sue for peace
before very long, therefore, he was determined that, in spite of
his age – he was 41 – he would prove himself to be the equal of
his comrades in arms, and although in the course of the next two
years his health was to be even further undermined by attacks of
dysentery and lung disease, illnesses which finally were to result
in his being invalided out of the army in 1917, he certainly conducted himself with exemplary courage at the front. After a
fruitless attempt right at the beginning of the war to enlist as an
aviator he consistently refused to take advantage of the many
opportunities that were open to him to escape from the life of
the trenches; instead he remained with his squad. During his
period of active service he was responsible for saving the lives of
a number of wounded men. He also received several citations for
bravery. In 1915 he was awarded the Croix de Guerre.

'He was amazing', commented one of the soldiers who knew
him during these years, 'at Crouy, which was a battle of horror
in which mud fought it out against blood, he was sublime.
Cool, calm and imperturbable he asked for and was given all
the dangerous missions. He went on to the very end.'[21]

And yet, in spite of the exaltation which he felt in the early
stages of the war and despite the deep satisfaction that he derived
from the friendship of his comrades at the front, the enthusiasm
that inspired him in the summer of 1914 was not to last for very
long. In the letters which he wrote to his wife he revealed the
increasing irritation with which he regarded the inefficiency of
the supply sections of the army and the growing sense of anger
that he felt when he thought of the number of men in Paris who
had succeeded in evading military service. Above all, he was
scandalised by the behaviour of the press; its glamorisation of
the tedious and murderous reality of war; the hysterical and
malevolent attitude that it adopted towards the enemy. The fact
that so many of his literary friends and acquaintances were now
involved in the field of official propaganda and 'information' work
served only to disillusion him even further, and as the winter of

1914 yielded to spring and spring to summer his innate pessimism
reasserted itself:

> The spectacle of the wounded and the dead, all this slaughter-
> house of war, is terrible. It is sunny and warm. The weather is
> very different from last winter when we were lost in fog and
> drowned in mud. And yet somehow everything which is asso-
> ciated with this part of the battle is ineffacably filthy and
> sullied: poor souls, poor playthings of the struggle and of life.
> The horror of war is something you cannot imagine unless you
> have seen it.[22]

Already by the summer of 1915, in fact, Barbusse was being
driven to the conclusion that the only possible benefit that the
war might bring in its train would be that men would be so
sickened by their experiences that they would refuse to go to war
ever again.

But in order for mankind to be converted to pacifism it was
necessary that the present conflict should be brought to an end,
and by 1915 the chances that this might happen were becoming
increasingly remote. It has already been seen that by the time the
war had entered into its second year it had completely changed
in character, and, if the extent of this transformation could most
clearly be seen in the sphere of military operations, the same
process was at work within the field of propaganda, too. By 1915,
indeed, each side in the war had convinced itself that it was
defending the basic values of European civilisation against the
assault that was being mounted against them by the barbarism in
the other camp. The Entente made great play of the atrocities
that had been committed by the Germans in occupied Belgium,
while the Central Powers pointed to the brutality with which the
British repressed the Indians and the Irish. Later on in the war
the British complained over the number of innocent lives that had
been lost as a result of the decision of the German government to
initiate a policy of unrestricted submarine warfare, while in
Berlin and Vienna the statesmen blamed the blockade which
England had imposed at the beginning of the war for the misery
and starvation that was making itself increasingly felt in Central
Europe in 1917 and 1918. The fact that there was an element of
truth in all these accusations only seemed to inflame the situation
further.

Meanwhile the war aims of the European powers became wider in scope. At the beginning of the conflict Germany may have been sincere in her claim that she was fighting a defensive war against Britain, France and Russia, but within a very short period of time she adopted a policy that went far beyond the demands of legitimate self-defence, a policy that involved massive territorial expansion. The Western Powers, too, adopted an ever-increasing series of claims. In the summer of 1914 their principal war aim had been to drive the Germans out of Belgium and prevent the Germans from over-running France, but very soon it became clear that, if France was ever again to feel secure from the German menace, she must demand a number of guarantees from Germany at the end of the war, guarantees that would involve far more than the restoration of Alsace-Lorraine to French sovereignty.

Already by the summer of 1915, therefore, it was becoming more and more obvious to Barbusse that, whatever the original ambitions of the nations had been in 1914, the war was rapidly turning into a war of attrition in which both sides were intent on total victory. And the most terrifying feature of the situation was that the hatred of the enemy that was being encouraged by the press and the enormous annexations that were being demanded by the politicians could only mean that, even if this war was brought to an end, other wars would surely follow in its wake. What, then, should mankind do? The only way in which Barbusse could see this vicious circle being broken was for the peoples of Europe to rise in revolt against their governments and to refuse to fight their wars. The one solution that measured up to the size of the problems that had been created by the war was socialism, 'the only political doctrine...where from the international point of view there is a glimmer not only of humanity but also of reason'.[23]

Barbusse's insistence that men must learn to overcome their suffering through an exercise of the will represented a new departure in his thought, and the emphasis that he now placed on the necessity for men to use their capacity to reason was to become increasingly marked in his work as the war progressed, a process that culminated in his foundation of the Clarté movement in 1919, a movement that was quite obviously inspired by Cartesian principles and 'l'esprit de géométrie'. Quite clearly

Barbusse had now decided that a major factor in causing the outbreak of the First World War had been the assault that had been launched on rationalism and positivism in the years before 1914, and it was in a desperate attempt to purge himself of his own sense of guilt in this matter that he was now prepared to make a complete return to the rationalist principles in which he had been reared; if necessary, he was prepared to force himself to believe in these principles if in this way he could make some contribution towards the greater good of mankind.

And yet, as he himself was aware, the best way in which he could serve the cause of peace in 1915 was not so much by attempting to convince men of the validity of the intellectual arguments against war but by expressing his sense of moral outrage at the events that were now taking place in Europe, by depicting, in as authentic a way as he could, the raw reality of the life at the front. It was by following this line of argument, therefore, that Barbusse came to produce *Le Feu*. In writing this novel he relied to a great extent on his own experiences in the war and on the notes that he had kept of the conversations of his fellow-soldiers. The leisure that he needed to finish the work he found, quite by accident, in the early months of 1916 when he was forced to convalesce from the illnesses from which he had suffered in the previous year. It was in the middle of 1916 that *Le Feu* started as a serial in *L'Oeuvre*. It was at the very end of that year that it finally appeared as a book.

2

TOWARDS COMMUNISM

It must be admitted that, partly because of the haste with which it was written, *Le Feu* is not the kind of book that can greatly impress the present-day reader. Despite the visionary power that the novel still retains, its style seems over-emphatic, its characterisation two-dimensional, and its plot difficult to follow. The propagandist element in the novel, an element which becomes particularly prominent in the closing chapters where Barbusse entirely abandons the techniques of Naturalism for a kind of Expressionism, is yet a further factor which helps to explain why it has lost much of its original appeal. Barbusse's contemporaries might have acclaimed *Le Feu* as the first successful attempt made by a writer to depict the First World War in truthful terms. What strikes the reader of today, however, is the way in which the book combines a great deal of indisputably authentic and realistic detail with passages of undisguised rhetoric, rhetoric which, far from enhancing the impact of the author's message, positively diminishes it. It is interesting to note that although one of the great masterpieces provoked by the war, Céline's *Journey to the End of the Night*, was strongly influenced by Barbusse, Céline drew his inspiration far more from *L'Enfer* than from *Le Feu*. Like so many other famous denunciations of the miseries of the First World War, in fact, like Remarque's *All Quiet on the Western Front* and Ernst Toller's play *Transfiguration*, *Le Feu* now seems to be of mainly historical interest.

But this is not to deny that in 1917 and 1918 the influence of *Le Feu* was considerable. In France large sections of the press praised it and Barbusse was awarded one of the most coveted French literary prizes, the Prix Goncourt, thus making it all the more difficult for the censor to delete passages which he considered to be dangerous for army morale. In England, too, the merits of *Le Feu* did not go unnoticed: Siegfried Sassoon thought highly of it and lent his copy to the poet Wilfred Owen who reported that it had set him alight as no other war-book had done.[1] Lenin read it shortly after his departure from Switzerland for Russia in 1917 and, according to his wife, Krupskaya, 'was deeply affected by Barbusse's book. . .to which he attached great importance'.[2] *Le Feu* was also read in Germany and Austria, despite the official ban that had been placed upon it by the governments of the Central Powers.

The book, in fact, was a tremendous popular success. Nearly a quarter of a million copies had been sold by November 1918, and Barbusse was particularly gratified by the reception that it was accorded by many of the ordinary people of France. One woman wrote to him that she had finished *Le Feu* with the feeling that she herself had been living in the trenches:

> It seems to me that my face is pale, muddy and strained, like the faces of the men who talked with one another during the dawn! This is the way in which I have lived through your pages.[3]

And men at the front were also amongst those who were quick to express their sense of indebtedness to the man who had shocked the civilians into an awareness of the conditions that the soldiers were being forced to bear. One of them wrote to him:

> You have cried out with the voice of truth. It is the picture of our life of Hell, of all that we endure, of all that we think. . .we thank you for avenging us, for denouncing the war and for recording our terrible epic for the benefit of posterity. . .You give us the courage to continue the struggle because, thanks to you, we know for what we are fighting.[4]

Barbusse himself was so impressed by letters such as these that he became convinced that the sentiments that he had expressed in his book were those of the French people as a whole. And yet there was another side to the picture and, for every expression of gratitude that he received after the publication of his novel, there was an equally hostile reaction from other sections of the French public who regarded his book as being pro-German in its implications. The abbé Sirech, chaplain-in-chief of the lycées of Lyons, thought that the author of *Le Feu* deserved the most drastic form of punishment:

> If the military tribunals condemn a poor soldier who refuses to

sacrifice his blood for his country to be stood up against a wall,
what punishment do *you* deserve, Monsieur Barbusse?[5]

And, although the authorities felt themselves to be powerless to
proceed against Barbusse in person, they certainly went to considerable lengths to counteract the influence of his book. Not only
did the French military mission in the United States take great
pains to assure the American press that the sentiments expressed
by the soldiers in *Le Feu* were not those of the French army as a
whole, the military censorship in French North Africa banned
any public discussion of the novel altogether.

The attitude that was adopted by the authorities is, of course,
understandable. It has already been seen that in the spring of
1917 the military position of France was gravely affected by the
mutinies that had followed the Nivelle offensive. The political
situation, too, was critical. In French politics 1917 was a year of
great tension and drama, a year in which there were growing
demands for a more vigorous prosecution of the war, while the
Socialists were becoming increasingly disenchanted with the conflict and defeatism was openly encouraged by newspapers like
Le Bonnet Rouge. On the one hand there was Clemenceau
arguing the necessity for France to follow a policy of total war:
on the other hand there were rumours that Joseph Caillaux, one
of the leading personalities in the Radical Party, was in favour of
negotiations with Germany and a French withdrawal from the
war. Meanwhile, both the Painlevé and Ribot ministries fell
because of their ineffectiveness. Months of political crisis were
only brought to an end in November 1917 when Poincaré, the
French president, at last overcame his personal dislike of
Clemenceau and summoned the latter to form a government.
Caillaux and his associates were arrested. Only then was France
fully re-engaged in the fight.

Given the kind of situation, then, it was inevitable that *Le Feu*
should have caused the controversy that it did. Unlike Barbusse
the French government saw no hope at all that the Germans
could be persuaded to entertain peace proposals. Why should the
Germans think in terms of peace, Clemenceau argued, when the
outbreak of the March Revolution in Petrograd and the demoralisation that set in within the Russian armies in the spring and
summer of 1917 made it possible for the Central Powers to think

in terms of a decisive victory in the East? And was it not true
that the civilian politicians in Berlin had lost overall control of
policy to the generals, thus making it even more unlikely that
Germany would agree to a compromise peace? If the German
army succeeded in defeating the Russians, Clemenceau maintained, the Central Powers would then launch a major offensive
in the West before the arrival of American troops in Europe
caused the balance of power to shift in France's favour. Throughout 1917, in fact, the great fear of the war party in France was
that, by agitating so vociferously for an end to the war, the Left
was paving the way, not for peace, but for a German hegemony
over Europe. Had the French authorities known for certain that
Caillaux was so committed to the idea of peace that he was
prepared to come to terms with Germany, allowing the Central
Powers to make territorial gains at the expense of the British and
the Russians on condition that France was treated generously in
return, they would have been even more concerned to counter
the influence of *Le Feu* than they were at the time of its publication.

Nevertheless, although Barbusse was associating with dangerous company in giving his support to the peace campaign, it
would be quite absurd to uphold some of the more extreme
charges that were made against him in 1917. It is true that on his
return from the army he had allied himself with the minority
section of the Socialist Party led by Marx's grandson, Jean
Longuet, who wanted the Socialists to withdraw their support
from the Union Sacrée in order to work for a peace without
annexations. But just because a small minority of those involved
in this campaign were outright defeatists, this did not mean that
either Longuet or Barbusse themselves were defeatists. While it
is correct to say that Barbusse insisted that the only reason why
the war was being prolonged was because it suited the nationalists in France and Germany that it should continue, and while it
is equally true that he believed that the only way in which the
war could be brought to an end was for the peoples of Europe to
defy their governments, the position adopted by Barbusse and
his friends must be sharply distinguished from the revolutionary
defeatism preached by elements of the so-called Zimmerwald
Left, whose position was close to that of Lenin. Barbusse was
never in favour of a French equivalent of the Treaty of Brest-

Litovsk, and was always insistent that Germany should evacuate all the French territory she had occupied since 1914 before any peace negotiations could commence.

Admittedly he was sufficiently naïve to place some faith in Caillaux: he took that devious and extremely ambitious politician at his face value and did not suspect the extent to which the latter was deceiving his Socialist admirers when he denied that he was prepared to come to a peace with Germany on terms that were humiliating to France. But no sinister significance can be read into that. Like the vast majority of those Frenchmen who were opposed to the war, in fact, Barbusse's motives were entirely honourable and, despite the abuse that was hurled against him by the Action Française, the author of *Le Feu* was *not* a German agent and the object of his novel had *not* been to spread enemy propaganda within the disaffected ranks of the French army. Indeed, as evidence to the contrary, he was able to point to the terms which the German government had employed when it had banned his book in 1917: it had condemned *Le Feu* as a 'danger-ous' work, a work that was likely to produce a cleavage between the German people and government. Barbusse declared that he felt honoured by this description:

> The spirit of my work is above all anti-imperialist and anti-militarist and it is logical that, in a country where militarism wears a crown on its head, they should stifle a serious attempt to bring to light the evils and suffering that are the result of these principles of oppression.[6]

Far from wanting in any way to create the conditions for a German victory over France, therefore, Barbusse was very firmly of the opinion that it was the existing structure of Imperial Germany that was the main obstacle in the way of peace and that, before the war could be brought to an end, the ruling clique within Germany must be overthrown. On this one issue, in fact, he was in agreement with the war party in his own country. Where he parted company with the war party, was over the methods by which this objective could be achieved. His oppo-nents believed that this could only be effected if Germany was made to suffer a military defeat, whereas he was convinced that a prolongation of the war was unnecessary. If the Socialists in all the warring nations could unite in common action in favour of peace, and if it was made clear to the German people that the peace conditions demanded by the Entente did not involve the annihilation or the dismemberment of their country, he argued, then it was possible that the German people themselves would rise in rebellion against the military régime which had seized control of their country. In this way, he hoped, the conflict could be brought to a speedy conclusion and millions of men would be spared slaughter at the front.

These expectations were not to be fulfilled, however. After the March revolution in Petrograd and the overthrow of Tsarism in Russia there was certainly a marked movement of opinion against the war amongst many sections of the European Left, and Barbusse's hope that the Left would unite behind a common policy seemed to be in the process of being realised when, on the initiative of the Russian Soviets, it was proposed that a conference of European socialist parties should be held in Stockholm to organise concerted action against the war. Barbusse's hopes rose even further when it became known that German Social Democrats were being allowed by their government to send a delegation to the Stockholm Conference. But this did not mean that Germany was seriously interested in the possibility of peace. Quite apart from the fact that the famous Reichstag Peace Resolution of July 1917 was largely a propaganda exercise and that a majority of those who signed it did not seriously intend that Germany should come out of the war with no annexations to her credit, the leaders of the German army were resolved to ignore the Peace Resolution completely. Hindenburg and Ludendorff calculated that, if Russia could be forced out of the war in the course of 1917, the prospects of a considerable expansion of German influence in Eastern Europe and the possibility that Germany could secure a decisive victory over France in 1918 would quickly silence any opposition there might be to their policies within the German parliament.

Just how correct these calculations were was to be shown only too clearly in the course of the next few months. The advent to power of Lenin in November 1917 led to Russia's acceptance of the draconian terms of the Treaty of Brest-Litovsk and to her withdrawal from the war. This, in turn, opened the way for Ludendorff's great spring offensive in the West in 1918, Germany's final attempt to break the resistance of the French. Despite the wave of industrial unrest in protest against the war that swept through Central Europe in the early months of 1918, therefore, the possibility that Germany might still secure a total victory over her opponents made it impossible for the Social Democrats to challenge the control that was exercised by the army over the direction of German policy, even if they had possessed the courage and the determination to make this challenge, which was doubtful. It was only after the High Command had lost its gamble in the West in the summer of 1918 that the German Left was able to assert itself, and by then it was too late to expect any of the Western powers to agree to a compromise peace.

This failure of the German Social Democrats to fulfil the rôle that he had assigned to them was a sad disillusionment to the author of *Le Feu*. But events in France, too, had bitterly disappointed him. In September 1917 the French government had refused to grant passports to the delegation selected by the Socialists to attend the Stockholm Conference, thus provoking the withdrawal of Socialist support from the ministry and the formal ending of the Union Sacrée. At the end of the year, by preferring Clemenceau to Caillaux, the French chamber had clearly demonstrated the fact that it was opting for a policy based on revenge. Clemenceau's policy was one of a fight to the finish, the defeat of the enemy, and then the imposition of a peace treaty that would meet the problems of French security by a harsh treatment of Germany. Barbusse was convinced that this kind of solution was no solution at all. Whilst the war was still raging it would only prolong the conflict by making the task of the German Social Democrats in opposing the ambitions of the High Command all the more difficult. Once the war was over it could only prepare the way for yet another European tragedy in twenty years' time.

And yet for a time at the end of the war it looked as if one could still entertain *some* hope for the future, for there was still the possibility that Wilsonian ideals would prevail. At least Wilson seemed to recognise that the sacrifices that the peoples of Europe had been called upon to make could only be given some kind of meaning if the peace that was signed at the end of the war was an exercise, not in revenge, but in reconciliation, and it was a sign of the confidence that Barbusse himself possessed in the integrity of the American president that, in October 1918, only one month before the end of the war, he sent a telegram to

Wilson expressing his support for the Fourteen Points.[7] In December of the same year Barbusse returned to the issue by publicly attacking those sceptics who claimed that Wilson would be unable to fulfil his pledges because secret agreements had already been made between the victorious powers.[8] All the greater was Barbusse's sense of shock, therefore, when the terms of the Treaty of Versailles were made public in May 1919.

Despite the fact that the hopes that Barbusse had placed in the ability of Wilson to secure a just and lasting peace were to be shattered he had already made it quite clear in the middle of the war that he did not intend to leave it to the politicians alone to decide what the fate of the world would be at the end of the conflict. He himself had learnt much from his comrades in the war:

> It was through them that I, a bourgeois writer, was able to abandon that kind of abstract idealism that is the particular sin of intellectuals. It was through them that I was put in direct contact with the working class.[9]

If the war had been possessed of any significance at all, he maintained, it had shown that Reason alone was the force that could save the world, and that the life of man as a collective being must now take precedence over his life as an individual. Between 1917 and 1919, therefore, he was busily engaged in founding two organisations – the Association Républicaine des Anciens Combattants (commonly known as the A.R.A.C.), and the Clarté movement – with which he hoped to make his own distinctive contribution to help solve the problems facing the post-war world.

As far as the A.R.A.C. was concerned, it was early in the war that Barbusse had first conceived the idea of setting up a veterans' organisation, but it was not until after the success of Le Feu that he possessed the financial resources to realise his ambitions, and it was not until November 1917 that the organisation was finally launched. Nevertheless, the movement soon made its influence felt. By 1917, of course, there were many organisations of war veterans already in existence, many of them concerned with the welfare of soldiers, the care of the wounded, and the provision of financial aid to the widows and orphans of those killed in action.

But although the A.R.A.C. was involved in the performance of
duties such as these, it differed from the majority of other groups
in this field in the extent to which it was politically motivated.
This, indeed, was a major reason for its success. By advocating a
policy of socialism and peace, by insisting that the sufferings that
had been endured by the soldiers during the First World War
were symbolic of the misery of the exploited sections of society
as a whole, the A.R.A.C. served as a kind of training ground for
many individuals who were later to become leading personalities
within the French Communist Party. Jacques Duclos, Jacques
Doriot (subsequently to be leader of the Fascist 'Parti Populaire
Français' in the 1930s) and André Marty (one of the leaders of the
mutiny that took place in the French fleet in the Black Sea in
1919 in protest against the Allied intervention against the Bolsheviks in the Russian civil war) were all members of the movement at the start of their political careers.

And yet Barbusse was still not satisfied. Despite the success of
the A.R.A.C. amongst the veterans he was particularly concerned
that intellectuals as well as soldiers should commit themselves to
the fight against militarism and war, and he soon came to realise
that it was only if he could manage to build up a series of *international* organisations that he could hope to transcend the rivalries
that had brought Europe to the verge of ruin. With the end of
the First World War, therefore, he founded not only the Internationale des Anciens Combattants – a movement to which were
affiliated veterans' organisations in France, England, Italy,
Germany and Austria – but also the Clarté movement.

The foundation of Clarté was largely due to the efforts of a
young man who had become a close friend of the author of *Le
Feu* in the course of the First World War. Like Barbusse,
Raymond Lefebvre was a man who felt completely alienated
from bourgeois society, an idealist who brought to his socialism
the same kind of fervour, and the same sense of guilt, that his
Calvinist ancestors had displayed in their religion. Before the
outbreak of the war Lefebvre's position had been one of Tolstoyan
anarchism, but after his experiences in the war he quickly
realised that something more positive was needed if the world
was to be spared another disaster like that of 1914. Even more
passionately than Barbusse he believed that it was the treason of
the intellectuals in the years before 1914 that had been respon-

sible for the catastrophe of the war, and, after he had been invalided out of the French army in 1916 (as a result of the wounds
he had sustained at Verdun), he issued an appeal to a number of
European writers including Romain Rolland, H. G. Wells and the
German pacifist Friedrich Wilhelm Foerster, in which he urged
the intellectuals of Europe to do penance for the sins committed
by the war propagandists:

> In the shipwreck of the European mind, more painful and
> degrading than the blind massacre itself, it is greatly to be
> wished that we should get to know one another. It is right that
> by such confessions the intelligentsia of Europe should
> proclaim its resurrection and purge the disgrace which its
> own greatest leaders have brought upon modern times.[10]

In December 1916 Barbusse wrote to Lefebvre expressing
interest in this idea and suggesting that a review published in
several languages would be the best method of uniting writers in
different countries. Although the difficulties of translating this
idea into reality proved to be insuperable in time of war Barbusse
regarded it as a matter of urgent priority and in May 1919 therefore, only six months after the Armistice, Clarté was finally born.

To celebrate the event Barbusse published a novel in which he
outlined the lessons that he himself had learnt in the course of
the years between 1914 and 1918. At first sight Simon Paulin, the
hero of the novel *Clarté*, is very similar to the leading character
of *L'Enfer* in feeling himself to be a victim of the soullessness
that characterised bourgeois society before 1914, a mere cog in a
social machine that destroys love and understanding between
human beings. But whereas *L'Enfer* ends on a note of despair
the atmosphere of the closing chapters of *Clarté* is quite different.
By now in fact Barbusse is an openly propagandist writer. Paulin
is caught up in the First World War and although he is at first
appalled by the brutality that he witnesses he eventually comes
to realise that his experience has been a blessing in disguise: by
uniting with his fellow soldiers in the struggle against militarism
he can at last experience that sense of human brotherhood that
had eluded him in the past.

True to the message of this novel Barbusse was determined
that the Clarté movement should be something more than a mere
forum for writers. If it was to avoid the self-centred nature of

most literary organisations, he insisted, it must emulate the achievements of the eighteenth-century Encyclopaedists and devote itself to the task of education and propaganda. The traditional divisions between workers and intellectuals had been broken down in the course of the war, and they must not be allowed to emerge again. By means of its publications Clarté must act as a 'living encyclopaedia', a 'large university' which would disseminate the teachings of rationalism and socialism to the masses.

This was an extremely ambitious programme for Barbusse to undertake, but, for a time, it looked as if it could be fulfilled. Within a couple of years of its foundation the Clarté movement had at its disposal an attractively illustrated weekly magazine, in addition to which it was able to sponsor the publication of books and the production of plays. And this was not all. The end of the First World War made it possible again for men to devote themselves to the task of international reconciliation, and the promulgation of the terms of the Treaty of Versailles convinced many writers that this kind of activity was both desirable and necessary. By 1920, therefore, Barbusse could count on the support of the flower of the left-wing intelligentsia of Europe for his movement. Writers of the calibre of Jules Romains and Georges Duhamel in France, E. D. Morel, Bertrand Russell and H. G. Wells in England, Heinrich Mann in Germany, and Stefan Zweig in Austria, were quickly enrolled into the cause. In the common revulsion against the débâcle of Western liberalism at the end of the First World War it seemed that Clarté might find a definite rôle and a coherent policy.

These hopes were not to be fulfilled, however, and by the end of 1920 the movement was in visible decline. One reason for its failure was its inability to attract the kind of mass audience for which Barbusse had hoped: according to one of the original members of the movement who eventually broke with Barbusse it never had more than 5,000 members even in France, and the kind of membership that it *did* attract was largely restricted to the radical intellectuals of the middle class.[11] Yet another reason for its final collapse was the fact that the aims of Clarté were far from being as clear as the title of the movement suggested: indeed, they were so vague that men of widely different viewpoints could subscribe to its programme, and the movement suffered from such chronic indiscipline that it was almost bound, sooner or later, to disintegrate. And yet the main responsibility for the failure of Clarté cannot be attributed to factors such as these. The truth of the matter was that the thin rationalist gruel that it offered mankind was hardly sufficient to appease the spiritual hunger from which Europe was suffering at the end of the First World War. Admittedly, after the insane horror of the war, the atmosphere in Western Europe was conducive to a neo-classical revival both in politics and the arts. But it was no more than a passing vogue. In the arts, Picasso and Stravinsky soon discovered that they were producing little more than pastiches. In the world of politics, the story was much the same. Maurras and his friends at the Action Française may have been sufficiently envious of the initial popularity of Clarté to issue a counter-manifesto, 'Pour un Parti de l'Intelligence', in Le Figaro in July 1919, but it was Gide who put his finger on the major weakness in Clarté when he complained that, although the programme of Barbusse's movement corresponded to the needs of the age, the terminology that it used was too doctrinaire and too naïve for it to be convincing.

With his public avowals of a renewed faith in Reason Barbusse could hardly agree with that. But he himself seems to have come to the conclusion that the programme of Clarté, although well-meaning, was too limited and vague, for within a few months of the launching of the movement he decided that it should move beyond a policy of opposition to militarism and war to a new policy that urged support for the Soviet Union and the need for world revolution. It was this decision that provoked the major crisis caused the movement to collapse in 1920.

The main reason why Clarté ended in failure was that it was killed by the man who had created it.

In some ways it is surprising that Barbusse should have moved to a position of support for Communism at the beginning of the 1920s, for in the past there had been considerable differences between his approach to the problems of war and peace and that of the Bolsheviks. In the years before the outbreak of the First World War, for example, at the same time that Barbusse was writing his articles pleading the case for pacifism in the columns of La Paix par le Droit, Lenin was confiding to Maxim Gorki that he believed that a war between Austria and Russia would be extremely useful for the cause of revolution in Western Europe, his only fear being that the Emperor Franz Josef and Tsar Nicholas would not fulfil his expectations.[12] And, during the First World War itself, at a time when Barbusse was making every effort to bring the conflict to an end, Lenin was again stressing the opportunities provided by the war for men to advance the cause of revolution. For Lenin was no pacifist. He wrote on 11 November 1914:

> War is no accident and no 'sin' as the Christian reverends think. They, like all opportunists, preach patriotism, humanitarianism and pacifism. War is an inevitable part of capitalism. It is just as much a legitimate part of capitalism as is peace. . .It is simply insane to talk about abolishing capitalism without a frightful civil war and without a succession of such wars. . .The only duty of Socialists, when an imperialist war breaks out between the bourgeois classes of different nations, is to transform this war between nations into a war between classes. Down with the sentimental hypocritical slogan 'Peace at Any Price'. Long live the civil war.[13]

While it is true to say that Barbusse himself abandoned his early pacifism in 1914 and later on in the war came to realise that the only way in which the conflict could be ended quickly was for the masses to support some kind of revolutionary action in order to overthrow the imperialistic governments that were in power, Lenin's appeals for a 'frightful civil war' and a 'succession of such wars' were not appeals to which he could instinctively respond.

It was, after all, with the necessity of opposing war by means of propaganda and education and not by means of internecine strife that Barbusse was primarily concerned when he launched the Clarté movement in 1919. Furthermore, throughout the war he had been insistent that it was only by means of concerted and *united* action that the forces of militarism and reaction could effectively be defeated. In accordance with this policy he had condemned the Bolshevik Revolution in 1917 for the 'deadly schism' that it had created within the ranks of Russian Social Democracy,[14] and the outbreak of the Russian civil war in 1918 only seemed to confirm his gloomy prophecies that the Bolshevik

Revolution was doomed to failure because of the divisions that it had caused within the Russian Left.

In founding Clarté, therefore, Barbusse was determined to cast his net as widely as possible and to avoid any strict identification of its purposes with those of any particular party. Indeed, so eclectic was he in his choice of contributors and supporters that he sometimes caused distress to his friends. On one occasion, for example, Romain Rolland sharply rebuked him for enrolling the Belgian poet Maurice Maeterlinck into the movement on the grounds that the latter had written a good deal of anti-German journalism in the course of the war. To Barbusse, however, these objections were irrelevant. What mattered to him was not the sins which an individual had committed in the past but the vision of the future to which that individual now aspired.[15] The horrific nature of war and the necessity for all men of good will to join in opposition to the idea of war seemed to him to be facts so self-evidently true that he hoped that the policies pursued by governments could be changed without the use of undue violence: 'The achievement of moral and social truth' he proclaimed in the manifesto of the Clarté movement, 'is being realised with a kind of fatality...A universal clarity is awakening.'[16] There was, he was prepared to concede, a small minority of individuals – capitalists, nationalists, clerics and generals for example – who stood in the way of the progress of humanity but he hoped that the final victory of Socialism and Reason would be accomplished in a relatively painless manner.

If Barbusse believed that widespread violence was unnecessary to achieve the aims of the Clarté movement in 1919, why, then, did he move so rapidly towards a Communist point of view in the course of the next few months? Undoubtedly it was the failure of Wilson at the Peace Conference and the continuing involvement of the Western Allies in the Russian civil war that were the main factors which prompted his sudden change of line. He was convinced that the terms of the Treaty of Versailles made a mockery of Wilsonian idealism. As for the western intervention in the Russian civil war this was even more sinister, for, although this policy might have been necessary when the First World War was still in progress – when it could be argued that it was in the interests of France, Britain and the United States to bring Russia back into the struggle against Germany – now that Germany had been defeated there was no possible justification for prolonging this interference in the internal affairs of the Soviet Union. The more Barbusse reflected on these issues, in fact, the more he was forced to conclude that Lenin had been right after all: the behaviour of the Western Powers towards Germany and Russia could only be explained by the fact that capitalism in its imperialist stage of development was bound by its very nature to lead to aggression and war. In these circumstances, Barbusse maintained, it was the duty of all those who were opposed to war to give their support to the Bolsheviks.

The author of *Le Feu*, of course, was not alone in thinking that the American president had betrayed the cause of peace at the Versailles conference. Raymond Lefebvre was so disillusioned with Wilson and so impressed by Lenin's analysis of the European situation that in July 1920 he left France illegally to attend the second congress of the Communist International. This action had a profound effect on the founder of Clarté, especially since Lefebvre was drowned on his return journey to France after the fishing vessel in which he was trying to evade the Allied blockade of the Russian ports was sunk in a storm off Murmansk. But although Barbusse was intensely distressed by Lefebvre's death, the author of *Le Feu* was in little need of further prompting to make him realise that he must change his views. He was already convinced that he had been living in a world of illusions and that something more drastic than Wilsonism or traditional socialism was needed if mankind was to be brought to its senses. And already, by the end of 1919, the events that he had witnessed in France and Germany in the months that had followed the end of the First World War – the murder of Rosa Luxemburg and Karl Liebknecht by forces under the nominal control of the Social Democratic government in Berlin in January 1919, the widespread criticism that was voiced in France that Clemenceau had made too many concessions to Wilson and Lloyd George and that the terms of the Treaty of Versailles were not sufficiently rigorous towards Germany – filled him with anger and contempt. In this situation an increasingly authoritarian tendency became apparent in his thought, a tendency that made it easier than it otherwise might have been for him to accept Communism. As one commentator on Barbusse's attitudes during this period has pointed out:

In his eyes socialism was 'the clarification of reason' yet the masses conspicuously lacked reason. Deeply as he shared their sufferings, he was apt to shower them with abuse as '*bêtes*', '*fous*', 'myopic', 'animal', as having short memories and poor judgement, as revering sacred objects and hating anything new. Liebknecht had been 'killed by the German people'. While his slogan 'Reason first. Sentiment ought to spring from the idea; the idea ought never to spring from the sentiment' appears to reverse the Marxist emphasis on life determining consciousness, and although Barbusse's 'eternal Reason' owed more to the Cartesian tradition than the Marxist, the spirit of Barbusse's thought came close in practice to that of the Bolsheviks. He too believed that only the enlightened could liberate the un-enlightened and he, like other French intellectuals, was driven to action as much by revulsion against stupidity as against injustice.[17]

This comment, although perceptive, lays too much stress on Barbusse's rationalism as an explanation of his conduct, and it may be thought that the driving force behind his conversion to Communism was a moral passion born of his Calvinist inheritance and his basic despair. Nevertheless, it must be admitted that it was in terms of Cartesian principles that Barbusse announced his change of position to the French public. In December 1919 he published a propaganda pamphlet entitled *La lueur dans l'abîme* which he had written to publicise the aims of the Clarté movement. In this booklet he still proclaimed that the guiding principles on which the movement was based were those of rationalism, and he still maintained that the aim of political action was to secure the greatest happiness of the greatest number. He was not yet committed to the view that the revolution that must transform the world must necessarily be violent in character: 'the revolution must be made in men's minds' was the motto of the Clarté movement, and these words appeared at the beginning of this pamphlet.[18] But to what specific policies was the reader committing himself if he accepted the general principles of Clarté? According to Barbusse they were policies which should ensure equality of rights and duties, equality of work for all, and the replacement of the existing class system by a single working class whose political institutions would be modelled on the lines

of the Russian Soviets. In other words, there should be a dictatorship of the proletariat.

A few weeks before the fateful congress of the Socialist Party
at Tours in December 1920 – a congress that was to result in a
permanent division of the French Socialist movement after a
majority of the delegates decided to accept the conditions that
had been laid down by Moscow for affiliation to the Comintern –
Barbusse went further. In *Le couteau entre les dents*, a new
pamphlet addressed to the intellectuals, he once again stressed
the fact that it was desirable that the revolution should be made
in men's minds, but in addition to this he now contended that the
Bolsheviks had been forced to kill their opponents because they
did not have the time to educate them. Although the social question was only one of the problems inherent in the human condition, it was the only problem that men could remedy. If the
revolution was to be successful, therefore, it was necessary for the
working class to use violence in order to achieve its aims:

> To change the course of events we must go back to the source.
> Order will not prevail unless it is imposed...We must face in
> our minds and in our hearts this great question of violence and
> find within ourselves the courage to master it. Let us make no
> mistake: the demagogic cry 'No violence on my account' is a
> sophistry to which feelings of compassion may lead us if they
> are weak, but which they will spurn if they are strong.[19]

From this point onwards the Clarté movement is doomed. From
the moment that Barbusse went beyond the stage of advocating
the use of reason to further the cause of revolution to the next
stage of advocating the use of force, the movement was subjected
to an increasing number of defections that finally resulted in its
collapse. It is true that for a number of years Barbusse was reluctant to take the final step of joining the new French Communist
Party on the grounds that he would be of more use to the party
by continuing his propaganda activities outside it. It is also true
that for a time he resisted the pressure of a number of his young
collaborators within Clarté who wanted the movement to affiliate
itself formally to the Comintern.[20] Nevertheless the fact remains
that it was in 1920 that Clarté received its coup de grâce. It was
in that year that most of the English section (including Wells and
Russell) resigned in protest against the growing influence of

Communism within the ranks of the movement. It was in the same year, too, that Barbusse finally alienated the pacifists who still supported him. In a sharp attack on what he described as their utopianism and naïveté he pointed out that pacifism had not succeeded in preventing the outbreak of the war in 1914 and that it would not succeed in preventing the outbreak of even more terrible wars in the future. By the faith which they contrived to place in the doctrine of non-violence the pacifists were playing into the hands of the militarists, and by the trust which they continued to place in the League of Nations they were doing nothing more than giving their support to a capitalist order that was bent on destroying the Soviet Union. However sincere they were in their ideals, Barbusse concluded, it was their policies and not his that constituted the major threat to world peace.[21]

Interesting though Barbusse's many quarrels with the non-Communist Left at this time were, perhaps the most revealing – and certainly the most spectacular – of the controversies provoked by Barbusse's conversion to Communism was the prolonged debate in which he became involved in the early 1920s with the writer Romain Rolland. This controversy was all the more important because the latter was regarded by many of his contemporaries as the most compelling voice of the European conscience.

Rolland had earned this reputation by his conduct during the First World War. At the age of 48 in 1914 he had not been under any obligation to do military service, and, at the outbreak of the war, he had decided to stay in Switzerland where he was on holiday. Whilst remaining in Switzerland, working for the Red Cross at the International Agency for Prisoners of War, however, he observed the events that were taking place in the rest of Europe with a growing sense of concern. His first reaction to the war was that of a patriotic Frenchman outraged by the German invasion of France and the German violation of Belgian neutrality, and it was in this spirit that he wrote his famous open letter to the dramatist Gerhart Hauptmann protesting against the acts of aggression that had been committed by the German army in Belgium. When Hauptmann ignored his charges and gave his support instead to the notorious manifesto of the 93 German intellectuals, a manifesto which defended the action of the

German government in invading Belgium and denied allegations that the German army had perpetrated atrocities in that country, Rolland was beside himself with anger.

Nevertheless by the September of 1914 Rolland's attitude had begun to change. In one sense it had been peculiarly appropriate that it should have fallen to him to protest against the crimes that had been committed by the German government at the beginning of the First World War, for more than any other French writer he had a profound admiration for German culture, and the danger of a war breaking out between France and Germany had been one of the principal themes of a long series of novels that he had published between 1904 and 1912 under the general title of *Jean Christophe*. On the other hand, the very fact he had been a notable advocate of Franco-German reconciliation in the years before 1914 meant that he could not repudiate this ideal now, and very soon he became convinced that his own country must bear part of the responsibility for the outbreak of the First World War. Although he was aware that as a result of his actions he would be an object of execration in France, therefore, he made it known in a series of newspaper articles (articles that were eventually published under the title of *Au dessus de la mêlée* in 1915) that he now believed that the war was a monstrous absurdity for which both sides were equally to blame. Rolland remained faithful to this position for the rest of the conflict. For a time he hoped, like Barbusse, that the triumph of Wilsonian principles might help to save Europe from the ruin that awaited it, but the provisions of the Treaty of Versailles were a source of bitter disillusionment to him. Whatever the statesmen might think that they had achieved in Paris, he protested, the treaty was in reality 'a sad peace' providing only 'a derisory interlude between two massacres of the peoples'.[22]

In the light of Rolland's attitude towards the First World War, then, it was only to be expected that he should have been broadly sympathetic towards the aims of the Clarté movement when it was founded in 1919. Already during the war he had expressed his conviction that the crimes against humanity that had been committed by the majority of European writers in welcoming the outbreak of the war in 1914 could only be expiated if they were willing to participate in an international movement to defend the basic principles of intellectual integrity and independence. And already in March 1918 he had published a manifesto entitled 'For an International of the Mind'. To this he added in July 1919 a 'Declaration of Intellectual Independence', a document that was signed by a number of prominent writers, philosophers and scientists including Croce, Einstein, Gorki, Tagore, Heinrich Mann, Bertrand Russell, Upton Sinclair, Jules Romains, Georges Duhamel and, inevitably, Henri Barbusse.

So similar indeed were the aims of Rolland and Barbusse at this time that at first sight it may seem surprising that they found it difficult to collaborate with each other. And yet there were a number of reasons why this was so. Rolland's disapproval of the lack of discrimination that was displayed by Barbusse in his search for supporters for Clarté had already been noted, and this was certainly one factor which helps to explain why the International Congress of Intellectuals which they hoped to gather together in Paris in 1920, did not in the end take place. An even greater source of tension, however, was the fact that these differences over method were only the expression of a much deeper incompatibility of temperament. Not only were both men rigid and unyielding in character, they were also equipped with a very different experience of life. Barbusse, it must be remembered, had observed the events of the First World War at close quarters while Rolland had commented on them from afar. Sooner or later therefore they were bound to clash. Sooner or later it was inevitable that they should quarrel over the lessons that were to be learnt from the war. The issues raised by the success of the Bolshevik revolution in Russia merely provided the occasion for this quarrel.

At first Rolland had enthusiastically welcomed the outbreak of the March Revolution in Russia in 1917, seeing in it the first act of that universal liberation of humanity from the tyranny of the past that he believed to be necessary if mankind was to escape a repetition of the sufferings of the First World War. Soon after the Bolshevik seizure of power in October of that year, however, he was greatly dismayed by the information that he received from his Russian friends such as Gorki concerning the terror that was being employed by Lenin's secret police, the notorious Cheka, and the atrocities that were being committed by both sides in the civil war. In the debate that took place within the French Socialist Party over the question of affiliation to the Third International, therefore, he refused to take sides. This reluctance to commit himself in the controversies of 1919 and 1920 did not mean that Rolland regarded the existing state of society outside the Soviet Union with any sense of satisfaction, and he was convinced that Europe would continue to be plagued with wars until the capitalist system had been overthrown. But, if he condemned the brutalities committed by the Right, he could hardly condone the atrocities committed by the Left, and, if he was distressed by the bloody way in which the Spartacist uprising was crushed in Berlin, he was equally disturbed by the excesses that were being perpetrated by the Bolshevik régime in Russia. Indeed, so appalled was he by the violence that was being committed in the revolutionary upheavals that followed the First World War that he was driven to the conclusion that European civilisation was doomed, and that the only solution to the problems of mankind lay in the philosophy and religion of Asia. Alienated from a Europe that was intent on destroying itself Rolland was increasingly attracted by the teachings of Mahatma Gandhi.

With his new-found faith in Communism Barbusse was bound to regard the evolution that had taken place in Rolland's attitude with extreme disfavour. In an attack on Rolland published in *Clarté* in December 1921, Barbusse, while praising the services that the author of *Au dessus de la mêlée* had rendered to the cause of humanity by denouncing the evils of the First World War, insisted that the position which the latter had now adopted would do nothing to prevent the repetition of such wars in the future. The task of a revolutionary, Barbusse proclaimed, was two-fold in nature: he must destroy, and he must create. Rolland had admirably performed the first part of this duty, but he now threw up his hands in horror at the methods that were necessary if the revolution was to enter the constructive phase of its development. Real and lasting progress could only be achieved if the revolutionaries equipped themselves with an exact analysis of the way in which society works, and this analysis was to be found in the programme of the Clarté movement. From the ideas contained in this programme it could be seen that since capitalism enabled a small minority of men to dominate the rest, liberty and fraternity are concepts that are too imprecise and too unreliable to be of any use in the strategy of revolution; equality alone must be the guiding principle that men should follow. As for Rolland's

objections to the use of violence, these, by definition, were
irrelevant: there could not be any errors of calculation in the
'social geometry of revolution' to be found in the programme of
the Clarté movement since there is no fundamental difference
between the laws of society and the laws of science. No one
within Clarté was advocating any unnecessary use of force to
achieve a just society, but it must be remembered that society, as
it was at present constituted, was itself an instrument of violence
in the hands of the capitalist classes; if anyone was inclined to
dispute this fact they had only to look at the origins and development of the First World War to see that this was true. The question at issue was not whether the exploited should be permitted
to use violence in order to achieve their aims, but whether they
should be permitted to use violence as a legitimate means of self-
defence against the forces which had plunged the continent into
war on one occasion and would do the same again unless the
peoples of Europe brought their activities to an end. The violence
of the masses, must be seen, not as an act of aggression, therefore,
but as the only means left to the people to disarm their leaders.
Seen in this light the use of force was only of short-term significance. It was only a marginal and provisional detail in the total
perspective of revolution.

Rolland's reply to this kind of argument was predictable. He
protested against 'the abstract conception of Man' that Barbusse
had introduced into the debate, a conception which, he complained, reduced 'the enigma of human evolution to a problem
in Euclidean geometry'. He reaffirmed the horror that he felt at
the cruelties that were being perpetrated by the Bolshevik
régime in Russia, and he expressed his fear that the terror being
conducted by the Bolsheviks would turn out to be not a temporary
expedient, as Barbusse had stated, but a permanent feature of
their rule: after all, he argued, this outcome seemed to be all the
more probable since the rigours of the Bolshevik dictatorship had
in no way been relaxed even with the ending of the Russian civil
war. Whilst expressing once again the sympathy that he felt for
many of the aims of the Russian Revolution, therefore, Rolland
did not hesitate to condemn the methods that were being
employed by Lenin and his supporters. He ended his statement
of position by saying that the attitude he had adopted towards
violence since the outbreak of the First World War had been a

consistent one, and that the guiding principle behind all his actions could be summed up in the words of Schiller's motto 'In tyrannos'. He was opposed to *all* tyrants, whatever their political persuasion.[23]

The debate between Barbusse, Romain Rolland and their various supporters was a lengthy one and it might have broken out again had not an event occurred which diverted Barbusse's attention to more pressing matters. This was the French occupation of the Ruhr in January 1923, an action that was deemed necessary by the French government after Germany had shown herself to be unwilling to fulfil her obligations under the terms of the reparations clauses of the Treaty of Versailles. The French Communist Party came out in opposition to this policy and urged the invading troops to fraternise with the German workers. The police then raided the party headquarters and the offices of the newspaper *L'Humanité*, which had come under the control of the Communists after the Tours conference in 1920. The entire Politburo of the party was incarcerated in the Santé prison.

Barbusse's reaction to all this was characteristic. 'Since I share their ideas', he declared, 'I must share the risks.'[24] Immediately he applied for party membership.

3

THE FIGHT AGAINST WAR

For some years after 1923 it seemed that the pessimism which Barbusse had expressed over the future of Europe in the course of his controversy with Romain Rolland had been somewhat excessive. Although the French occupation of the Ruhr seemed seriously to imperil the prospects for peace at the time that it happened, the period after 1923 was marked by a significant relaxation in European tensions. Franco-German relations were greatly eased by the economic boom which Western Europe (particularly Germany) enjoyed between 1924 and 1929. The advent to power of Stresemann in Germany in 1923, and the election of a left-wing ministry in France in 1924, further helped to improve the international atmosphere. Even the Soviet Union made some attempts to break out of her isolation in the middle of the 1920s: whilst remaining intensely suspicious that the capitalist powers might launch a counter-revolutionary crusade against her, Russia seemed, for a time, to be in favour of some kind of peaceful coexistence with the West. By 1924, then, it seemed to many observers that for the first time in twenty years the danger of a major war was receding. Indeed, it was indicative of the new mood that prevailed in Europe by the middle of the decade that the strength of the Communist parties tended to diminish and that of the Socialists to increase. This could be seen very clearly in France where, after the crisis years of the early 1920s the Socialists made a spectacular recovery, while the Communist Party experienced a sharp decline.

The optimism of the Locarno era did not last for very long, however. In 1929 the Wall Street Crash set in motion that progressive decline in international financial confidence that was to result in the Great Depression. And, with the onset of the Depression, Europe was faced by the growing menace of Fascism. By 1932 the Nazis had emerged as the largest single party within the Reichstag. By January 1933 Hitler had been nominated as chancellor of Germany. Ever since the end of the war Barbusse had prophesied that the forces of capitalism would inevitably lead to militarism and war. Now with the intensified crisis of capitalism and the emergence of Fascism all his most gloomy predictions seemed about to be fulfilled.

But was Barbusse correct in his further assertion that the only effective solution to the problems that now faced Europe was for men to adopt Communism? Certainly the record of the European Social Democracy in the inter-war years does little to disprove this claim, for, despite the revival in their fortunes during the period of stability in the middle of the 1920s, the non-Communist Left were ill-prepared to meet the situation that confronted them at the end of the decade. The leaders of the Socialists might protest that the spirit of Marxism was being completely perverted inside the Soviet Union. They might also protest that Bolshevism did violence to the libertarian principles inherent in Socialism. But at least the Communists were aware that the world of Hitler and Mussolini was very different from the world that existed before 1914, while the Socialists still clung to the illusions that had led to the downfall of the Second International. As a result of their inability to meet the challenge of the Right the German Social Democrats were destroyed by Hitler in 1933, while the Austrians went down in defeat before Dollfuss in 1934.

In France, it is true, the Socialists did not suffer any comparable reversal of fortune in the course of the 1930s. Indeed in 1936 French Socialism enjoyed a kind of Indian Summer when Léon Blum emerged as the leader of the largest single grouping within the Popular Front. But not only did this alliance end in failure, from the very inception of the Popular Front the Socialists found it impossible to resolve the contradictions that existed at the very heart of their ideology. Were they a Marxist party, or were they a party of revisionists? Were they pacifists, or were they prepared to sanction the use of force? The Socialists could never decide. Already in 1933 a crisis had occurred within the ranks of the French Socialists that boded ill for the future. It was in that year that the brilliant Marcel Déat (regarded by many as Blum's eventual successor) left the Socialists after losing patience with the reluctance of his colleagues to face the drastic economic and political changes that were necessary if Europe was to pull itself out of the Depression. In the same year Pierre Renaudel left the party because he feared that the pacifism of the Socialist rank and file would prevent Blum from taking any positive action against the increasing danger that threatened France from Nazi Germany. Déat was undoubtedly wrong in maintaining in later years that it was only by imitating the methods and ideology of the Fascists that the Socialists could achieve their aims, and yet much of his attack on the outdated character of party dogma was perfectly justified. As for Renaudel's criticisms of the Socialists, these were to prove to be more than well-founded when, in 1938, the party, in deference to the pacifist element within its ranks, voted in favour of the Munich agreements. Clearly it was not from the French Socialists that one would expect the most resolute resistance to the growing menace of the dictators.

What political grouping, then, *did* offer the best hope that Hitler and Mussolini would be stopped in their tracks? Perhaps the most interesting evidence of the appeal that was to be exercised by Communism in the course of the 1930s is to be found, not in any analysis of the weaknesses of the Socialists, but in the change that took place in the attitude of independent supporters of the Left such as Romain Rolland. Already by 1927 the latter was somewhat disenchanted with the wisdom of the East and was beginning to look with increasing favour on the Soviet Union, but it was the rise of Fascism in the early 1930s that finally convinced him that he must accept the validity of many of the arguments that Barbusse had used against him in the previous decade. In the preface that he wrote to his *Quinze ans de combat* which appeared in 1935 Rolland made it plain that, while still refusing to join the Communist Party, he had now abandoned many of the reservations that he had formerly held on the use of revolutionary violence. Proclaiming his disillusionment with the Gandhian ethic, he now reproached himself for his lack of realism in his appreciation of the situation of Europe at the end of the First World War. In the years immediately after the Treaty of Versailles, he confessed, he had clung to an abstract idea of liberty that did not take into account the fact that liberty, if it is to be meaningful, must be closely related to the world as it is. In the early 1920s, he lamented, he had been a victim of that kind of bourgeois ideology which maintains that intellectuals can retreat into their ivory towers and isolate themselves from the common struggles of mankind. Now he had come to realise that it was only in the Soviet Union that real liberty had been achieved. Now he had come to appreciate that this could only have been accomplished by means of a temporary resort to violence. In any case, he argued, the violence that had appalled him in the early years of the Bolshevik régime had now been eliminated, and with the rise of Stalin the moderate forces within the Soviet Union had reasserted themselves.[1]

In response to the situation that had been created in Europe in the early 1930s there were many individuals like Rolland who now abandoned the scruples that had prevented them from accepting Communism ten years earlier. But whether they were wise to do so is a question to which there is more than one answer. For, if they themselves believed that by joining forces with the Communists they were allying themselves with the most determined and the most effective opponents of Fascism, others might reply – as Rolland himself had argued in the early 1920s – that the Communists must bear a considerable burden of responsibility for the rise of Fascism in the first place. After all, it can hardly be denied that, by resorting to a policy of revolutionary violence in 1917 in the years that followed the Bolshevik Revolution, Lenin and his followers were teaching the rest of the world a lesson from which the international communist movement was not the only force to benefit. Nor can it be denied that Lenin's creation of the Comintern was largely responsible for that tragic division between Communists and Socialists that was so to weaken the European Left in the 1920s and 1930s. Would it be too much of an exaggeration to say that Lenin, by deliberately splitting the Italian Socialist movement in 1921, and Stalin, by the absurd policy of vilification that he directed against the German Social Democrats in the years between 1928 and 1934, both played important rôles in creating the conditions that were favourable for the victory of the dictators? To most observers the truth of this statement is beyond dispute.

It would, of course, be foolish to claim that Lenin should be held responsible for all the crimes and follies committed by his successor. Despite the cynicism that he displayed in his choice of tactics Lenin was uncompromising in his revolutionary idealism, and towards the end of his life he showed himself to be deeply concerned by the growing evidence that the Communist régime in Russia was being transformed into a bureaucratic system that was prepared to resort to terror on a colossal scale. On the other hand, the policies that were pursued by Stalin – the creation of a tyrannical régime inside Russia and the subordination of the foreign Communist parties to the dictates of the Third International – were not entirely the result of his own personal whims but were partly determined, at least, by the legacy that had been bequeathed to him by the founder of the Soviet Union. Lenin, it must be remembered, had justified his seizure of power in Russia in 1917 by arguing that, in the circumstances of the First World War, the Bolshevik revolution would trigger off a series of socialist revolutions in the highly industrialised countries of the West, and that it was from these countries that the Bolsheviks would receive the help they needed to transform the Soviet Union into a socialist society. Far from being in accordance with any determinist view of history, therefore, Lenin's action in 1917 was a tremendous gamble with destiny. The tragedy of Lenin's career was that this was a gamble that was only partially successful. The use of revolutionary violence certainly enabled the Bolsheviks to consolidate their hold on Russia, and at the end of the First World War there were a number of attempts at communist revolution in the rest of Europe outside the Soviet Union. But, with the failure of these attempts in Berlin, Munich and Budapest, and with the defeat of the Red Army at the gates of Warsaw in 1920, the chances of revolution in Europe became increasingly remote. From this moment the character of the Russian revolution began to degenerate – as it was bound to degenerate in a country that was economically so backward and where there were so many difficulties involved in any peaceful attempt to undertake a programme of rapid industrialisation. From that moment, too, there began that process by which the leaders of the Soviet Union were to sacrifice the interests of the foreign Communist parties to the exigencies of Russia's domestic and foreign policies, a process that was to enable the Fascist dictators in the rest of Europe to claim, rightly, that the Communists were agents of Moscow, and, wrongly, that it was in Fascism alone that the peoples of Europe could find their way towards Socialism.

For Communist parties outside the Soviet Union, then, the situation which confronted them in the 1930s was indeed a tragic one. Ardent in their commitment to fight against the forces of Fascism they were compelled to throw away countless opportunities for extending their influence within their own countries by the sudden switches of policy that were decreed by the Comintern. Containing within their ranks many of the most idealistic and self-sacrificing elements within the European Left they found themselves forced into that sycophantic adulation of the achievements of Stalin that was to blind them to the enormities that were being committed by the Russian dictator in the name of Socialism.

But if this was the fate that awaited men like Romain Rolland when they announced their support for the Communists in the early 1930s, this was the fate to which Henri Barbusse was already condemned.

Of course it would be quite wrong to conclude from this that the French Communists lost *all* their independence in the years that followed the First World War. It must be remembered that it was with the prospects of revolution in Germany, and not in France, that the Soviet Union was primarily concerned in the period before 1933, and of all the foreign Communist parties it was the German party that was subjected to the most intensive forms of Comintern surveillance during these years. A further factor that prevented the French Communists (or, at least, the rank and file) from becoming totally Bolshevised in the 1920s was the persistence of specifically French ways of thinking within the party: the outrageous Anatole France may only have been speaking for himself when he confided to the Belgian Socialist Vandervelde that the only reason why he supported the Communists was that he was attempting to preserve the Franco-Russian alliance,[2] but the strength of the indigenous revolutionary tradition in France, the widespread feeling that the Russian Revolution owed its inspiration to the ideas of the French Revolution, and the inability of large numbers of French Communists ever really to understand such foreign concepts as 'dialectical materialism', and 'democratic centralism' meant that, behind the façade of discipline and unity that the party presented to the outside world, many different ideological tendencies could be found.

All this can quite clearly be seen in the case of Barbusse, for it has already been seen that, despite the sharp words that he had used in his controversies with Rolland and the pacifists in the early 1920s, the main reason why he supported Communism was his belief that it offered the best chance of securing human brotherhood and avoiding war, and he was always reluctant to accept the limitations that might be imposed on his activities by party divisions. As far as he was concerned, therefore, the fact that he had finally joined the Communist Party in 1923 did not mean that any fundamental change had taken place in his attitudes. Immediately after he joined the party he was at pains to convince the leadership that he could be of more use to them by continuing to play the rôle to which he had become accustomed than by attempting to follow a new career, and in 1924 he refused the party's suggestion that he should stand as a candidate in a safe seat in the parliamentary elections, arguing that such a move would unduly restrict his freedom of manoeuvre.

His one fear was that another terrible war might break out in Europe and his one concern was to rally as large a body of opinion as he could in favour of revolution. In 1925, therefore, he gathered together a large number of intellectuals to protest against the war which the French army was fighting against the Rif in Morocco. In 1927 he went further and attempted to enrol Jesus Christ within the ranks of the enlightened. In *Jésus* and *Les Judas de Jésus* (and in the unpublished play *Jésus contre Dieu* which he wrote at the same time) he attempted to demonstrate that a distinction should be made between the idea of 'the Christ', a theological abstraction invented by St Paul in order to prove that the founder of Christianity had been the Son of God, and Jesus the man who was a revolutionary atheist and rationalist whose primary concern had been that of alleviating the lot of the poor and the downtrodden. Once this essential distinction is made, Barbusse argued, the activities of Jesus became more comprehensible to modern man. Jesus appeared at a point in time when the corrupt and evil society of the Ancient World was in the process of disintegration – just as the capitalist world was moving towards its final collapse in the twentieth century. Seen in this light there were many parallels between the early Christians and the present-day Communists: both were groups of men who were determined to overthrow the existing order and to replace it by one founded on justice.

Such a comparison was obviously intended to be flattering to Barbusse's fellow-Communists, and the explanation that he offered for publishing this analysis of Christianity – his desire to combat the renewed vigour that was being displayed by the

Catholic Left following the papal condemnation of the Action Française – showed that he had no desire or intention to appear to be unorthodox. Nevertheless the incident very clearly demonstrates both the incorrigibly un-Marxist nature of his thought and his impatience with the niceties of party dogma, and it is not surprising that in the aftermath of this excursion into biblical exegesis there were a number of demands from party members that the author of *Le Feu* should be disciplined for such a blatant exhibition of bourgeois idealism.

The fact that Barbusse was not punished for his offences is a revealing comment both on the nature of the French Communist Party in the middle of the 1920s and on the flexibility which the party was still able to exercise in its handling of the policies laid down by the Comintern. This freedom of manoeuvre was severely circumscribed at the end of the decade, however, for in 1928 the Sixth Congress of the Comintern, in response to the downfall of Bukharin and the switch to the Left in the domestic policies of the Soviet Union, decided that the principal enemies of the international Communist movement and the principal agents of Fascism were not the forces of the Right, but the Social Democrats (or Social Fascists as they were then called). Immediately a witch-hunt began against right-wing deviationists within the French party – the Trotskyists had been expelled several years earlier – and a series of purges took place which resulted in the membership falling to under 20,000 compared with the 131,000 supporters which it claimed in 1921.

For a time Barbusse himself could have been in danger because of the eclectic nature of his thought, and perhaps the only reason why the party leadership was reluctant to take action against him was their desire to retain his name and prestige for propaganda purposes, a desire that was particularly understandable in the lean years that the party experienced in the period between the disintegration of Clarté and the emergence of a new generation of Communist writers at the beginning of the next decade. But, with the advent of Maurice Thorez as the dominating personality within the party leadership in 1931, there was a slight alleviation in the rigidity of the party line. Thorez might be a faithful follower of Stalin and a cautious bureaucratic functionary – so cautious that when at the end of 1933 the Comintern itself began to look with favour on the policy of a Popular Front, he refused for many months to take any initiative in the matter until Stalin's attitude was made abundantly clear – but he was also possessed of a genuine respect for men of culture (provided they were harmless) and was deeply anxious to extend the appeal of Communism in France. In these circumstances Barbusse was given a fairly free hand to proceed with his activities, provided that he did not offend against the guiding lines of party policy.

The author of *Le Feu* made the most of this opportunity. Already before the emergence of Thorez as the leading force within the Central Committee of the French party Barbusse had shown his capacity to interpret party policy in a more liberal way than was approved by Moscow. This was over the question of socialist literature, an issue that was closely related to the major change that had taken place in the Soviet Union in the late 1920s when Stalin had jettisoned the New Economic Policy and had embarked on the first Five Year Plan and the collectivisation of Russian agriculture. One result of this change was a growing insistence in Moscow that writers should devote themselves to themes connected with the economic development of the Soviet Union: it was also decided that the future of Communist literature could best be assured by encouraging the emergence of a new type of writer drawn from the ranks of the proletariat. Barbusse agreed with these proposals in theory, and yet his own preoccupation with the personality of Jesus Christ was totally opposed to the spirit of the first, and his attitude towards the second was one of some scepticism. He decided, therefore, that he would try to water down these proposals. He sent a tactfully worded message to the Second International Congress of Proletarian writers held at Kharkov in 1930 pointing out that there were many difficulties involved in achieving the end that they desired:

> In my opinion it is not a good idea to seek to create the new literature by citing the case of proletarian journalists. The activity of these journalists is interesting, and they can provide the movement with a strong element of proletarian common sense, but they lack the resources necessary to form a worthy basis for proletarian revolutionary literature.[3]

And, in order to protect himself from the general attack that was launched by the conference on 'bourgeois literature' (an attack which, inside the Soviet Union, had already led to the persecution of Pilnyak and Zamyatin and had been a contributory factor in the suicide of Mayakovsky) he used his influence within the French Communist movement to see to it that the resolutions of the Kharkov congress were not implemented in France.[4]

This episode is revealing in itself of the degree of independence that Barbusse still attempted to retain after his conversion to Communism, but it is quite overshadowed in significance by the idiosyncratic way in which he implemented the decisions taken by the Sixth Congress of the Comintern on the tactics to be employed in the fight against Fascism. Whereas the Comintern decreed that it was the Social Democrats who were the principal harbingers of Fascism, Barbusse was convinced that it was men like Mussolini and Hitler who represented the major threat to the cause of world peace. In this situation he believed that it was imperative to rally as much support as possible against the danger of war. Already in 1929, he had played a leading part in organising a Congress against Fascism that was held in Berlin. Three years later he helped to found the most famous of all the organisations with which his name was to be associated, the World Committee against Fascism and War. Two great congresses of intellectuals were gathered together by this committee, in Amsterdam in 1932, and in the Salle Pleyel in Paris in the following year. Although it would be straining the evidence too far to say that, by concentrating his energy on the struggle against the Right, and by inviting to these congresses representatives from all sections of progressive opinion, including Social Democrats, Barbusse was anticipating the policy of the Popular Front, it is clear that he was interpreting the Moscow line with a considerable degree of flexibility.

Admittedly he was far from reckless in the pursuit of his aims. The Comintern was anxious to use the Amsterdam–Pleyel movement to rally public opinion in Western Europe against a possible attack on the Soviet Union by Japan or Germany, while party leaders like Thorez wanted to use the movement in order to detach many of the Socialist rank and file from their party machine. In the course of his campaign against Fascism, therefore, Barbusse appealed for all men of good will to defend the Soviet Union whilst simultaneously making the ritual attacks on the leaders of Social Democracy that Communist orthodoxy demanded. Furthermore none of the organisations that he founded were quite what they might appear to the politically uninitiated. Although Barbusse repeatedly denied that his campaigns were controlled by the Communists, the League against Imperialism which he helped to found in Brussels in 1927, the Congress against Fascism that was held in Berlin in 1929, and the Amsterdam–Pleyel movement itself, were all in fact masterminded by the celebrated German Communist Willi Münzenberg, the arch-exponent of the front organisation, a man who, according to Arthur Koestler, produced committees as a conjurer produces rabbits out of a hat.[5] In running his many organisations Münzenberg was careful to avoid the weaknesses that had destroyed Clarté by seeing to it that resolutions of which the Communists disapproved were quietly dropped or side-tracked, and that persistent objectors to the tactics employed by the Communists were eventually forced out of positions of prominence.

Nevertheless it would be quite wrong to imply that, by manipulating their organisations in the way that they did, Barbusse and Münzenberg were only concerned to force their supporters into a slavish acceptance of the Communist party line. On the contrary, it would be easy to refute such a charge simply by examining some of the opinions expressed in Barbusse's newspaper *Monde*, the main propaganda organ that he used to publicise the aims of the Amsterdam–Pleyel movement. The fact that the author of *Le Feu* had only been able to establish this newspaper with the aid of subsidies from Moscow did not deter him from opening its columns to an extraordinary variety of individuals. Among the contributors to *Monde* were not only Socialists such as the Belgian Henri de Man – whose *Au delà du Marxisme*, published in 1927, had been a devastating critique of the antiquated nature of Marxism – but also ex-Communists such as the Italian writer Ignazio Silone. Indeed, in some ways it seemed that Barbusse had a weakness for renegades: in the spring of 1933, at a time when the Comintern was attributing the entire responsibility for Hitler's triumph to the treachery of the German Social Democrats, yet another ex-Communist was pointing out in the pages of *Monde* that the Communists themselves must bear a considerable share of the blame.[6]

This was heresy of a rather serious kind, and throughout 1932 and 1933 Barbusse and Münzenberg were regarded with some suspicion and hostility in many influential circles within the Soviet Union (where *Monde* was, in fact, banned). How, then, did they survive? The skill which Münzenberg displayed in maintaining a position of some influence within the German Communist Party and the Comintern is certainly one factor that helps to explain this situation, and the support that he and Barbusse received from Thorez is another. But the main reason must surely be that, despite Münzenberg's growing misgivings, Barbusse at least was determined never to fall foul of Stalin.

Quite early in his career as a Communist, in fact, Barbusse was clear that Stalin was the man of the future. In 1927, for example, after his first visit to Russia, he published *Voici ce qu'on a fait de la Géorgie* which described the events that had taken place in Georgia since the overthrow of the Menshevik régime in 1921: in Barbusse's hands the brutal and treacherous way in which Stalin had treated both the Mensheviks and the Bolsheviks was completely glossed over, despite the fact that the methods which had been employed by Stalin had greatly disturbed the dying Lenin. In 1928 Barbusse returned to the Soviet Union and spent a year there, travelling and writing up his impressions: the result, *Russie*, which was published in 1930, included even more flattering references to Stalin. In 1932 Barbusse agreed to write a biography of Stalin, a biography which appeared in 1935 and in which Stalin is described as a man 'with the head of a scholar, with the figure of a worker, and with the dress of a simple soldier'.[7] Stalin is also portrayed as the only true heir of Lenin. Trotsky, with whom the author of *Le Feu* had had friendly relations in the middle of the 1920s, is depicted as an intriguer who had opposed the Bolshevik seizure of power in the first place, a troublesome deviationist who had always remained a Menshevik at heart.

This, then, was the price that Barbusse had to pay in order to pursue his campaigns without too much interference from Moscow, and to posterity it cannot but seem that the price was far too high. Of course for all Communist sympathisers in the 1930s the achievements of the Soviet Union under the leadership of Stalin was a subject that evoked deep respect and veneration. To Charles Vildrac, a friend of Romain Rolland and the author of *Russie Neuve*, the Soviet Union in 1935 appeared as 'a great free road on free soil, towards distant perspectives, along which a whole people audaciously advances'.[8] In *Quinze ans de combat* Rolland himself praised 'the firm yet gentle hand' of Stalin who was guiding the Russian Revolution towards an even greater comprehension of the 'rights of the spirit'.[9] And, at a time when the capitalist system in the West seemed to be far gone in decline, at a time when Fascism was rapidly extending its influence throughout Europe, such an attitude was at least understandable. Even by Communist standards, however, there was an egregious quality about the adulation that Barbusse was prepared to lavish on the Russian dictator, and, when the unctuous terms in which the author of *Le Feu* was accustomed to praise Stalin are contrasted with the former's constant denunciation of the evils of the West, it is clear that more than most party members Barbusse was vulnerable to the charge of pharisaism.

Barbusse tried to counter this charge by explaining in his book on Russia that since the capitalist press lies continually about conditions in Russia it is legitimate for Communist sympathisers themselves to tell lies in defence of the Soviet régime, but there is considerable evidence to show that his own personal integrity was gradually corrupted by his involvement in this kind of activity. Like so many writers whose early inspiration had faded and whose continuing reputation had come to depend on their membership of the Communist Party, like so many Western moralists who were flattered by the way in which they were lionised by their hosts in the Soviet Union, Barbusse, in fact, became the victim of his own vanity in the years that followed the First World War.

Many observers have borne testimony to this. While Louis Fischer's recollections of Barbusse in Moscow are that he talked for most of the time about Jesus Christ,[10] the Hungarian Communist Ervin Sinkó describes Barbusse in extremely unflattering terms in his memoirs as an accomplished and devious practitioner of literary politics, using the German Communist Alfred Kurella to write the biography of Stalin that later appeared under Barbusse's own name, and then insisting that Kurella should hand over half the receipts from this publication.[11] Margarete Buber-Neumann, the sister-in-law of Willi Münzenberg, contrasts Barbusse's public eulogies of the achievements of the Soviet Union at the official opening of the Dnieper dam in 1932 with his behaviour back at his hotel, and paints a satirical picture of the author of *Le Feu* complaining about the inadequacy of the accommodation that had been provided for him:

> I was very surprised that my idol Barbusse displayed such traits of the bourgeois and the prima donna in his character and that, despite the great socialist achievement that had just been accomplished, he was not prepared to forgo his creature comforts. It is particularly ironical in view of the fact that once when someone reproached him for not telling the truth about conditions in the U.S.S.R. Barbusse replied that a Communist had the duty to remain silent about any difficulties in the Soviet Union because these difficulties would be overcome.[12]

And, if these comments are thought too trivial to be significant, there is the evidence of Barbusse's dealings with Victor Serge in a far more serious matter. After holding a number of important posts in the Comintern in the early 1920s, the latter (who was of Russian origin) subsequently became involved with the Trotskyist opposition to Stalin within the U.S.S.R. When he tried to make Barbusse aware of the terror that was already being employed against the opposition, however, he found that he had undertaken an impossible task:

> When I told him about the persecution, he pretended to have a headache, or not to hear, or to be rising to stupendous heights: 'Tragic destiny of revolution, immensities, profundities, yes... yes...Ah my friend!' My jaws juddered as I realised that I was face to face with hypocrisy itself.[13]

Whether by the time of his death Barbusse really believed that all the conflicts and wars that afflicted the world could be attributed to capitalism and imperialism, however, whether he really believed in the infallibility of a system of 'social geometry' that could produce a figure such as Stalin – these are questions to which there is no certain answer. In one sense it might seem that he was protected from despair:

> Social truth is simple. Things that are complicated are those which have been buried beneath the accumulation of errors and prejudices created by generations of tyrants, parasites and lawyers...The man who wants to arrive at the truth must simplify. He must have a brutally simple faith or else he is lost.

People of the world, you will never possess this simplicity
unless you take hold of it. If you want it, take it in your hands
yourselves. I give you the talisman, the magical and extraordinary words: you can.[14]

Already by the end of the First World War, therefore, there was
a pronounced tendency for Barbusse to escape from unpleasant
facts by seeking refuge in high-sounding phrases, and this was a
tendency that became more pronounced as the years went by. At
one moment his search for a panacea for the ills of the world led
him to launch a campaign in favour of Esperanto. At another
moment his passion for flying could be used to avoid any discussion of awkward problems that might arise on the ground:

When you fly in an aeroplane you have a new vision of the
world, a new vision which is superimposed upon the one you
have held up to that time. . .the pedestrian is limited to details
and is condemned to see little things. When you rise above the
world, above the inhabited world, there is silence, immobility
and grandeur. This grandeur is made up of little things all of
which you can take in at one glance. No longer is one confined
to the sentimental, individual or egotistical point of view.[15]

But it is impossible to maintain an attitude like this for very
long. Clearly Barbusse himself was not satisfied by the 'brutally
simple faith' that he urged on others. The very importance that
he attached to the rôle of clarity and reason in human affairs
betrayed the extent to which he suffered from inner anxieties and
doubts, and, even if his later writings never exhibit the same
pessimism (or the same literary quality) that is apparent in
Pleureuses and *L'Enfer*, there is ample evidence to show that he
never really emancipated himself from the despair that had
dominated his youth.

'It is difficult enough to fight capitalism, but even more difficult
to fight oneself', he once remarked to the Russian writer Ilya
Ehrenburg,[16] and even Serge, in his otherwise hostile portrait of
Barbusse, describes him as a man who had known suffering.
Perhaps it was in *Jésus* and in the collection of short stories that
he published in 1925 under the title of *Force* that Barbusse most
clearly revealed the nature of the fear that haunted him. In *Jésus*,
which he dedicated 'to all the troubled and tormented souls of

our time,' he makes it plain that even if all the material problems
of the poor were capable of solution men would still be lonely
and unhappy, and in *Force* he gave an even more unambiguous
statement of his conviction that the misery of the human condition is irremediable. The first story in this collection, *La Force* is
the story of an inventor living in the days of the Roman Empire
who discovers a new source of energy which he is able to harness
for the benefit of mankind but is then faced with the problem of
to whom he should entrust his discovery. The main part of the
novel shows the way in which the inventor is progressively disillusioned with all the political factions and social groupings with
whom he comes in contact, for all of them want to make use of
his discovery for purely selfish ends. Eventually he is obliged to
destroy his invention. Admittedly Barbusse indicates that at some
time in the future humanity might be ready to take advantage of
the blessings that this inventor had been prepared to bestow on
it, and yet the main impression that is left by the novel is that
such an outcome is unlikely.

'Every state except one is moving through Fascism towards
ruin', Barbusse lamented in his biography of Stalin.[17] Of *one*
thing the author of *Le Feu* does seem to have been certain in the
last years of his life – another world war was on the horizon
unless the peoples of the world organised themselves against this
danger. This, no doubt, was the main reason why he clung so
tenaciously to his faith in the Soviet Union and Stalin. With the
advent of Hitler to power in Germany, therefore, he redoubled
his efforts to combat Fascism. In 1933 he went to the United
States to found an American league against capitalism and war.
Back in Europe he played an important part in the successful
fight to save the life of the Bulgarian Communist Georgi Dimitrov
(who had been put on trial by the Nazis on a charge of complicity
in the Reichstag fire), and led a fruitless campaign to secure the
release of the German Communist leader Ernst Thälmann from
the concentration camp into which he had been thrown. In 1934
Barbusse's attention shifted to his own country where, with the
outbreak of the February riots in Paris, he became convinced
that the Fascists were attempting to seize power.[18] In order to
combat this he strove to gather as many writers and intellectuals
as possible in an anti-Fascist front. In this enterprise he achieved
considerable success: the French delegation at the Congress in

Defense of Culture that he organised in Paris in 1935 was a particularly distinguished one, with Gide, Malraux, Aragon and Rolland in attendance.

1935, indeed, promised to be an unusually busy year for Barbusse. On 14 July he took a prominent part in the traditional workers' rally held in the Place de la Bastille, a rally which attracted an unusually large number of supporters following the agreement that had at long last been reached between the Socialists and the Communists to work together in a Popular Front. That evening he attended another rally at the Buffalo Stadium at which, arm in arm with Thorez, Blum and Daladier, he pledged himself to the fight against war. By the end of July he was in the Soviet Union where he proposed to start work on a film based on the life of Stalin.[10] Meanwhile his efforts to alert mankind to the Fascist danger were acclaimed by the Seventh Congress of the Comintern.

At this point, however, the physical weakness from which he had suffered since the First World War now took its revenge on him. After contracting pneumonia, Barbusse died in Moscow on 30 August.

One year after his death there began the public trials of the Old Bolshevik leaders in Russia, trials which prompted Romain Rolland to declare that he believed in the complete guilt of the accused and that he had no reason to doubt the impartiality of the judicial system that condemned them.[20] In 1939 Stalin agreed to the Non-aggression pact with Nazi Germany that left France at Hitler's mercy. In 1940 Willi Münzenberg, who had broken with Moscow after the onset of the purges, was murdered during the fall of France – probably by members of the French Communist Party or agents of the N.K.V.D.

The author of Le Feu was spared the final acts of the tragedy of European Communism in the 1930s, however. After an impressive funeral ceremony in Moscow on 2 September 1935 his body was brought back by train through Nazi Germany to Paris where it was laid to rest in the cemetery of Père Lachaise. Crowds lined the streets as the coffin passed slowly by. Despite his controversy with Rolland in the early 1920s Barbusse could never resolve his own doubts and anxieties over the problem of violence and throughout all his peace campaigns in the 1920s and 1930s there had been a major contradiction between his appeals for resistance

to Fascism and his simultaneous demands for universal dis-
armament. But the illusion that words were a substitute for action
was almost universal within the French Left in its fight against
Fascism in the early 1930s, and it would be churlish to criticise
Barbusse too harshly for his efforts to spare mankind another
holocaust like the one that had taken place between 1914 and
1918. There is a certain poignancy in the fact that even during
his final illness he telephoned to France every day in order to
organise yet another campaign in favour of peace:

> 'Abyssinia', he told his secretary, 'can lead to a major war and
> that can only be avoided if we do something big, very big.
> Certainly we have already increased our efforts, but that is not
> enough. We must expand. . .expand. . .expand.'[21]

Perhaps it was fitting, therefore, that accompanying the cortège
at his funeral there was a group of men whose fate had never
been far from his thoughts – invalids from the First World War
in their wheelchairs.

PART II

DRIEU LA ROCHELLE AND FASCISM

The army began to break up. Under the first fury of fire one
part became separated from another. Already they could hardly
see each other: in a very short space of time they could not see
each other at all. And for four years their efforts and their
sufferings took place parallel with each other without their ever
meeting. Artillery and infantry looked for each other, but never
met. And the generals were somewhere else. Already we were
nothing more than groups of men lost in the abominable
solitude of the modern battlefield.

La Comédie de Charleroi, p. 45.

4

THE DECADENT

It would hardly be an exaggeration to say that a feeling that Western civilisation was in a process of total disintegration was widespread in Europe at the end of the First World War, for if the most striking expression of this view was Spengler's *The Decline of the West*, which was published in 1918, there were many other writers who were of a similar opinion. In his poem 'The Scythians', written in 1918, the Russian poet Alexander Blok announced that the civilisation of humanism had been destroyed by the war and that a new civilisation based on the masses had taken its place, and it has already been seen that Romain Rolland himself was amongst those who came to the conclusion that Europe was dying and that the only hope for the world lay in Asia. Asia exercised a considerable fascination on the young André Malraux, too. After his first journey to Indo-China in 1923 he attacked the sterility of European culture in his essay 'La Tentation de l'Occident' (1926), and in the next few years he moved from the realm of theory to that of practice by devoting himself to the Nationalist and Communist revolt against Western imperialism that was developing in Saigon and Canton.

The case of Malraux is spectacular enough in itself to show the appeal that was exercised by the idea of the decline of the West in France in the 1920s, and yet perhaps the most radical expression of this idea is to be found, not in anything written by Malraux, but in two essays that were published in 1927 by a writer who, seven years older than Malraux, had fought in the First World War and was eventually to become a Fascist. This writer was Pierre Drieu la Rochelle, and the title of the book was *Le jeune Européen*.

The first essay in this book, 'Le sang et l'encre', tells the story of a young European who examines the various stages of his life after his return from the First World War and then analyses the reasons that have led him to become a writer. The second essay, 'Le Music-hall', consists of a meditation in which the same young

European reflects on the nature of the civilisation in which he is living. Not surprisingly, in view of his experiences during the First World War and its aftermath, he comes to the conclusion that this civilisation is dead: the war has destroyed everything, society has lost its meaning, and the only way in which men can communicate with one another is for them to accept the fact that their lives are theatrical and unreal. In this music-hall atmosphere each European nation has lost its sense of identity – the Italians are enthusiastic and empty, the Spaniards forgotten, the French anaesthetised, the English bereft of their power, the Scandinavians preserved in ice, and the Germans stupefied with work. It is only the young Slav nation who possess any vigour, but it is their misfortune to have been born too late into a world that has grown old. In the years between the end of the First World War and his conversion to Fascism, in fact, Drieu's pessimism was cosmic in its implications: If Europe was in decline, he maintained, so too was Asia, America, and the planet as a whole.[1]

Drieu la Rochelle was well equipped to investigate the phenomenon of decadence. He was born in 1893 into a wealthy bourgeois family, but the near-ruin of the family fortunes by his father was to haunt him for the rest of his life. Already as a child he was obsessed by a constant fear of failure, and already as a child he tried to overcome this fear by indulging himself in heroic, romantic fantasies; he was fascinated by the Napoleonic legend, and dreamt of a career as a soldier commanding a fort in the Sudan. The fact that at school he did not display in athletic pursuits the same proficiency that he showed in his academic work only intensified his desire to incarnate the heroic virtues.

As a result of this background it was almost inevitable that he should have been greatly attracted by the nationalist revival that was taking place in France in the years before 1914, and in the doctrines of Maurras he was able to find, not only a critique of liberalism that he greatly admired, but also a quality of extremism that influenced him profoundly throughout the rest of his career. In the combination of individualistic aestheticism and political commitment to be found in the work of Maurice Barrès, Drieu discovered something that was even more important to him. In his capacity as a public figure Barrès preached a romantic nationalism and Bonapartism that was in revolt against the narrow rationalism of the nineteenth century. In his writings Barrès analysed the problems of a soul divided between impulses towards anarchy and a deep-seated desire for discipline. Both these themes made an irresistible appeal to the young Drieu la Rochelle.

Significantly enough in the light of his later career, however, it was to a German and not to a French writer that he was most deeply indebted for opening his eyes to the reality of the world. Drieu was fourteen years old when he lost his faith in Catholicism and it was in the same year that he read *Thus Spake Zarathustra*. Nietzsche was to remain the formative influence on him for the rest of his life. From this point onwards Drieu became convinced that, with the decay of traditional religious values, there was an urgent need for men to discover some new Myth that would save Western civilisation from the destruction that awaited it. And from this point, too, Drieu was fascinated by the idea of self-annihilation. It was through his reading of Nietzsche that he discovered Schopenhauer, and it was through the latter that he came in contact with Eastern philosophy and religion. Already as a young man he experienced in an acute form the temptation of despair: in 1913, when he failed his examinations at the École des Sciences Politiques, he seriously considered the idea of suicide.

At the outbreak of the First World War he was in the army completing his period of military service, but, as he confessed many years later in his autobiographical short story *La Comédie de Charleroi*, the initial stages of his contact with army life had been a tedious and exasperating experience:

I went into the war like a civilian – so little had I been a soldier in the unmilitary life of an army penned up in barracks in the Paris garrison. All we knew was the theory and the ridiculous performances on the parade ground. We knew nothing about life in the field. We remained immobile throughout the winter, trying to keep ourselves free from epidemics. In the spring the regiment exercised itself a little, but I avoided unimaginative gymnastics. The only thing I liked was marching when I could escape into daydreams. And throughout all this time I was caught between the nationalism to which I had subscribed before coming into the army and my practice of slipping away and dodging the column to seek refuge in a book or in my own thoughts. I did this even though I was shocked if others did the same thing.[2]

From this kind of existence, therefore, the declaration of war was at first an act of liberation:

> What did I feel when war was declared? Freedom from the barracks, the end of old ideas, the opening up of new possibilities for me. . .It was so marvellous that I did not think it could happen. I was sceptical. I thought that all this mobilisation in Europe was nothing but a bluff and that men would be so frightened by the scale of the operation they had mounted that, after going through some kind of manoeuvres, they would call it off before they came to blows. Even if they *did* come to blows I thought that the enormous armies of troops would get out of control and would eventually have to disperse for lack of munitions and provisions. . .I was prepared to wager that this would happen and promised to give my friends three bottles of champagne even if the regiment only got as far as leaving the barracks. Soon I had to take note of what was happening. The fight was on. When I read the first news of the battles in Russia and in Alsace my hopes surged up again.[3]

But soon the attractions of war began to pall as his regiment was forced to take part in interminable marches and countermarches near the Belgian frontier, and once again Drieu began to think about the possibility of committing suicide. He was overwhelmed by a sense that he was only a small cog in the vast and anonymous machine of war, and he was afraid that if he were put to the test he would prove to be a coward.

His first encounter with the enemy reassured him on this score, however. Under the stimulus of battle he realised that he was capable of reacting with courage and determination, and at last, towards the end of August 1914, all things were revealed to him. In the course of a bayonet charge at the battle of Charleroi, the first major battle between the French and the Germans in 1914, he discovered what for him was the real significance of human existence:

> Suddenly I knew about myself, I knew about life. This strong free hero was me. This game that went on without end was my

life. . .Who was it who suddenly came forth? A leader. Not merely a man, a leader. Not merely a man who gives of himself, but a man who takes. . .In my hands I held victory and liberty. Liberty. Man is free, he can do what he wants. Man is a part of the world and, in a moment of paroxysm, in a moment of eternity, each part of the world can realise within itself every thing that is possible.
Victory.
The victory of men. Over what? Over nothing; beyond everything. Over nature? It is not a matter of conquering nature or even of surmounting it but of expanding it to its maximum since the power to do is within us. It is not a question of conquering fear by means of courage, but of mixing fear with courage and courage with fear so that one can lift oneself up as far as one can go. . .In this moment I felt the unity of life. . .
The same gesture for eating and loving, for acting and thinking, for living and dying.
Life is a continuous flow, a continuous flow.
I wanted to live and die at the same time.[4]

This description of Drieu's reactions at the beginning of the First World War was written twenty years afterwards in 1934 when he had just been converted to Fascism, and yet from the evidence of the poetry that he wrote during the First World War itself it is clear that in later years he did not exaggerate the impact that the experience of battle had originally made on him. In these poems (published in 1917 under the title of *Interrogation*) Drieu celebrates the spirit of struggle and combat in which life must be lived if it is to be possessed of any grandeur. He is insistent that without suffering and danger and without the qualities that men must develop in order to fight against suffering and danger human existence would be doomed to futility:

Comme l'été flambait par toute l'Europe dans les
Champs de blé et les sombres entrailles de usines
Une force renaquit
La force du soldat
Notre vie alourdie en fut secouée et mise en branle, l'ivresse
versée par la coupe ensoleilée des trompettes
Nour reprit tout d'un coup
Se sentir mille et mille et adorés de son peuple

Les femmes avec leurs bouches rouges dirent: 'Nous sommes
vos femmes
O, nos mâles, allez tuer!'[5]

Nevertheless by the time that *Interrogation* was published
Drieu's attitude towards the war was much more complicated
than might be indicated by pretentious juvenilia such as this. At
the beginning of the war he regarded the struggle between the
nations in terms of a conflict between two opposing forces of
Nietzschean Supermen who would perform great deeds of
heroism, and, after the bayonet charge at Charleroi, he did not
hesitate to claim that the kind of exultation that he had felt in the
course of the battle was comparable with the ecstasy that had
been experienced by the religious mystics of the past. But he
reacted in this way because he had little experience of the kind
of mass slaughter that is the inevitable accompaniment of modern
technological warfare. He had been slightly wounded at the
battle of Charleroi (a battle which, despite Drieu's heroics, had
actually resulted in a French defeat) and he was stricken down
with dysentery when he was sent to the Dardanelles in 1915, but,
until he sustained severe injuries from an enemy shell shortly
after his arrival in Verdun in 1916, he was not called upon to take
part in a battle in which individual acts of courage and endur-
ance were rendered meaningless by the changing character of the
conflict.

Once he did experience the reality of modern warfare, however, he rebelled against it, as he made clear in yet another of
the poems published in *Interrogation*:

Ce cri qui sortit de moi, ce cri que je mis au monde dans une
déchirure d'accouchement.
Ce cri né dans un repli de ma chair si intime.
Je ne pouvais l'extirper de l'ordre des faits accomplis par aucun
reniement
Il ne faudra l'avouer jusqu'à la fin de ma vie.
Ce cri de révolte
Ce jour-là à Verdun, je fus celui qui crie non à la douleur.
Je fus parmi ceux qui crient non à la douleur.[6]

And from now on Drieu's attitude towards the problem of war
was profoundly ambivalent, so ambivalent that the censor made

an unsuccessful attempt to prevent the publication of *Interrogation* in the summer of 1917.

By the time that this had happened, however, Drieu's period of active service was virtually over: the injuries that he sustained at Verdun necessitated a long period of convalescence, and, although he managed to return to the front as an interpreter with an American division in the autumn of 1918, by that time the end of the war was already in sight.

Nevertheless, the conclusion of the Armistice did not afford him great satisfaction. Already during the war he had been haunted by the fear that the world to which he would return if he survived would not be worthy of the sacrifices which his generation had been called upon to make, and the reality of peace, when it arrived, was to be worse than he had anticipated. Very soon after his demobilisation he was appalled by the ease with which so many of his former comrades allowed themselves to forget the lessons that they had learnt in the war, and unutterably dismayed by the eagerness with which men lost themselves in that mad scramble for money and power that had been characteristic of European society in the years before 1914. In reaction against the materialism of the post-war world, and in reaction against the unhappiness caused by the failure of his first marriage, therefore, he plunged into all the distractions that Paris had to offer in the 1920s. The fact that he was sufficiently wealthy not to have to worry about earning his living made his pursuit of pleasure particularly frenzied. These were the years in which Drieu belonged to the society of 'le Tout-Paris', in which he patronised the celebrated 'Le Boeuf sur le Toit', the years of his friendship with the poet Louis Aragon, and of his involvement with Surrealism.

Surrealism had developed out of Dadaism, an intellectual and artistic movement that had been founded in Switzerland during the First World War in protest against the madness and futility of the slaughter that was taking place in the rest of Europe. In the arts Dadaism became synonymous with a frenetic concern for novelty. Politically it was anarchist. The aims of the Surrealists were very similar to those of their parent movement, but where they differed from their predecessors was in the degree to which they attempted to provide a more sophisticated basis for their repudiation of the existing order of things: while sharing the same destructive urges that had been apparent in the work of the Dadaists they were also concerned to utilise all the recent discoveries that had been made about the rôle of the subconscious in order to emphasise the absurdity of conventional values.

All this, of course, was something to which Drieu was bound instinctively to respond, particularly after the disillusionments that he had experienced in the years after 1914. Like the Surrealists he, too, had come to the conclusion that life is inherently meaningless, and that the only kind of truth that men can discover is fundamentally subjective and irrational in character. And yet it is important to note that he never committed himself totally to the Surrealists and that by the middle of the 1920s, he had broken with the movement completely.

The reasons behind this development were various. In a political sense Drieu's revolt against existing society had never been identical with that of the Surrealists: politically he was a man of the Right with leanings towards anarchy, a revolutionary position but one which inevitably led him to repudiate the Communist tendencies that were latent in Surrealism, tendencies that finally made themselves manifest in 1925 when a number of the movement's sympathisers (including Aragon) expressed their support for the Communists at the time of the French involvement in the Moroccan war. In any case by 1925 it had become clear to Drieu that many of the activities of the Surrealists affronted his deepseated pessimism. Unlike many of the Surrealists, for whom the appeal of the movement's doctrines lay in the fact that they provided the most effective method of shocking the bourgeoisie, he could not take so frivolous a view of the problems of the postwar world. What particularly appalled him about the action of the Surrealists in giving their support to the Communists was that this seemed to indicate that they believed that the anxieties and the miseries of the individual human being could be forgotten in the service of some collective good. This was an attitude that seemed to him to smack of escapism.

Indeed, it was the profound sense of despair that led to Drieu's break with the Surrealists in 1925 that was also to provide the one great theme in the fictional work that he was to produce in the years that followed the First World War. Like Drieu himself, in fact, all the 'heroes' of his novels are creatures of torment, victims of the nihilism inherent in the society of the modern great city. And again like Drieu himself, all these heroes are perpetually haunted by the idea of self-destruction. Alain, for example, the principal character of Le Feu Follet (1931) is a gigolo who lives on the income that is provided by his wealthy mistress, but he is also a drug-addict and the novel is a description of the last days of his life before he decides to commit suicide. After his adoption of Fascism in 1934 Drieu was still preoccupied with the theme of decadence and death. The son of the unhappy middle-class family described in Rêveuse bourgeoisie (1937) may seem to escape from the curse of heredity and the misery of his family background by joining the army at the outbreak of the First World War, but his death in the course of the war can be seen to be just as much an act of suicide as an act of true heroism. Even in Drieu's most ambitious novel, the semi-autobiographical Gilles (1939), which traces the career of a Parisian intellectual from his return from the First World War to his conversion to Fascism in the 1930s, it is not clear whether the action of Gilles in joining the Nationalist forces in the Spanish civil war is prompted by his hope that the Fascist cause will be triumphant, or whether he is consumed by an overriding desire to get himself killed.

On the other hand, if it is true to say that even after his espousal of Fascism Drieu's outlook on the world was characterised by despair, it would be a complete misrepresentation of his position to neglect or to ignore the positive element in his work, an element that was to find particular expression in the political writings that he produced in the years after the end of the First World War. As Maurice Martin du Gard has pointed out in his memoirs of Parisian life in the 1920s, the author of Le Feu Follet and Le Jeune Européen was a much more complicated personality than one might at first think:

If I wrote that Drieu went to Maxim's to think about the war, no one would believe me. Nevertheless when he went into the bar it was always for him the first evening of his seven days leave. In the morning he had been in the mud and cold of the trenches. Now he was enjoying a period of convalescence after being wounded. . .Smart and well-washed he was now leaving hospital in a uniform that he had designed for himself – an adjutant's uniform with a lot of stripes on his arm, a simple ribbon of the Croix de Guerre on his chest and, discreetly, in a semi-circle below this a small scale replica of the glorious insignia of the 146th regiment of infantry.[7]

The fact was that, like so many of the followers of Barrès, Drieu was a narcissist but a narcissist who was continually engaged in an attempt to escape from the prison of the Self. Although in the 1920s he found it difficult to abandon his individualism and follow other disciples of Barrès like Malraux and Aragon who were moving closer to Communism, he, too, was searching for salvation through some kind of political commitment.

Throughout the 1920s, in fact, Drieu's overriding concern was to resolve the contradictions that existed in his view of the world, to reconcile his Nietzscheanism with the lessons that he had learnt at Verdun, to overcome the conflict between the nationalism that he had supported in the years before 1914 and his hatred of modern technological warfare. Indeed, it would hardly be an exaggeration to say that it was because of these very tensions that Drieu was to prove such an acute observer of French society in the years that followed the First World War, for, as a decadent constantly engaged in an attempt to triumph over decadence, who was better equipped than he to analyse the problems of the French nation in an era of decline? And as a patriot who believed that the age of the nation state had now come to an end, who was better qualified than he to examine the state of Europe in the 1920s? If events were to demonstrate that it was only by identifying his own fate with that of his country that Drieu could give a meaning and a purpose to his life, time alone was to show that it was only a writer with Drieu's temperament and experience who could fully reveal the weaknesses of France in the post-war world.

It would be difficult to deny that the decline of France was one of the major political facts of the nineteenth century. At the time of the Revolutionary and Napoleonic wars France had dominated the rest of Europe, not only because she produced skilful generals, but also because in social and economic terms she was the most advanced nation on the continent, a nation which, in addition to these advantages, was possessed of a revolutionary message of wide appeal. By 1914, however, all this had changed. In terms of population France now ranked fourth in Europe after Russia, Germany and Great Britain. Politically she was ruled by the weak and unstable system of the Third Republic. In terms of industrial power it has been estimated that by the time of the outbreak of the First World War the relative strength of Germany, Britain and France could be expressed in terms of the ratio of 3:2:1. If this state of affairs boded ill for England, traditionally the greatest industrial and naval power in Europe, even more serious were the implications for France.

In view of all this it is not surprising that long before the outbreak of the First World War there were a number of Frenchmen who felt nothing but despair when they contemplated what the future might hold for their country. 'France is dying. Do not disturb her agony.'[8] These were the terrible words with which Renan had chided Déroulède for his activities in the Ligue des Patriotes towards the end of the nineteenth century. And, with the increasing tension that became evident in Europe in the years after the first Moroccan crisis, there was always a subconscious fear amongst Frenchmen that in any contest with Germany their country was inevitably doomed to defeat. And yet, if the basic facts of French decline were beyond dispute, there were very few Frenchmen who were potential defeatists in the years before the outbreak of the First World War. On the contrary, it was in the years between 1905 and 1914 that the influence of the nationalist revival made itself increasingly felt.

The presiding spirits of this nationalist revival, it is true, were not united over the methods by which they hoped to restore their country to its rightful position in the world: the political ideal of Barrès was essentially Bonapartist in inspiration – he accepted many of the ideals of 1789 but wished to see them expressed in a more authoritarian and much more inspiring régime than that of the Third Republic; Péguy, for his part, wanted to combine a revitalised republicanism with a revitalised Catholicism; while Maurras, in contrast to the other two, was an irreconcilable opponent of both republicanism and romanticism and wanted France to embrace his own intensely personal (and intensely ungenerous) solution to the nation's ills, a solution that united royalism and classicism with the positivist philosophy of Auguste Comte. Nevertheless, in spite of these differences, it would be difficult to exaggerate the influence of the nationalist ideologists on a whole generation of French middle-class youth in the years before 1914. Repeatedly they urged the necessity for Frenchmen to overcome their divisions and stand firm against the overweening ambitions of the Second Reich. Repeatedly they proclaimed that, if only France would have confidence in herself, the days of retreat would be ended and the days of glory would return.

In a certain sense the days of glory *did* return, for although the arguments of the Nationalists did not go unchallenged, and although the battle between Nationalists and Socialists over questions of foreign policy was to become increasingly bitter in the years before 1914, with the outbreak of the First World War, and, even more, with France's eventual victory at the end of that war, it seemed as if the wildest dreams of the Nationalists had been fulfilled. At the beginning of the war, despite the assassination of Jaurès by a Nationalistic fanatic in July 1914, the formation of the Union Sacrée seemed to indicate that Frenchmen were at last uniting against the German danger. At the end of the war the German menace seemed to have been entirely removed. In 1919, for the first time since the fall of Napoleon III, France appeared to be the greatest military power in Europe.

And yet there was another side to the picture, and the position of France was not really as secure as it seemed in the immediate aftermath of the First World War. As far as the internal situation of the country was concerned it has already been seen that the political and social divisions that had been surmounted by the promulgation of the Union Sacrée had reasserted themselves once again by 1917, and these divisions were to become even more pronounced with the emergence of a powerful Communist party in 1920. Then there was the cost of the war to the French people to be taken into consideration: 1·7 million of France's able-bodied men had been killed between 1914 and 1918, and 740,000 were seriously injured. But this was not all: the loss was qualitative as well as quantitative since the proportion of fatalities was greatest within the officer class. Maurice Barrès once pointed out that of the 161 students of the 1911, 1912 and 1913 promotions to the École Normale Supérieure (the pinnacle of the French educational system) who had been conscripted in 1914, 81 were dead or missing and 64 wounded by the end of the war.[9] With figures such as these it is hardly surprising that pacifism was to make the appeal that it did in France in the period between the wars or that the quality of leadership in all sections of French public life was to be a subject that provoked constant concern. For twenty-five years after 1919, at a time when their country needed all the resources of courage and initiative she could find, the French people were determined that they would never again be forced to endure another experience like that of the First World War, and for a whole generation after the signing of the Treaty of Versailles effective power was in the hands of men who were either too old or too exhausted to match up to their responsibilities.

The situation might not have been so dangerous had the nation's external position been reasonably secure, but this was far from being the case. The truth of the matter was that France had only been able to emerge with victory at the end of the First World War because she had received the support of powerful allies, and in the course of the next twenty years she was to discover that it was impossible to reconstruct the coalition of forces that had triumphed in 1918. In Europe she had already lost her traditional ally to contain the ambitions of Germany in the East as a result of the Bolshevik Revolution and Russia's withdrawal into isolation, and the system of alliances that she was to build up in the 1920s with the nations that comprised the Little Entente was hardly to prove to be an adequate substitute for the strength that had formerly been provided by the Tsar. In the West, too, the situation was problematical for, although the defection of Russia might not have mattered had France been able to find sufficient support from Britain and the United States to restrain Germany from embarking on yet another war against her, events were to show that this support was extremely difficult to secure. Already at the time of the Peace Conference the Anglo-Saxons had rejected Clemenceau's argument that the annexation of the left bank of the Rhine was essential for French security. And, in the years that followed the Peace Conference, not only did the Senate of the United States refuse to ratify the agreements that had been entered into at Versailles by President Wilson, but even Britain was reluctant to support any rigorous interpretation of the Versailles settlement. The terrible truth about the French situation, then, was that despite all the sacrifices that France had made in the course of the First World War, and despite all the delusions of grandeur to which her victory at the end of the war had given rise, the events that took place in Europe between 1914 and 1918 were to mark yet another stage in the process of French decline. Once Germany had recovered from the political and economic chaos into which she had been plunged as a result of her defeat, she would soon discover that in many ways France was in a weaker position than she had been a generation or so earlier.

The true gravity of France's position was not, of course, to become fully apparent until the rise of Hitler in the following decade, but already in the aftermath of the First World War Drieu was aware what the realities of the French situation were. Despite the fact that he had been a supporter of the Right before 1914 and was still to regard himself as a man of the Right in the years after 1918, it was not long before he became convinced that the only hope for his country lay in her making a radical break with the policies she had pursued in the past. In particular, he became convinced that French policy must no longer be influenced by the kind of nationalism propagated by Barrès and Maurras.

This did not mean that he no longer respected his former masters. He was always deeply moved by the sense of total commitment that Maurras displayed in his devotion to the idea of French greatness, and he was always impressed by the trenchant nature of Maurras's attacks on the weakness and instability of the republican system in France. Barrès, too, was a figure whom he continued to venerate. When, for example, in May 1921, the Dadaists held a mock trial in Paris at which they found Barrès guilty of intellectual treason for his propaganda activities during the First World War, Drieu, who was called upon to testify as a witness for the prosecution, refused to lend his support to any attack on the reputation of a man whom he had idolised ten years previously. It was not the personalities of the Nationalist leaders that he now criticised, it was their policies. And, even as far as their policies were concerned, it was not their aims but the methods by which they intended to pursue their aims that he now repudiated. He still regarded himself as a patriot, and he still believed that his primary duty was to see to it that the interests of his country were properly safeguarded, but two events that had occurred in the war, the success of the

Bolshevik revolution in Russia and his own experiences as an interpreter with the American army in the final stages of the conflict, had caused him to modify his views considerably.

From now on Drieu was convinced that the old Europe was doomed. The theme that dominates his first major political essay, *Mesure de la France*, which was published in 1922, therefore, is the problem of how the greatness of France can best be assured in the new set of circumstances that operated in the post-war world. As the title of this essay implies Drieu's main concern was to demonstrate to his fellow countrymen that France's position was not as secure as it might have seemed in the flush of victory in 1918. The roots of French weakness, he reminded his readers, went far back into the past. In the second half of the nineteenth century France had not expanded her industrial base sufficiently and she had not produced enough children for her to pursue a truly independent policy.[10] In these circumstances it was foolish to believe that France could pursue her aims in isolation from the policies and interests of other powers. The Maurrassian doctrine of 'La France seule' might have made sense in the age of Louis XIV or Napoleon Bonaparte, but it was clearly not suited to the situation in which France now found herself.

In any case, he maintained, the events that had taken place in Europe between 1914 and 1918 had shown that Maurras's obsession with the eternal rivalry that he believed to exist between France and Germany no longer bore much contact with reality.[11] If the war had been possessed of any meaning at all it had shown that the era of the nation state was drawing to a close and that the age of the superpower was close at hand. Was it not significant that in 1917 and 1918 it had been Wilson and Lenin who had taken the initiative in appealing for peace? And, by addressing their appeals over the heads of the other statesmen of Europe, were they not demonstrating the contempt which they must feel for the traditional enmities that divided the smaller powers of the continent? Already it was clear that the decline of Europe was proceeding at an accelerating rate as a result of the growing revolt of Asia and Africa against European imperialism, a revolt that was being encouraged by both the United States and the Soviet Union. And already it was evident that the rivalry between France and Germany must be settled amicably if Europe was not to be dragged into another war that would reduce her influence

in the world even further. The only way in which France and the
rest of the continent could escape from the doom that awaited it,
Drieu was convinced, was for the states of Western and Central
Europe to unite:

> This is not a cosmopolitan dream or the product of an over-
> fertile imagination, it is an urgent necessity, a sordid question
> of life or death. If Europe does not federate she will destroy
> herself or be destroyed by others. And the war generation, who
> do not seem to have realised this, will have to do it or else it
> will be too late.[12]

This need for Europe to unite against the power of the United
States and the Soviet Union which provided the central message
of *Mesure de la France* was put forward with an even greater
sense of urgency by Drieu in a second essay, *Genève ou Moscou*,
which appeared in 1928. By this date, in fact, he had come to the
conclusion that in his earlier work he had underestimated the
degree to which the continent was falling under foreign domination. As far as the United States was concerned he was prepared
to admit that there had certainly been a diminution in her *political*
involvement in Europe as a result of the growth of isolationism,
but American *economic* power was making itself increasingly felt,
and it was only because there had been a considerable influx of
American money into the continent that Europe (particularly
Germany) had been able to enjoy the economic boom that had
been evident since 1924.

This, he believed, was an extremely serious situation, but it
was rendered even more dangerous by the fact that, if the
capitalist system should ever run into serious difficulties, Europe
would not simply be ruined but would then fall into the hands
of the Bolsheviks. Drieu, in fact, was much more concerned by
the threat which menaced Europe from Moscow than that which
was posed by the economic strength of the United States, for it
was not the military power of the Soviet Union that he feared
(although he realised that this would be a factor that would have
to be reckoned with once Russia had gone through the process of
industrialisation) but the appeal that was exercised on many
elements within the European working class by Communism.

How could this danger be overcome? Despite the élitist nature
of his approach to politics Drieu had long been aware that the

active support of the masses was necessary for the stability of any political system in the twentieth century, and for many years before 1928 he had been searching for some way in which the working class could be integrated into the national community. Already in the period before the outbreak of the war, for example, he had been greatly influenced by Sorel's denunciation of the decadence of the bourgeoisie, and for a time during these years he had been a member of the Cercle Proudhon, that remarkable, if short-lived, organisation that had been founded by the younger members of the Action Française in an attempt to widen the appeal of Maurras's doctrines of integral nationalism by uniting them with Sorel's ideas on the heroic mission of the working class. Once the First World War had broken out Drieu's belief that it was possible to achieve some kind of synthesis between nationalism and socialism was further strengthened. In 1914, he was fond of pointing out, the overwhelming majority of the European workers had ignored the decisions of the Second International and had obeyed the appeals of their governments to support the war. And in the course of the war the experience of the trenches had shown that all men were brothers in the face of death. Surely, he argued, this could only mean that the class divisions that had existed in Europe in the nineteenth century were now obsolete and redundant.

In the years that followed 1918, therefore, Drieu was insistent that the challenge of Communism *could* effectively be defeated, but he was convinced that this could only be done if the rulers of Europe were not afraid to carry out a policy of sweeping social reforms. Unlike the leaders of the Action Française who, in the course of the 1920s, increasingly came to identify themselves with the defence of bourgeois interests, he could understand the reasons why so many members of the working class had been attracted by Communism. He was aware that during the war a great opportunity had been lost by the Right to win the masses permanently to their side, and he was perceptive enough to realise that it was the serious inequalities that still existed within Western society that blinded the workers to the much greater injustices and inequalities that were present within the Soviet system. But, while demonstrating his readiness to sympathise with the aspirations of the workers, Drieu refused to believe that Communism was the best solution either to the problems of the proletariat or to those of European society as a whole. The tragedy of the situation as he saw it was that, by placing their faith in a movement whose policies were determined from Moscow, the workers were limiting the effective power that they could wield within the political systems of their own national communities, and, by allowing themselves to become the tools of Russian foreign policy, the Communist parties were helping to prevent the creation of a united Europe. All this simply played into the hands of the reactionaries.

What the masses really *did* desire, he believed, was a new and enlightened form of capitalism that would seek to create more wealth for society as a whole and to distribute that wealth in a more equitable way than had been done in the past. What men must try to create was a new kind of society that would transcend the divisions that existed between the people who possessed money and the workers who were dominated by the power of money. This, he thought, was what Mussolini had been trying to do when he seized power in Italy in 1922.[13] The one hope that he could see for the future was that Europe might produce more figures like Mussolini, more up-to-date versions of Bismarck and Disraeli, more men of the Right who could steal the thunder of the Left.[14]

The need for such figures was all the greater, he maintained, because the First World War had revealed the extent to which Europe was in the throes of a profound spiritual crisis, a crisis in which the beliefs and attitudes of the past were no longer relevant. Already in the nineteenth century men like Nietzsche had inveighed against the destruction of culture by the forces of science and technology, but it had taken the outbreak of the war to arouse the peoples of Europe to the magnitude of the danger by which they were faced. For a time, he was prepared to concede, it might have seemed as if the Russian Revolution might offer mankind some radical alternative to the materialism of the West, but these hopes had been dispelled when Lenin had been converted to the view that the only way in which the Soviet state could survive was for it to outstrip the productive capacity of the United States.[15]

In what way, then, could Europe hope to defend its civilisation against the forces of materialism that were intent on destroying it? On this point Drieu was quite clear. On the political plane

Europe must unite itself round the League of Nations at Geneva
to stand up to the development of the superpowers. On the
spiritual plane her writers and artists must work together to produce a new Renaissance:

> The whole tragedy of the period in which we live can be
> summed up in the question: how is man to come to terms with
> the fact that he is wedded to the machine? Will he be able to
> control it and learn to live with it? For he cannot repudiate it –
> this would be to destroy all the efforts that have been made by
> our ancestors since the discovery of fire. We must learn how
> we can avoid misusing it, and this attempt, which is only part
> of the endless attempt to protect the quality of life, must be
> made in the sphere of morals and not that of politics. It must be
> made by intellectuals, perhaps grouped in a circle like the
> great philosophers of Antiquity. Perhaps indeed our enthusiasm
> will be sufficiently ingenious for us to found a church. . .What
> we must aim at is a reintegration of mankind, intellectually,
> morally and bodily.[16]

It was by following this line of argument, therefore, that Drieu
hoped to save Europe from the destruction that otherwise awaited
it. It was by outlining this solution to the problems of the world
that he hoped to triumph over his own despair.

5

THE FASCIST

The views that Drieu expressed in *Mesure de la France* and *Genève ou Moscou* were, of course, prophetic. With the Great Crash on Wall Street in 1929 his warnings that the European economic system was too dependent on that of the United States proved to be only too well-founded and, with the political crisis that developed in Europe in the aftermath of the Depression, his predictions that the stability of the mid-1920s was illusory and that new ideologies would emerge to challenge the discredited principles of nineteenth-century liberalism were more than borne out by the course of events.

And yet the fact that Drieu's analysis of the situation had so quickly been proved to be accurate was of little comfort to him. He was appalled by the harm that the Depression inflicted on the cause of European unity, and he was angered by the way in which the onset of the economic crisis only intensified the feelings of hatred and suspicion that divided one nation from another. He himself was still convinced that the only effective solution to the problems of Europe lay in some kind of federation, and in *L'Europe contre les patries* (1931) he argued in favour of this policy with a power and a conviction that was now born of desperation. In a part of the essay that was obviously prompted by his anxiety over the rise of Nazism he pleaded with the German people to fight against the nationalist hysteria that was being exploited by Hitler and his allies, and in order to demonstrate his good faith to the German people he declared that he himself was now ready to repudiate all the obligations that might be laid upon him by his country – even to the extent of disobeying any mobilisation order that might be promulgated by the French government in the event of war.

Indeed, so ardent was Drieu's desire for peace in the early 1930s that, disillusioned with the unrepentant nationalism of the Right, he was even prepared to consider the possibility of supporting the Left: one evening in 1932 he telephoned the local secretary of the Socialist Party to find out what the conditions for membership were; and on another occasion he allowed himself to be taken by a friend to a meeting that had been organised by the Amsterdam–Pleyel movement. This flirtation with the Left was only short-lived, however. Although the Socialists were sincere supporters of the principle of international collaboration, Drieu was soon disillusioned by their naïveté and lack of effectiveness and, as far as Barbusse's organisation was concerned, the one meeting that he attended afforded him no sense of pleasure. As he afterwards commented:

> I am as uneasy in an exclusively proletarian meeting as I am in a salon of millionaires, I hate everything which is totally self-sufficient and which is content to withdraw ferociously into itself. In spite of my good manners I would have created a certain amount of uproar if I had spoken.[1]

Several years later he recalled the lifeless nature of the proceedings of this meeting in his novel *Gilles*, where he satirised the mechanical way in which the assembly mouthed Communist slogans and monotonously intoned the verses of the Internationale.[2]

Opposed as he was to the Communists and alienated as he was from both the traditional Right and the Socialists, therefore, it looked by the early 1930s, as if Drieu was condemned to political limbo. But then, just at the moment when he felt most isolated, he was able to extricate himself from his difficulties by discovering a political doctrine that fitted the facts of his experience. This process of renewal was initiated in the course of a journey that he made to the Argentine in 1932, a journey that made it possible for him to see the problems of Europe in a new perspective.[3]

What struck him immediately when he was able to see the situation in Europe from this new vantage point was the fact that, although the most significant development that had taken place on the continent since the end of the First World War was the battle between Communism and Fascism, a battle that was now being fought with increasing fury as Europe slid further and further into the crisis of the Depression, the similarities that united Communism and Fascism were greater than the differences that divided them. Seen in this light the events that had taken place in Europe since the outbreak of the First World War took on a new meaning. The world was obviously moving into a new epoch of revolutions, revolutions which, unlike the liberal and parliamentary movements that had dominated the nineteenth century, were both socialist and nationalist in character. Russia had experienced such a revolution in 1917, and Italy had gone through something similar in 1922. Even the advent to power of Roosevelt in America in 1932 could, at least partially, be fitted into the same pattern: by its repudiation of the principles of laissez-faire that had been the prevalent ideology of the Hoover era the New Deal emphasised the role of government intervention in the economy; and the growth of isolationism in the United States in the course of the 1930s indicated that America was moving towards a nationalist, as well as a collectivist, solution to its problems.

But it was not merely in Russia, Italy and the United States that these revolutionary developments could be seen to be taking place. With the Nazi seizure of power in Germany and the rioting that took place in Paris on 6 February 1934 the process that Drieu had first observed in the course of his journey to South America could now be seen to be world-wide in its implications. It will be seen at a later point in this essay how great was the impact made on Drieu by the triumph of Hitler in Germany, but at the time it was the events that took place in Paris at the time of the February riots that made the greatest impression on him. The fact that the disturbances that took place in the aftermath of the Stavisky Affair were disturbances in which both the extreme Left and the extreme Right demonstrated their opposition to the Third Republic seemed to afford final proof that the party distinctions that had divided the French nation in the past were now redundant. This being the case, Drieu argued, it seemed that what the French people needed was a new political movement that would rally together all those who were discontented with the Third Republic by uniting nationalism with socialism.

From this point onwards, Drieu was clear where it was that Fate was now leading him. Although he had to wait for another two years until the founding of Jacques Doriot's Parti Populaire Français seemed to present him with the political movement that he desired, he knew as soon as the Stavisky riots had ended what political ideology it was that he now wished to adopt. Almost overnight he announced his conversion to Fascism.

It goes without saying that, as far as Drieu was concerned, Fascism was much more than a mere *political* movement. What it really taught, he believed, was that life must be lived in terms of heroism, risk and adventure. What it really provided was the sense of human brotherhood that the peoples of Europe needed in order that they could overcome the temptation of despair. It was no accident that it was in the same year that Drieu became a Fascist that he published *La Comédie de Charleroi*, for in his view Fascism was the only political doctrine that measured up to the experience of life that had been gained by the soldiers who had fought in the First World War.

Stated in these terms it might seem that it was largely as a result of nostalgia and a belief in élitism that Drieu decided to support the Fascists, but, although he could hardly deny that there was some truth in this accusation, he was convinced that there was more to his decision than that. Fascism, he asserted, was an ideology that was extremely relevant to the needs of the modern world. It was not at all what the Marxists claimed it to be – a piece of ideological camouflage devised by the ruling classes in order to disguise the fact that capitalism had now entered into its last, and most desperate, stage of decline. The reality of the situation was quite different. It was only by means of Fascism that mankind could be led towards socialism:

I have come to the conclusion that Fascism is a necessary stage in the destruction of capitalism. For, despite what is believed by the antifascists and despite what is believed by the majority of those who support it, Fascism is not the friend of capitalism. Without doubt Fascism brings a temporary respite to certain social categories and certain classes, but at the same time it detaches them further from their economic roots. Fascism creates a civilisation of transition in which capitalism as it existed in its period of high prosperity is rapidly destroyed.[4]

Yet another weakness in the Marxist interpretation of Fascism, according to Drieu, lay in the inability of the Left to grasp the significance of the heroic myth that lay at the heart of Fascist ideology. The great mistake of both the Socialists and the Communists, he was convinced, the reason why they had failed before Mussolini in 1922 and Hitler in 1933, was that they were unable to appreciate the extent to which the masses are moved by passions and emotions that are infinitely more complicated than Marxist ideology will allow. Lost in despair in the bewildering complexity of modern civilisation, human beings need not only material but also spiritual satisfaction: they need some kind of ideal that will give meaning and grandeur – even a tragic meaning and a tragic grandeur – to the drab reality of their lives. It was this psychological dimension of politics that had been understood by Lassalle, Bakunin, Proudhon and Fourier – the great non-Marxist socialists of the nineteenth century. It was this dimension of politics that had been neglected by the European Left ever since it had come to accept the mechanical and superficial analysis of human motives that had been put forward by Marx and Engels. The heroic myth was far more than a piece of petit-bourgeois sentimentality, therefore: it was the main factor that had contributed to the Fascists' success.

Drieu was aware, of course, that most of the blame for the sterility of contemporary Marxism must be borne by men like Engels and Kautsky who had modified the teachings of Marx to suit their own 'scientific' and gradualistic approach to the problem of Socialism. He was also aware that many of the criticisms that he made of Marxist Socialism could not be applied to Communism, especially to Communism as it was practised in the Soviet Union. Indeed, it would not be an exaggeration to say that from the time he became a Fascist Drieu's attitude towards Communism was one of pronounced ambivalence – in 1935, for example, only one year after his conversion to Fascism, he was forced to admit that the atmosphere of freshness and youth that he had encountered in the course of a visit to Moscow was particularly enchanting to someone who was accustomed to the decadence of Paris.[5] But this did not mean that his devotion to Fascism was in any way diminished, and he was quick to point out that the success of the Bolsheviks was quite compatible with his main argument. For was it not because Lenin had been prepared to reject the passivity of orthodox Marxism that the Bolsheviks had been able to seize power in Russia in 1917? And was not Lenin as much as Hitler or Mussolini a product of the revolt against rationalism and positivism that had been so important a feature of the European intellectual scene in the years before the outbreak of the First World War?

Is not the genius of Lenin, so tactical, so much at ease in his writings as a polemicist, impregnated with something resembling this philosophy of mobility and action propagated at the same time by both Vilfredo Pareto and Georges Sorel in philosophy, by Poincaré in science, a philosophy later to appear in the arts under the forms of Futurism, Cubism, Surrealism – all doctrines founded on the negation of reason and being, on an idealistic phenomenalism commanding pragmatism in ethics?[6]

As far as Drieu was concerned, therefore, Lenin's achievement must be seen for what it was – a Fascist achievement. What the success of Lenin had really demonstrated, Drieu maintained, was that Socialist leaders, in order to achieve their aims, need qualities of determination and resolve, qualities that can only adequately be described as being Nietzschean in character. In many ways Lenin was the first of the Fascist dictators. By creating the Bolshevik party in 1903 he was the first European politician to make an unequivocal break with the liberal assumptions on which nineteenth-century civilisation had been built. By openly advocating the use of duplicity and force to further his ends he was the precursor of Hitler and Mussolini.

But this was not all. What the victory of the Bolshevik revolution had further illustrated, Drieu maintained, was the necessity for any successful revolution in the twentieth century to be both nationalist and socialist in character.[7] This might not have been apparent in 1917 when Lenin had held that the fate of the Bolshevik régime in Russia depended on the prospects for revolution in the rest of the world, but when Stalin had abandoned the policies of the founder of the Soviet Union and had decided to come out in favour of the doctrine of 'Socialism in one country' the nationalistic character of the Bolshevik experiment was plain for all to see. The pity of the whole situation, according to Drieu, was that the Communists in the rest of Europe could not appreciate the realities of the situation in which they were now placed, and this was the reason why their efforts were eventually doomed to failure. But at least the Fascist parties had now been founded and Drieu was confident that at length the masses themselves would come to appreciate the fact that outside the Soviet Union it was Fascism and not Communism that most faithfully represented the different national traditions of European Socialism.

From a statement such as this it might seem as if Drieu had abandoned the ideas on European unity that he had put forward in the years that followed the First World War. But he himself saw no contradiction between the views that he supported before and after 1934. By the middle of the 1930s it is true, he accepted it as inevitable that, under the impact of the Depression, the nations of Europe would pursue their own narrow ambitions without regard to the consequences that followed for the rest of the world. He also thought it to be inevitable that in these circumstances the activities of the League of Nations would be increasingly ignored. But this represented only a change of emphasis and not of principle on his part, and in *Socialisme Fasciste*, the collection of essays that he published in 1934, he was at great pains to refute the charge that Fascism was necessarily opposed to the idea of European unity. In these essays he not only reiterated his opposition to modern technological warfare, claiming that the heroic virtues that were implicit in Fascism could be realised in the domain of sport,[8] he also expressed the hope that, once the majority of the nations of Europe had adopted a Fascist solution to their problems, then the way would be open for some kind of Fascist internationalism.[9]

He knew, of course, that there would be many difficulties involved before this ideal could be translated into reality, and he was aware that one of the most serious problems that must face any Fascist government that might come to power in Paris would be that of establishing friendly relations with Hitler's Germany and Mussolini's Italy, two Fascist régimes whose foreign ambitions conflicted with the interests of France. But at first he was reasonably hopeful that these difficulties could be overcome. Mussolini might have plans for an Italian Empire in the Mediterranean, but he was surely enough of a realist to recognise that France was stronger than Italy. As far as Hitler and the Germans were concerned, they certainly presented a much more serious danger to France than did the Italians, but perhaps a policy aimed at Franco-German reconciliation might persuade the German dictator to moderate his demands.

All in all, therefore, Drieu was confident that the advent to power of a Fascist party in France would represent a major step forward for the cause of European unity and a great act of liberation for the mass of the French people. For far too long, he proclaimed, the revolutionary aspirations of the French working class had been thwarted by the inability of the Marxist parties to identify themselves with the nationalism inherent in the Jacobin tradition. For far too long the spontaneity and the imaginative capacity of the French people had been stifled by a political and cultural system that was the product of rationalist and positivist doctrinaires. Now at last in Doriot's movement the masses were offered a real opportunity to decide the destiny of their country. No longer were the people of France condemned to accept a bourgeois system of values which placed a premium on avarice and resulted in alcoholism and a declining birth-rate. Of proletarian origin himself, Doriot was well-equipped to understand the frustrated idealism of the common people of France, and the fact that he had left the French Communist Party in 1934 because he disagreed with the sterile 'class against class' policy pursued by the Comintern since 1928 meant that he put the interests of France before those of any foreign power. In place of the rigidity of a Marxist ideology that was alien to the deepest instincts of the people of France, therefore, the P.P.F. was reasserting the principles of the *French* revolution. In place of the decadence and stagnation of the Third Republic the aim of the P.P.F. was to create a régime that would begin the process of French regeneration.

Once they were given a lead in this way, Drieu maintained, the French people were bound to respond, for they must clearly recognise that the situation of France was becoming increasingly precarious in a Europe in which the rivalry between Germany and the Soviet Union was becoming daily more bitter. Already, as a result of the participation of the Communists in the Popular Front, the Soviet Union was in a position to exert a growing influence over French foreign policy. And already the spectacle of France's weaknesses and divisions was tempting Hitler to increase his demands still further. The only way in which France could escape from a situation in which her freedom of action was being constantly eroded was for her to transform herself by means of her own kind of national revolution. Fascism was the sole means by which France would be able to break through the deadlock between Left and Right that paralysed her internal development, the sole means by which she could become sufficiently strong and united to resist the ambitions of the dictators.[10]

Whatever the merits of this apologia for Fascism – and Drieu's exposition of this ideology was infinitely more lucid and intelligent than anything that was produced in Italy and Germany in the 1930s – it is quite clear that embodied in it was a great deal of wishful thinking. It can hardly be doubted, for example, that Drieu's hopes that Hitler might be prepared to cooperate with a Fascist France in order to further the cause of European unification were greatly affected by the fact that he himself had long been an admirer of Germany. Perhaps it would be useful at this point to look in greater detail at the extent to which Drieu's Germanophil sympathies affected his political judgement in the course of the 1930s.

It has already been seen that it was the philosophy of Nietzsche that was the most important influence on Drieu's adolescence, and the way in which German civilisation combined within itself an intense romanticism with a ruthless concern for the pursuit of power was something that always fascinated him. This fascination had only been increased by his experiences during the First World War. In one of the poems published in *Interrogation* (one of the poems that had caused the censor so much anxiety in 1917) it was in terms of profound admiration that Drieu had addressed the German people:

A vous Allemands – par ma bouche longtemps taciturne d'ordre militaire – je parle.
Je ne vous ai jamais haïs.
Je vous ai combattus avec le vouloir roidement dégainé de vous tuer. Ma joie a jailli dans votre sang.
Mais vous êtes forts. Je n'ai pu haïr en vous la force, mère des choses.
Je me suis réjoui de votre force.
Hommes, par toute la terre, réjouissons-nous de la force des Allemands.[11]

And after the war, too, he was full of sympathy for the problems which faced his former enemies. True to his ideal of European federation he repeatedly urged the necessity for a rapprochement between France and Germany from 1922 onwards, and in 1923,

at the time of the French occupation of the Ruhr, he advocated a
policy of Franco-German economic collaboration as the only way
in which the bitterness that divided the two nations could be
removed.[12]

In view of this background, then, it is not surprising that Drieu
should have been excited by Hitler's advent to power in Germany
in January 1933. Nor is it surprising that, a year later, at the
invitation of Otto Abetz, he should have been the first French
writer of any note to take part in a conference in Nazi Germany.
When he visited Germany again in 1935 to observe the Nazi
party rally in Nuremberg he was overwhelmed by the new sense
of purpose with which the German nation was inbued, and, just
as on his visit to Moscow in the same year, he was constantly
struck by the contrast that existed between the atmosphere that
prevailed in France and the dynamism that was to be found in
countries that were ruled by totalitarian régimes. Admittedly, he
could not help feeling some anxiety when he read the nationalist
slogans that were printed in the German newspapers, and both
as a Frenchman and as a European he was forced to ask himself
whether National Socialism was a movement that was attuned to
the needs of the present time, or whether it was a force that
remained trapped in the hatreds and rivalries of the past. But on
the whole he was greatly impressed by what he had seen. Like
an over-civilised Athenian who had come into contact with Sparta
he was forced to admit that it had been a fascinating experience.
'It is marvellous and terrible', he wrote after his return from
Nuremberg, 'it seems to me more and more certain that in one
way or another the future will not be peaceful.'[13]

The racialist element in Nazi ideology particularly appealed to
him. Already in 1928 in the preface that he had contributed to a
volume of poems published by the Norman writer Jean-Louis Le
Marois, Drieu had spoken of the importance of the 'Nordic'
element in the French racial mixture, an element which, he
believed, had been unduly neglected in the past.[14] But this was
an expression of Drieu's romanticism, an aesthetic and not a
political judgement, and in his other writings in the 1920s he was
at pains to attack racialist ideas as being contrary to the idea of
European federation. In any case, since Drieu's first wife had been
Jewish and he had moved freely in Jewish circles in the years after
the war, he could not seriously accept a policy of anti-semitism.[15]

After 1934, however, his opinions underwent a profound change. It is true that he never accepted the more lunatic aspects of Nazi racialism: he was careful to point out that ethnography was as full of uncertainties as the other social sciences, and he was scornful of any attempt to use the word 'Aryan' in a racialist rather than in a linguistic sense. On the Jewish question, too, he was not entirely orthodox: whilst maintaining that Zionism must be encouraged as the only possible solution for those French Jews who felt themselves to be more Jewish than French, and whilst agreeing with the Nazis that Marxist Jews should be expelled from the national community, he never excluded the possibility that *some* Jews might be assimilated into the population of Europe. Nevertheless, once all these qualifications are made, the evolution of Drieu's opinions on the question of race is one of the most striking, and one of the most lamentable, indications of the extent to which he came under the spell of Nazi doctrines in the period after 1934.[16] Already in many of the articles that he wrote in the course of the 1930s, in fact, there were plenty of indications that Drieu's fascination with racialist ideology – a fascination, incidentally, that was not shared either by Doriot or by the bulk of the P.P.F. – might eventually lead him to throw in his lot with Hitler.

In fairness to Drieu, it must be said that he himself was aware of some of the dangers that might result from his infatuation with German ideas. He was dishonest enough to attack the Jews as harbingers of decadence whilst ignoring his own oft-repeated testimony that the decline of France was very largely the fault of the French people themselves. He was also sufficiently disingenuous to claim, in reply to those who objected that the position he had now adopted on racialism was in conflict with his basic Europeanism, that any movement such as Nazism that was attempting to unite the various Nordic elements in Europe was working towards the ultimate federation of the continent. On the other hand he was forced to admit that Hitler himself might not see things in quite the same way as he himself did, and he could never forget for long that National Socialism was a product of German, and not of French, conditions:

The Germans are wrong to make a goddess out of Germany and the German race. They are wrong in believing that any human entity can express everything that pertains to the phenomenon of Man. Only the divine can enable human beings to express themselves completely. And a goddess is not God. It would be wrong if Fascism, which has been a profoundly human reaction against the narrowness of Marxism, should itself retreat into another kind of narrowness. The cult of the goddess 'Germany' or the goddess 'Italy' might be more comprehensive than the cult of the proletariat: it can never be sufficiently comprehensive to incorporate all the mystery by which Man is surrounded.[17]

Despite the attraction that he felt towards many aspects of Nazi ideology, therefore, Drieu's sympathy for the Nazi régime was to wane rapidly when it became clear to him that Hitler did not interpret the doctrines of Fascism in quite the subtle way that he did himself, and it was with a growing sense of urgency that, from the time of the German remilitarisation of the Rhineland onwards, he was to exhort the French Fascists to beware of the danger of becoming the creatures of either the Italian or the German dictators. 'We in the P.P.F.', he wrote, 'are increasingly opposed to Moscow, and if there was a party that represented Berlin or Rome we would be irrevocably opposed to them.'[18] The quarrel between Fascism, Communism and Democracy, he maintained, was not a conflict between different creeds, but a battle between nations, nations who used ideological arguments in order to disguise the real nature of their ambitions. 'Stalin deceives us with anti-fascism,' he proclaimed, 'London deludes us with the defence of democracy, Hitler and Mussolini would very much like to dupe us with anticommunism.'[19] In this kind of situation it was essential that France should take care to preserve her independence. There might be a case for France attempting to appease Italy with colonial concessions in order to detach Mussolini from the camp of the Axis. There might be cogent reasons for France allowing Hitler to acquire an overseas empire or to expand eastwards at the expense of the Soviet Union if he was prepared to renounce his other territorial ambitions in Central Europe.[20] But whatever course of action the French statesmen adopted towards the other European powers they must obey the dictates of French national interest.

Already by 1937, however, Drieu was pessimistic over the

future. He was certain he knew what the ultimate objectives of
the German dictator really were:

> Hitler wants Austria and Bohemia, he wants to unite them into
> the German state. That means he rejects the real and subtle
> possibility of European unity, in which the powerful German
> element could act freely as a unifying factor, in favour of the
> summary and brutal idea of a hegemony exercised by Berlin. . .
> And when Hitler is in Vienna, he will dominate and soon
> absorb Hungary and the divided Balkans. Hitler, who for
> several years showed that he possessed the wisdom of the war-
> veterans, is leading Germany along a road that will lead to
> war. He is leading the German people to what will possibly be
> a fruitless victory over a heap of ruins.[21]

When the Czechoslovakian crisis finally came to a head in
September 1938, therefore, Drieu was firm in his conviction that
France should not abandon the Czechs to their fate. It was not
out of sympathy for Beneš and his people that he took this view –
indeed, he believed that many of Hitler's claims to Czech territory
were fully justified – but the point that he wished to stress was
that France had given certain guarantees to the Czech government and that if they did not keep to these promises the French
people would be dishonoured before the world. As for himself he
was clear where his duty lay. He would fight to the end:

> We have no choice other than that of never losing hope in our
> country. Certainly it is a terrible fate to see our country slowly
> dying before our eyes. But we must remind ourselves that, if
> we do not know how to avert death, it is because we do not
> know how to preserve life. If we do not know how to conquer,
> it is because we do not know how to fight. It is our country
> which gives us our life, but it is also we who give life to our
> country. We must die with her. And, to the extent that we
> remain by her side, to the extent that we remain faithful to the
> ideas that we believe to represent the only possible future for
> her, she is not dead, she still manifests herself to the world.
> And after all, miracles of the blood are always possible.[22]

But at Munich there were no miracles of the blood: France
capitulated before Hitler; Jean Cocteau expressed the reaction of
his fellow countrymen when he exclaimed, 'Long live the shame-

ful peace'; and Drieu was beside himself with anger. In an open letter to the prime minister, Daladier, he expressed his deep sense of shame at the humiliation that his country had been forced to endure, and in a passage of particularly savage polemic he bitterly attacked the Radical Party for the responsibility that they must bear for preparing the French nation for the disaster that had now overtaken it. For half a century the Radicals had ruled over France, and for half a century they had indoctrinated the youth of France with rationalism, anti-clericalism and the worship of bourgeois values:

> And after fifty years this is what you have done with one of the
> most noble peoples in the universe. You have created a race
> that is miserly, anaemic and stupid. The Frenchman has
> become stupid. He looks at events with surprise and stupe-
> faction. He is unable to understand them, even though they are
> events that are common to humanity. In the face of the
> constant threat of calamity he vainly stammers out the words
> that he has been taught, words that have been emptied of all
> meaning: peace, security, disarmament, union of the peoples.[23]

Was it any wonder that the dictators now regarded French states-men with contempt?

By the autumn of 1938, then, Drieu had been forced to the con-clusion that France was doomed. But this was not the only sorrow that he had to bear, for another bitter truth that he had to accept at this time was that French Fascism was doomed as well.

There were many reasons why this had happened. The lack of cohesion displayed by the French Right was one factor, a lack of cohesion that was reflected in the very multiplicity of Fascist and quasi-Fascist groupings in France in the 1930s. It can hardly be denied that there was something absurd about a situation in which, in addition to Doriot's P.P.F., there was Colonel de la Rocque's 'Croix de Feu' (later to be renamed the 'Parti Social Français'), Marcel Bucard's 'Franciste' movement, François Coty's 'Solidarité Française', Pierre Taittinger's 'Jeunesses patriotes', Paul Clémenti's 'Parti Français National Communiste' and Jean Boissel's 'Racisme International-Fascisme' – all com-peting for Fascist support. But even this list is by no means exhaustive, for while a number of these groupings were virtually moribund by the middle of the decade, new parties were continually in the process of being organised. In addition to the movements mentioned above, for example, there was the group of former socialists around Marcel Déat who were moving towards an increasingly authoritarian and pro-Fascist position in the 1930s, a tendency that culminated after the defeat of France in the founding of Déat's 'Rassemblement National Populaire' in February 1941.[24]

The situation might not have been so confusing had there been any real cooperation between the various parties, but not only was an extreme disregard for discipline one of the besetting weaknesses of the French Right as a whole, the rivalries that existed between the different Fascist groupings were extraordinarily bitter: de la Rocque was suspicious of the other Fascist leaders; the followers of Déat and Doriot were irreconcilably opposed to de la Rocque; and the hatred that existed between Doriot and Déat was a hatred that was maintained until the last weeks of the Second World War when both were in exile in Germany. Clearly this was not a set of circumstances that augured well for the victory of Fascism in France.

But the fact that the 'Croix de Feu' was numerically the strongest of the groups on the extreme Right indicates that there were even more important reasons for the failure of French Fascism than the chronic disunity from which it suffered. The truth of the matter was that Colonel de la Rocque enjoyed the success that he did because he was far too much of an ex-officer to be labelled as a revolutionary, and far too much an upholder of the privileges of the middle class to countenance any radical policies within his ranks; while believing that the parliamentary system should be replaced by a more authoritarian type of régime, he was much closer in spirit to Maurras and Pétain than to Mussolini or Hitler. The popularity of the 'Croix de Feu' is an indication, therefore, that it was the strength of the forces of conservatism that was the main obstacle in the way of any major Fascist breakthrough in France in the 1930s.

The number of genuine Fascists in France was, in fact, extremely small. Just as the French Left was inspired by anti-Fascism rather than by Communism, so the French Right was motivated by anti-Communism rather than by any positive adherence to Fascist principles. A pacifist horror of war and a desire to see France possess a planned economy were the main reasons why Déat became sympathetic to Fascism in the 1930s. Doriot, too, was extremely vague about the political principles that inspired his movement. Whatever Drieu might claim on behalf of the P.P.F. the leader of that party consistently refused to describe himself as a Fascist in the 1930s, and, with the benefit of hindsight, it is clear that the driving force of Doriot's 'Fascism' was neither Nationalism nor Socialism but that kind of virulent anti-Communism that is only possible in someone who has formerly been a party member.[25]

By German, or even Italian, standards, therefore, the French Right was conservative rather than revolutionary, and this conservatism was characteristic not only of the propertied classes but of the French nation as a whole. Unlike Germany, France had not been subjected to a series of dramatic upheavals in the period after the First World War. She had not been defeated in 1918 and, despite the economic difficulties that she experienced in the middle of the 1920s, she suffered far less than Germany from the initial effects of the Great Depression. It was out of a sense of national humiliation and economic distress that Hitler was able to build National Socialism. Neither factor operated so powerfully on the other side of the Rhine.

On the contrary, what France *did* have to fear in the 1930s was not the revolutionary overthrow of her society but the atrophy of her political institutions and her increasing inability to act as a great European power. These two problems were closely related since her lack of success in pursuing a coherent foreign policy was partly due, at least, to her own internal divisions. When, for example, she attempted to bring Mussolini into play against Hitler – as Laval did at the time of the Abyssinian war – this infuriated the anti-Fascist Left. And if the Popular Front had dared to try to revive the alliance with Russia, the alliance that had been so successful in helping France to resist the German onslaught in 1914, this would have been thwarted by the anti-Communist Right. With the hatred of war that was to be found in all sections of her society, therefore, and with the impasse that had been reached in every aspect of her policy, France was condemned to drift helplessly towards catastrophe.

Nevertheless, if it is true to say that *all* the political parties in

France share some of the blame for the way in which this situation had been created it is clear that the Fascist groupings must bear a particularly heavy burden of responsibility, for by the end of the 1930s their early efforts to overcome the divisions between the classes had been transformed into a negative and sterile hatred of the Left, and their early ambition to restore the greatness of France had degenerated into a policy of appeasing Hitler and Mussolini. By 1938, indeed, it was evident that, despite the stridency with which the Fascists asserted their rôle as the standard-bearers of a French renaissance, all that they could now offer to the French people was a policy of abject surrender to the dictators. This was the final reason why Fascism failed in France in the years before the outbreak of the Second World War. This was the final reason why Drieu himself was to break with the P.P.F. in the months that followed Munich.

Of course long before the Munich crisis finally erupted Drieu was acutely aware that there were many weaknesses inherent in the position of the extreme Right in French politics. During the Second World War, for example, he was to claim that within a very few months of its foundation he had realised that the P.P.F. was not an effective instrument for implementing Fascist principles in France: in Doriot's party, he admitted, there had only been 'a few dozen Fascists, ex-Communists for the most part', while the rest had been 'old fashioned Royalists, vague Catholics, vague nationalists without mentioning pacifists and other eccentrics'.[26] And as early as 1934 he had been perceptive enough to realise that in the changed political circumstances of the 1930s the traditional patriotism of the French Right might come under an increasing strain: if a general war broke out between Russia and Germany, he asserted, it would be difficult to prevent it from turning into a European civil war in which the bourgeoisie would be sympathetic towards Germany while the workers would support the Soviet Union.[27]

What he did not expect, however, was that the French Fascists, too, would desert their country in her hour of need. And yet this is what happened in 1938. When the P.P.F. supported a policy of appeasement at the time of the Czech crisis, and when it was revealed at the end of 1938 that for over a year the leader of the P.P.F. had been in receipt of subsidies from Mussolini, Drieu felt that his position had become untenable. He resigned from the party immediately. In his letter of resignation he reproached Doriot in bitter terms for the betrayal that he had committed:

> You have deceived us, you did not want to save France. You have remained inactive, cloaked in infidelity and bad faith. There were Frenchmen who wanted to liberate France from the fate that has been hers for the last hundred years, who were ready to throw themselves into the fight once the first sign of encouragement was given to them. You have left them burdened with their former irony and doubt.[28]

Little did he suspect when he wrote this letter, however, that within the space of the next eighteen months he himself would come to the conclusion that it was only through the agency of the foreigner that Fascism could be brought to France.

As was only to be expected the months between France's declaration of war against Germany in September 1939 and the French collapse in May and June 1940 were extremely difficult for Drieu to bear. He was deeply concerned by the low state of French morale, and he was particularly worried by the fact that his country had entered the war with no allies except England.

This did not mean that he disliked England – indeed, ever since he had paid a visit to Shropshire in his youth he had regarded that country as his second home and in the 1920s and early 1930s he had a number of English friends particularly in the circle round Aldous Huxley. But he could never think of England as an entirely satisfactory partner for his country in time of crisis. He had been irritated by the way in which the English had sabotaged France's early efforts to secure an alliance with Mussolini by refusing to accept the provisions of the Hoare–Laval pact, and he could never forget that, by failing to support the French when they had wanted to oppose Hitler's remilitarisation of the Rhineland, the English had sanctioned the first major infringement of the terms of the Treaty of Versailles. By the end of the 1930s, it is true, England had at last woken up to the realities of the German danger, but by that time she had sanctioned so many concessions to Germany and had so confused and demoralised the French people that France had virtually to be dragged into the war against Hitler at the time of the Polish crisis. Even though England was now fighting in the war on France's side, therefore,

Drieu was doubtful that she could provide the kind of assistance that France so desperately needed. During the First World War, he pointed out, it had taken the British two years or so to make their full contribution to the cause for which they were fighting, and there was every prospect that the same thing would happen again. Once the Second World War started in earnest it was France that would have to bear the brunt of the German attack.

It was in a mood of deep pessimism, then, that Drieu contemplated the future of his country in the autumn of 1939. Everything that he had worked for seemed to have failed. Fascism had not been successful in restoring French greatness, and the nation was still burdened with a political system that inspired little confidence. At both ends of the political spectrum there were elements who refused to give their whole-hearted support to the war effort. The Communists, in accordance with the Nazi–Soviet pact, were maintaining that the war was an imperialist war in which the workers must refuse to become involved. On the anti-Communist Right it was widely held that it was not Hitler but Stalin who was France's principal enemy. Although Doriot had been urging the necessity for France to resist Hitler ever since the latter's occupation of Prague in March 1939, Déat openly proclaimed that he was reluctant to die for Danzig. Drieu was in despair.

This despair is reflected in *Notes pour comprendre le siècle*, the long political essay that he wrote in the early months of the Second World War. In this essay he maintained that the only good that might come out of the war was that the French people would be forced eventually to admit the validity of the arguments that he had put forward in the course of the 1930s. The Western Powers must now be forced to realise that their outlook on the world was hopelessly outdated, and that a new approach to their problems was a matter of urgent necessity. No longer was it realistic for the English and the French to think of the German threat in purely military terms. A man like Maurras who believed that most of the evil in the world could be attributed to the unification of Germany and that the only solution to the German problem lay in the undoing of that unity was obviously living in the past. The French had tried to deal harshly with Germany at the end of the First World War, and the only effect of that policy had been that it had helped to create the conditions that enabled

Hitler to come to power. If, by some miracle, the French were to be victorious again, and attempted to impose another Treaty of Versailles on Germany, it would only mean that other Hitlers would emerge in the future. Whatever the differences that seemed to divide them, the Soviet, Nazi and Fascist régimes had this one factor in common – they fulfilled the needs of the masses in the twentieth century by attempting to unite socialism with nationalism. Only by following their example and then surpassing them could England and France hope to come to terms with the crisis by which they were now faced, and only then could they create the conditions in which a new Europe could be built. France in particular must drastically alter her outlook on life. She must discard the outmoded principles of rationalism and individualism which had for so long been the dominant forces within her civilisation. She must turn instead to the task of creating a new type of human being, a human being who would combine political idealism with physical strength. The Frenchman of the future, Drieu proclaimed, must be both a militant and an athlete.[29]

But the Frenchman of the present was sitting in the fortifications of the Maginot Line, and Drieu was to spend the months of the phoney war fretting with impatience at the inactivity of the Western Allies. The publication of his novel *Gilles* was to afford him a certain amount of pleasure, but he felt middle-aged, childless and lonely – his second marriage, to the daughter of a Parisian banker, had ended in divorce in 1933, and his current mistress was temporarily out of Paris – and he was embittered by the failure of his attempt to secure any kind of useful employment in the war-effort. 'My poor novel will appear too late or it will not appear at all', he had written just before the publication of *Gilles*. 'My best work will be engulfed. For my part I have predicted all that. But it is no consolation to be right in matters such as this.'[30]

Although he was to be amazed by the speed with which the French armies collapsed before the onslaught of the German panzer divisions in May 1940, therefore, this was a development for which, in a psychological sense, he was not entirely unprepared. His first reaction was to declare that he would escape to England and that, if he could not do this, he would commit suicide. But this was a mood that did not last for very long and he soon came to the conclusion that the important thing for

France to do was for her to react in a positive way to the catastrophe that had now overtaken her. He welcomed the advent to
power of Marshal Pétain, and he was conscious of the fact that
Pétain's acceptance of the Armistice agreement would be useful
in preserving a limited degree of French independence. On the
other hand he was doubtful whether the conservative and reactionary elements that had come to power in Vichy were the
elements that were needed if the French nation was to be
revitalised.

What then, was the best solution to the problems that now
confronted France? One possibility was that of supporting the
Resistance and, for a time, Drieu was attracted by the idea of
joining de Gaulle. The leader of the Free French had left French
soil, however, and his organisation was only just in the process of
being formed; in any case the prospects for de Gaulle's ultimate
victory hardly seemed favourable in the summer of 1940 when
Hitler's grip on Western Europe seemed so secure that it looked
as if it could never be shaken. In this situation, the only alternative policy that seemed to offer itself was one of close collaboration with Germany, and this was the policy that Drieu was
eventually to endorse in October 1940.

In publicly announcing his support for such a programme
Drieu was aware that he was contradicting everything that he
had said in the 1920s and 1930s on the necessity for European
federation to be based on the principle of the equality of nations,
but he defended himself by saying that recent events had forced
him to change his mind. It was inevitable that the strong should
triumph over the weak. For centuries men had talked about the
need for European unity and for centuries nothing had been
done until one nation had found itself in a position to impose
this policy by force. Now the way was open for the creation of a
new international order. It was up to the nations of Europe to
decide what kind of order this was going to be.[31]

6

THE COLLABORATOR

'Everything begins in mysticism and ends in politics.'[1] It was in these terms that Péguy pointed to the dilemma caused by the conflict between ideals and reality, and to men of conscience this conflict has always been very real. And yet in the case of those writers who declared their sympathy for Fascism in the course of the 1920s and 1930s it might seem that such a problem could never arise, for, by denigrating the rôle of the intelligence were they not already encouraging the wildest forms of irrationalism, and by worshipping the use of force were they not condoning in advance the appalling cruelties that were to be committed by the dictators? 'Our strength is our quickness and brutality', Hitler told his generals when they were about to march into Poland in September 1939, 'Ghengiz Khan had millions of women and children killed by his own will and with a gay heart. History sees in him only the builder of a great state.'[2] Could it not be said that this was only a more extreme expression of certain views that were held by all Fascist intellectuals in the years that followed the First World War?

In one sense the answer to this question must clearly be, yes. However much the leaders of Fascism may have perverted the aims of their followers, and however much the leaders of Fascism may in their turn have been corrupted by the example of Adolf Hitler, the fact remains that, by demanding a rebirth of the heroic virtues and by romanticising the nature of violence, writers such as Malaparte in Italy and Drieu la Rochelle and Robert Brasillach in France were paving the way for barbarism.

And yet this is a matter about which it is dangerous to generalise. It may very well be true that, by talking about the aims of Fascism in terms of a Nietzschean Will to Power, a number of writers helped to provide the Fascist dictators with the intellectual respectability they so desperately needed. Nevertheless, the relationship of many of the 'Fascist' intellectuals to the dictators was infinitely more complicated than appearances might

suggest. In Germany, for example, there was a whole generation
of writers in the 1920s and early 1930s, the so-called 'linke Leute
von Rechts', who believed like Drieu that the only way in which
they could remain faithful to the experiences in the war and its
aftermath was for them to adopt a philosophy which combined
within it elements of nationalism, socialism and Nietzschean
activism. But although this brought them close to Hitler, the
more intelligent members of this generation – men like Ernst
Jünger and Ernst von Salomon – held themselves aloof from the
Nazis, and by the end of the 1930s were completely alienated
from the German régime. By the outbreak of the Second World
War, in fact, it was clear to them that the Nazis, far from being
the representatives of any true élite, were products of the de-
humanised technological battles – the Materialschlachten – of
1916–18, and that the advent to power of Hitler, far from repre-
senting the triumph of the Superman, was the victory of that kind
of demagogy and 'herd mentality' against which Nietzsche had
so passionately inveighed. 'In the previous war we told one
another about those wounded and killed in battle, in this one
about those deported and murdered', Jünger commented in his
diary during the Second World War,[3] and one of the ironies of
Jünger's career during these years was that, in the course of his
duties on the staff of the German military commander in Paris,
he, who had so long ago become disillusioned with Hitler, was
brought into frequent contact with French collaborators who
were still in the first flush of their enthusiasm for the German
New Order.

The case of Jünger, then, is a useful reminder that the attitude
adopted by many 'Fascist' intellectuals towards a régime that
claimed to embody the principles of Fascism was often much
less simple than appearances might suggest. And yet this in a
sense only increases the mystery that surrounds Drieu's actions
after the fall of France, for the most intriguing feature of his
decision to throw in his lot with Hitler in 1940 is that he did this
in the full knowledge that the idealists of Fascism would be
betrayed by the politicians of the movement and with a clear
awareness of what Hitler's objectives really were. Already after
his break with Doriot, in 1938 for example, he had spoken of the
'abyss' that separates the ideas of an intellectual and the ideas of
a man of action.[4] And during the phoney war, after reading *Hitler*

Speaks, Hermann Rauschning's famous denunciation of the Nazi régime, he expressed his full agreement with Rauschning's thesis that Hitler's movement was the product of spiritual nihilism: Nazism, he proclaimed, was neither nationalist nor socialist in character; rather it was the expression of a ceaseless desire for domination that would only be checked at the furthest edges of the world unless it was halted first by the fortifications of the Maginot Line.[5]

If Drieu was possessed of such a clear-sighted appreciation of the realities of Nazism by 1939, why, then, did he subsequently agree to support a policy of collaboration? One explanation is that it was a manifestation of his basic despair. In his reminiscences of Drieu in the summer and autumn of 1940 Jean Grenier refers to the importance that the former attached to the 'necessities' of the historical process:

> He came back to this idea that fascinated him: the bets are now being placed, let us play our part, things are being decided now for centuries to come, let us not lose too much time, let our country take the place which is its due immediately lest other countries get there first. In one sense he went further than the military in accepting the facts of the situation: they reacted to their defeat in war as players react to the losing of a game; as an intellectual he saw one civilisation being buried by another and saw no hope of a revanche either in two years or in two hundred years.[6]

But Drieu himself advanced another explanation. In a passage in his diary written in 1943 he explained that in declaring his support for the collaboration he had been affirming, not his fatalism, but his hope – his hope that Nazism would evolve beyond the demands of German nationalism to embrace the cause of Europe, his hope that France would emerge from her ordeal revitalised. His action in 1940 had been motivated by optimism and not by despair:

> There are always two men inside me. One of them is a pitiless observer who is only too inclined to strip away the superficial aspect of things in order to reveal the seeds of decay that exist in every being and every situation. The other is characterised, not by intelligence, but by sensibility. He is moved by passions

and rages, by pity and unfailing hope. At times it is he who emerges to defy the warnings of disaster that are given by the observer and to engage in activities of which he thought himself to be no longer capable.[7]

Whether this provides a really adequate explanation of his conduct in 1940 is open to some debate, however. 'My enemies have brought out well – it is sufficiently obvious – the inverted and feminine nature of my love of force', he wrote in his diary in 1940,[8] and the element of self-torture in Drieu's reaction to events must not be underestimated. Throughout his career he had denounced the phenomenon of decadence, and yet he himself had long been a self-avowed decadent. As a Fascist he had praised the heroic virtues, and yet there had always been a defeatist element even in his most passionate pleas for a reinvigorated France. Perhaps it was this element of masochism that was responsible for his behaviour in 1940, for although the guiding principle behind his actions may not have been immediately apparent in the immediate aftermath of the French defeat, by 1944 it was unmistakably clear. By 1944, in fact, it was obvious that the main reason why Drieu supported Hitler was not that he was ignorant of the suicidal impulses that lay behind Nazism, but that subconsciously he had known for some time what these impulses really were. By 1944, indeed, it was evident that, whatever hopes that Drieu may have entertained for a policy of collaboration in 1940, it was his own urge towards self-destruction that was now the driving force behind his actions.

Lasting as it did only from October 1940 to the autumn of 1941, the period of Drieu's closest involvement with the collaboration was relatively short in its duration, and, although he mixed quite freely in the circles that were frequented by the leading personalities of the collaboration in Paris, his main sources of information tended to be former colleagues of his in the P.P.F., such as Pierre Pucheu (later to be Pétain's Minister of the Interior and eventually to be executed by the Free French in Algiers), and Paul Marion (later to be Secretary-General for Information and Propaganda at Vichy). With the Germans he had relatively little contact, apart from his longstanding friendship with Otto Abetz who had now become the German ambassador to France. 'I was never the author', Drieu commented in later years to explain the part that he had played in the collaboration, 'at most I was the prompter or the man who was called in to patch up the scenario.'[9]

Nevertheless, the fact that he was prepared to take over the editorship of the renowned *Nouvelle Revue Française* in order to attract other intellectuals into the collaboration indicates that, for a time, at least, he took seriously the rôle that he had chosen for himself as an active propagandist for Hitler's New Order. And, at first, there seemed a lot to be said in favour of this policy. After the British evacuation at Dunkirk and the action of the British navy in causing the death of 1,500 French sailors in the notorious engagement at Mers-el-Kebir in July 1940, a bitter hatred of England was widespread in France. Anti-German feeling, by contrast, was somewhat appeased by the tactful behaviour of the occupying forces.

Although Drieu was aware that this state of affairs would not last for very long, therefore, he was convinced that there was now a real opportunity that a policy of Franco-German cooperation might succeed:

> This time, whether they like it or not, the French have made a start. This time they have not been able to sit and wait. The Germans were there and they have had to come to an accommodation with them. That has been done, it is being done, and nothing will be able to prevent it from happening. Shocks, misunderstandings, reverses, gnashing of teeth, despair, listening to the English radio – none of these matter. We are collaborating, and that is a guarantee of life.[10]

As for the Germans, everything that he saw of them in war-time – their strength, their calmness, their self-confidence – he found to be immensely reassuring. 'Germany is in the process of making herself European,' he announced in the columns of the *Nouvelle Revue Française*. 'We can only guess at the dimensions of the effort that she is now making to acquaint herself with all the expanses and frontiers of Europe.'[11] The stress that was being laid by the Nazis on the supremacy of the Aryan race he found to be particularly comforting: already in *Notes pour comprendre le siècle* he had pointed out that the term 'Aryan' was so vague that nearly all the peoples of Europe could be considered to be members of this racial élite – with the exception of the Jews.[12]

And yet, at the very moment that Drieu was exhorting his fellow-countrymen to cooperate with the Germans in the task of building a united Europe, the Polish people were being subjected to every kind of Nazi brutality on the grounds that they were racially inferior, and it was not long before Drieu himself was driven to doubt the wisdom of his initial reaction to the German victory. More and more it became apparent that Hitler was not interested in creating a united Europe on a Socialist basis. More and more it became clear that the ideas of a man like Abetz were being ignored, and that Germany was only concerned to further her own narrowly conceived ends with no intention of treating the nations she had conquered as potential allies to be won over to her side by a policy of reconciliation.

Admittedly France escaped some of the worst excesses that characterised Nazi rule in the territories that were now under Hitler's control. Even though the country was divided into two, the Vichy régime was, for a time, allowed some semblance of an independent existence, and, since Hitler never had the time or the inclination to pursue any consistent policy towards France once the Russian campaign had started in the summer of 1941, Laval was able to a certain extent to exploit this situation to his country's advantage. On the other hand the Germans never accorded the French people the kind of respect that might have won over a substantial number of them to support a policy of active, rather than passive, collaboration. The territorial integrity of France, for example, was subjected to considerable German interference – not only was the country divided into an occupied zone as well as the unoccupied area that was left to Vichy, but Alsace-Lorraine was annexed outright by Germany, and there was even talk of detaching further areas such as Brittany and the region near the Belgian frontier from French control. By 1941 it was obvious even to an observer who was temperamentally so sympathetic to the Germans as Drieu that France was being reduced to the status of yet another vassal state, yet another occupied nation whose resources were to be exploited for the greater good of the Third Reich.

Some of the Nazis, indeed, were quite open about their attitude. As Goering said on one occasion:

It is Herr Abetz who operates in terms of collaboration. I do not. I only think of collaboration in the following way: if the gentlemen of France become our generous providers to the extent of having nothing left for themselves, then I will collaborate. If they eat everything themselves they must be made to understand that this is not collaborating.[13]

And, if anyone was inclined to doubt the fact that Goering meant what he said, they had only to look at the kind of blackmail that was used by the German government to keep the Vichy régime in order. Whenever it looked as if the opponents of collaboration were gaining the upper hand at Vichy Hitler closed the border between the unoccupied zone and the rest of France. Yet another powerful weapon that the Germans possessed in their dealings with Marshal Pétain was the control that they exercised over the 1,500,000 French prisoners of war who had been captured in the campaign of 1940. It was indicative of the contempt with which Hitler regarded France and her political leaders that, despite the most strenuous efforts that were made by Laval to secure their release, only a small number of these men were allowed to return home in the course of the war.[14]

By 1941, then, many of the hopes that had been placed by the collaborators in a policy of genuine cooperation between France and Germany had been shown to have been misguided. It is true that once the war had been extended to Russia there were elements within the Nazi régime who believed that the Second World War should be regarded as a crusade against Bolshevism, a crusade in which *all* the European nations should be called upon to unite. It is also true that by 1943 and 1944 one of the themes on which the Nazi propaganda machine was to lay its greatest stress was the necessity for *all* Europeans to stand together to resist the domination of the continent at the end of the war by American capitalism and Russian Communism. But, although a number of Fascists in the occupied countries (including Doriot) were determined to prove their fidelity to the European Idea by volunteering to serve alongside the German army in the war on the Eastern Front, this did not mean that Germany was sincere in her claim that she was now defending the cause of European unity against the forces that were opposed to it. The major Russian counter-offensives in 1941 and 1942, together with the appalling casualties that were now being inflicted on the German army, provide convincing evidence that there were less disinterested motives behind the change of policy. In any case, this was a change of policy of which Hitler himself never really approved.

Drieu was quick to appreciate the realities of this situation. Already by December 1941 – the month in which Germany declared war on the United States and the month in which the German armies reeled before the onslaught of the first major Russian counter-offensive in the East – he was prepared to admit the possibility that Hitler might eventually be defeated. And already he had decided who it was who would benefit from this defeat. If Germany were to be beaten, he maintained, it would be better that Europe should fall to the Russians than that it should be liberated by the Anglo-Saxons. The Bolsheviks, like the Nazis, might have abandoned the cause of revolutionary Socialism, and the Russian political system might have degenerated into a bureaucratic tyranny, but if Europe became Communist she would at least be forced to accept a political system that fitted the circumstances of the twentieth century, whereas if she was conquered by the West she would suffer again from all the weaknesses which had been characteristic of the democracies in the 1930s.

He still *hoped* that Germany might emerge victorious from the conflict, of course, and in 1942 he travelled to Germany to take part in a Congress of European writers that was organised at Weimar.[15] But by the beginning of 1943 he could delude himself no longer. In October 1942 the British defeated Rommel at El Alamein, and in January 1943 Field Marshal von Paulus and 300,000 German troops surrendered to the Russians at Stalingrad. Meanwhile, the situation inside France was rapidly deteriorating. In November 1942 the Americans took over control of French North Africa, and, as a reprisal, the Germans invaded the unoccupied zone in France. From now on the authority of Vichy was largely fictitious: the government was progressively purged of all but the most ardent collaborators; both the Germans and the Milice embarked on a campaign of reprisals against the Resistance; and although Laval was able to save about a half of the French Jews from transportation to the extermination camps, and had considerable success in protecting the French people as a whole from the full fury of the German demands for 'labour volunteers', the end of French independence was clearly in sight.

In July 1943 the Western Allies, having completed the conquest of North Africa, invaded Sicily. On 25 July there was a meeting of the Fascist Grand Council in Rome at which Mussolini was deposed from power. Analysing the failure of Italian Fascism in the pages of *La Révolution Nationale* Drieu gave more than a hint that the reasons that had led to the downfall of Mussolini were equally relevant to the plight of European Fascism as a whole:

1. From the political point of view he [Mussolini] neglected the task of maintaining the popular basis of his authority. At an early stage he abandoned the device of consulting the people by means of the plebiscite, a device that had originally constituted part of his political strength.
2. From the social point of view the Fascist position has always been profoundly unsatisfactory. Corporatism is not a solution. The fact that for the last two years it has proved to be no solution for France helps us to understand why it has been so impotent in Italy as well. Corporatism is only of value to the extent that it is a means towards the establishment of socialism. When it ends in an impasse it causes the worst kind of discontent to accumulate.
3. From the international point of view Fascism has been the victim of a drama that is developing in all the countries of Europe, a drama which demonstrates the fact that we in the continent have found no solution to the serious problems involved in holding the balance between nationalism and internationalism. Fascism has not been able to reconcile its violent nationalism, its deepseated impulse towards imperialism with the need for it to recognize its position of inferiority vis à vis other powers, with the need for it to subordinate its policies to those of empires greater than its own.[16]

Already in June 1943 the *Nouvelle Revue Française* had ceased publication. The public explanation that Drieu had given for this development was that it had been made inevitable by the shortage of printing paper, but there can be little doubt that there was a more important factor than that behind this decision.

'I have been completely wrong about Hitlerism', he remarked to one of his friends in January 1943. 'On the whole I was a much better judge of Germany in 1933 and 1934. When I became a partisan my vision was obscured. As much as any other nation Germany shares in the decadence of Europe.'[17]

For a time he thought of joining the Resistance – he was particularly attracted by the idea of becoming a member of the Alsace-Lorraine brigade which was commanded by André Malraux. But as soon as he thought of this possibility he realised that such a solution to his problems was out of the question, for, apart from the fact that the Communists would never permit it, he was not convinced that the Resistance was a credible political force. At one moment he considered that de Gaulle might be nothing more than a 'mixture of Colonel de la Rocque and Alexander Kerensky',[18] a figure of the Right who would prove himself to be unable to resist the pressure of the Left. The next moment he was excited by the possibility that de Gaulle might be a secret Fascist, a more successful version of Doriot, an inspired leader of men who was playing off the Russians against the Anglo-Saxons and the Anglo-Saxons against the Russians in order to reassert the position of France as a great power.[19] But whatever the principles that inspired the leader of the Resistance the issue was really irrelevant. Drieu was convinced that the Americans and the British would never allow de Gaulle any real degree of independence, and he was firmly of the opinion that at the end of the war the Communists would succeed in frustrating any efforts that de Gaulle might make to overcome the bitter divisions that existed in French society, divisions that had been greatly exacerbated by the events that had taken place since 1939.[20] It was only too obvious what was going to happen in France at the end of the war. Once France had been liberated from the Germans, the adherents of Vichy would be persecuted by the Communists and the Resistance would undertake a bloody purge of the collaborators. The country would then slide even further into the decadence and defeatism from which she had suffered in the 1930s, and Frenchmen would soon discover that the Fourth Republic was no improvement on the Third. Finally, some time after the defeat of Germany, there would be another world war, this time between East and West to decide who should dominate Europe. After two or three years in which she

would be able to enjoy the latest American films, France would
be overrun by the Russians and the Communists would be in-
stalled in power.[21]

In these circumstances the only course of action that Drieu
believed to be open to him was for him to remain faithful to his
principles and to accept the doom that was awaiting him, for,
although Fascism had been betrayed by the dictators, and
although Fascism in practice had never been anything more than
a façade to disguise the manoeuvrings of politicians who had an
insatiable lust for power, he could not deny the hopes that it had
once aroused within him:

> I cannot live except in this dream of a reassertion of the
> principles of virility and asceticism [he wrote in his Journal
> in 1945]. I believed in a dream as an intellectual should, and I
> remain faithful to this dream. The half realisation of this dream
> was the final expression of everything that I love in life: a
> certain physical attitude; a certain kind of aristocratic
> behaviour. It was a dream that was ruined by bureaucracy, by
> the verbalism of the propagandists, and by bourgeois half-
> measures, but it excited me for ten years and it made me realise
> what my true nature was.[22]

The extermination of six million Jews could hardly be described
as a 'bourgeois half-measure', and a passage like this certainly
illustrates the extent to which Drieu, like so many French
Fascists, was incapable of understanding the truly revolutionary
(and satanic) nature of Nazi irrationalism. But even if Drieu *had*
been aware of this it would hardly have deterred him from the
course of action on which he was now engaged. Towards the end
of his life Barrès confessed that his one remaining desire was to
live in 'an Escorial of dreams'.[23] This was something that Drieu
experienced, too. The fact is that by the final years of the Second
World War he was deliberately shutting his eyes to the events
that were taking place around him and was moving ever more
rapidly into a private world of his own imagination. To emphasise
the fact that he was prepared to die with Fascism, he had already
rejoined the P.P.F. in November 1942, and, although he was only
to stay with the party for a few months, by this action he had
effectively cut himself off from any possibility that he might
escape the vengeance of the Resistance.

From now on, his behaviour was dominated by a kind of death-wish. More and more he came to identify his own fate with that of the German people. More and more the spectacle of the Third Reich moving towards its final Götterdämmerung was something that he found to be profoundly moving. Despite his disillusionment with Hitler he was fascinated by the scale of the tragedy that was now being enacted by the German people. Towards the end of the war he wrote:

> Certainly I like all the peoples of Europe in equal measure,
> but amongst these peoples, apart from the English – whom I
> shall never forget, any more than I shall ever forget my first
> mistress – it is the Germans whom I am beginning to appreciate
> . . .Their physical presence in Paris exasperates me; I see little
> of them; but in the end I am won over by their solitude in the
> middle of the world. They, too, are a minority people. And in
> addition they are more courageous than the rest.[24]

But was it really true to say that all Germany's efforts since 1933 had been in vain? Could it not be argued that both Hitler and Mussolini had played a vital rôle in preparing Europe for its eventual unification by the Communists? There were questions that were posed by Drieu in his last major piece of political journalism, an article that he wrote for the *Révolution Nationale* in July 1944. In this article he openly admitted that Hitler had gravely damaged the cause of European unity by the policies that he had pursued in the occupied territories. He also conceded the fact that the German dictator had based his support far too much on reactionary forces such as the Wehrmacht rather than on the revolutionary enthusiasm of the working class. But, if Mussolini and Hitler had rejected and misunderstood Marxism, was it not equally true that they had created the conditions for its final victory?

> Fascism has been the most wonderfully effective camouflage
> for a great social movement of the petite bourgeoisie, a move-
> ment that has been furiously romantic like everything that is
> produced by this class wherever it still flourishes, and this
> movement is the vanguard of the real socialist revolution.
> From this point of view we have not been mistaken. We
> European Fascists will prove to be just as revolutionary as we

always wanted to be. We can die contented. We have performed a task in Europe that other people were unable to
accomplish. Later on the Communists will see that we opened
up the way for them in an area where their own advance had
been relatively slight.[25]

These views were so obviously defeatist in character that the
article was banned by the German censor. A few weeks later the
Western Allies entered Paris. Drieu remained unrepentant, however. Not only was he unperturbed by the prospect of a Russian
hegemony over Europe, he welcomed it. 'I want to see the
triumph of totalitarian man over the world', he wrote in his
Journal. 'The era of the divided man has ended. The era of the
integrated man is returning.' His only fear was that Stalin might
not have a successor who was worthy of him.[26]

The story of the remaining months of Drieu's life is briefly told.
After the Allied liberation of Paris in August 1944 he refused to
follow the example of many of the other collaborators by seeking
refuge in Germany: instead he chose to lead the life of a fugitive
in the French capital, moving from one address to another to
avoid being arrested by the Resistance. He knew that eventually
he must be caught, but he had already decided that he would
commit suicide rather than face the humiliation of a trial.
    Meanwhile he devoted himself to the task of composing his
spiritual testament. Critics like Brasillach had undoubtedly been
justified in claiming in the 1930s that, despite its apparent
sophistication, a great deal of Drieu's fictional work suffers from
a tawdry and sentimental romanticism (although whether Brasillach was the most suitable person to make this kind of criticism
is another matter).[27] And in his political writings, too, Drieu's
achievement was often an uneasy amalgam of the intelligent and
the facile. In his final work, however, Drieu achieved an economy
of style and a consistency of tone that had hitherto eluded him.
In 1943, in the novel L'homme à cheval, he offered a moving
commentary on the disillusionment of his hopes for European
unity by describing the rise and fall of a South American dictator
whose ambitious schemes for federating the subcontinent had
eventually ended in failure. In 1944 there appeared Les chiens
de paille, another valedictory work, in which he defended his

activities during the occupation by comparing the rôle that he had played with that of Judas: just as the latter had been compelled to commit a terrible crime in order that the rest of mankind should be saved, he argued, so the collaborators had been called upon to betray their country in order that France might be reborn. But it was in *Récit Secret*, the document that he wrote during his months of hiding in Paris in 1944 and 1945, that he most successfully conveyed the essential starkness of his final vision of the world.

The major theme of *Récit Secret* is the loneliness of the human condition. Drieu confesses that he himself had first experienced this sense of loneliness during his youth and during the early weeks of the First World War. But then he had taken part in the bayonet charge at the battle of Charleroi, and from this moment he had realised that Indian philosophy and religion was correct in asserting that the Self is an illusion:

> The things that I felt to be spiritual, immortal and inextinguishable in me were precisely the things that were not particular to me. In my moments of fulfilment and lucidity I have always felt that what was important for me and in me was the element that was not me, the element that was part of something other than me, something quite foreign and opposite to me.[28]

For a time it had seemed that Fascism might offer him a means of escaping from the trammels of the Self into the realm of the Infinite, but Fascism had failed and now there was no other alternative except for him to destroy himself. What attracted him in Buddhism, he confessed, was that it repudiated the idea of the immortality of the soul: when a person dies he is released from the world completely and the Self is annihilated. What frightened him about Buddhism, he admitted, was its teaching that if a person is not sufficiently detached from the world at the time of his death he will be made to undergo another incarnation and forced to live out another life as meaningless and futile as the first.

The immediate problem for Drieu, however, was to find the most effective method by which he could bring his present life to an end. In the early days of August 1944 he had taken a fatal dose of luminal, but his cook had returned unexpectedly to his flat and summoned an ambulance to take him to hospital. While he was in hospital he had cut his veins, but again he was saved. Finally on 16 March 1945, however, he succeeded in committing suicide.

Many harsh judgements have been passed on Drieu, most of them justified. As an egocentric who regarded the destiny of others as being peripheral to his own concerns, he was often totally irresponsible. As an aesthete who placed himself beyond Good and Evil, he advocated solutions to the problems of the world that immeasurably increased the sum of human suffering. And yet no one could deny that his career was a tragic one. Perhaps it was Mauriac who passed the most charitable verdict on him when he said that Fate would have been kinder to Drieu had he been permitted to die when his illusions about the world were still intact: he should never have returned from the Dardanelles in 1915.[29]

PART III

GEORGES BERNANOS AND THE KINGDOM OF GOD

Who would deny that Evil is organised, that it constitutes a universe that is more real than that which is apparent to our senses, with its sinister landscapes, its pallid sky, its cold sun, its cruel stars? A kingdom that is spiritual and at the same time carnal, of a tremendous density, of an almost infinite heaviness, in comparison with which the kingdoms of earth are like images or symbols. A kingdom that can only really be countered by the mysterious kingdom of God which we talk about, alas, without our being able to understand or even imagine, but the advent of which we await.

Les grands cimetières sous la lune, p. 81.

7

'THIS CENTURY DECEIVES US'

By the end of the 1930s many European intellectuals had come to repudiate the various forms of authoritarianism that had established themselves in Europe in the years that had followed the First World War: in 1936 André Gide announced his disenchantment with Communism in his *Retour de l'U.R.S.S.*; Malraux had fallen out of sympathy with the Communists by 1939; and, after his return from Catalonia in 1937, George Orwell was to spend the rest of his life in attacking all the 'smelly little orthodoxies'[1] that menaced the cause of freedom. But it was not merely on the Left that men came to oppose tyranny in the course of the 1930s, for there was no more spectacular volte-face than that performed by Georges Bernanos during the first twelve months of the Spanish civil war. A life-long, if an extraordinarily anarchical, supporter of the extreme Right in French politics, he had settled in Majorca in 1934, and, in the summer of 1936, he had given enthusiastic support to the rebellion of the Spanish generals against the republican régime. By 1937, however, he was a bitter opponent of Franco and, in the course of the next year, he was to publish one of the most passionate attacks on tyranny ever to be written – *Les grands cimetières sous la lune*.

It is important to note that Bernanos's primary aim in writing this book was not so much to attack the principles of the original Spanish Fascists grouped round José Antonio's Falange movement as to direct the attention of his readers to the rôle that had been played by the army and the middle class in perverting these principles. Nevertheless this in no way diminishes the impact of his work. On the contrary, in this book Bernanos enumerates the ways in which, with the outbreak of the civil war, the Spanish Right abandoned all moral scruples. He shows how the Spanish army, which had traditionally been a stronghold of freemasonry, now put itself forward as the defender of Catholicism. He shows how the middle classes came to adopt the principles of the Fascists so that they could more effectively preserve their own selfish interests. He analyses in detail the process by which the Falange in Majorca, only 500 strong at the beginning of the war, was transformed into a force of 15,000 men within the space of a couple of months. Finally he describes the way in which, in the course of the war, the Falange was reduced to the status of an auxiliary force of the army, its leaders ignored or forced into submission, and its rank and file encouraged to commit the most terrible atrocities against the civilian population.

In a place like Majorca the change that came over the Spanish middle class at the outbreak of the war was particularly striking. The bourgeoisie, who before the outbreak of the civil war had continually professed a pious horror of violence, now sent their sons into the Falange movement and took the initiative in selecting the people who were to die in the purges:

You must see. You must understand. There is a small island, very calm, very snug, with its almond trees, oranges and vines. The capital is hardly of more importance than an old town in our French provinces. The second capital, Soller, is nothing more than a market town. The villages, isolated from one another, clinging to the mountainside or scattered on the plain, are only linked together by bad roads and infrequent and unreliable public transport. Each one of these villages is a closed world with its two parties, that of the 'Priests' and that of the 'Intellectuals', with which the workers timidly associate themselves. There is still a lord of the manor, whom one does not see except on rare occasions, but who knows his people, and who a long time ago, together with his ally, the parish priest, has taken note of the bad ones. Never mind!
The pleasant nature of Spanish customs has meant that this world has lived in harmony and danced together on feast days. Until the day when practically all these villages had its committee to carry out the purges, a secret and benevolent tribunal generally composed of the following people: the landowner or his bailiff, the sacristan, the parish priest's housekeeper, several peasants of property and their wives, and finally the young men hastily recruited into the new Falange, all too often very recent converts, impatient to show their mettle, intoxicated by the fear they inspire in poor devils when they see a blue shirt and a bonnet with a red pompom on it.[2]

The terror was not confined to the villages, however, and, even if Bernanos had wished to ignore the reality of what was happening elsewhere in the island outside Palma, he soon found this to be impossible, for the murder squads transported their victims through the main streets of the capital to their place of execution:

I have seen down there in Majorca lorries full of men passing along the Rambla. With a noise like thunder they rolled along at the same level as the terraces that had just been painted in many different colours, terraces that have the gay murmur of a travelling fair. The lorries were grey with the dust from the roads. The men sitting in them were grey as well. They were sitting in groups of four with their grey caps on their heads and their hands discreetly stretched out over their cloth trousers. Each evening, when they returned from the fields, men like these were taken away from their far-off villages; they left for their last journey with their shirts sticking to their shoulders with sweat, their hands still dirty from the day's work, leaving the soup laid out on the table and a breathless woman arriving too late at the end of the garden with a bundle of personal belongings wrapped in a clean napkin: Goodbye! Best wishes![3]

In view of all this, Bernanos maintained, it was no wonder that a number of the original members of the Falange wanted to leave its ranks; his own son had torn up his Falange shirt in disgust after being forced to take part in a punitive expedition like this.

But this was not the most terrible feature of the situation. For how had it been possible for the Nationalists to know which were the people to be taken away and shot? In one of the passages that has just been quoted Bernanos had already made a pointed reference to the fact that the tribunals that were set up in the country villages included a fair number of individuals who were associated with the Church. When the purges became more frequent in the early months of 1937, however, even Bernanos was to be amazed by the extent to which the ecclesiastical authorities now became directly involved in the machinery of terror. Several weeks before the Easter week of 1937, for example, the churches in Majorca issued forms to their parishioners, forms which were to be filled in by the faithful after they had taken their Easter communion and were then to be handed back to their

parish priests. It was clear to the inhabitants of the island for
what purpose these forms had been distributed. Immediately the
churches of Majorca was packed with terrified penitents.

As a Catholic Bernanos was particularly scandalised by incidents such as this one. This, then, was the reality behind all the
propaganda that was being put out by many Catholics in the rest
of Europe, propaganda which claimed that the Franquist rebellion was a 'crusade' to defend the principles of Christianity
against the attack that was being mounted against it by its
enemies. In one of the most remarkable passages in his book on
the Spanish civil war Bernanos imagines an address that might
be delivered to the Church by an intelligent agnostic, an address
upbraiding the Christians for their spiritual mediocrity and lack
of genuine faith. The agnostic points out that it had not been
Communists or atheists who had originally decided that Christ
should be crucified, and it was not Communists and atheists who
were crucifying Jesus Christ at the present time. If Christians had
tried to put the teachings of St Francis into practice instead of
merely applauding them, then Europe would have been spared
the Reformation, the wars of religion, and all the terrible events
that had taken place since. Only by emancipating itself from the
worship of power and money, only by attempting to recover the
spirit of childhood could the Church hope to recapture the
allegiance of modern man:

> The purposes of God, as you say, are beyond our comprehen-
> sion. But it is still difficult to believe that you are not being
> given your last chance. Your last chance and ours as well. Are
> you capable of rejuvenating the world? Yes or No? The Gospel
> is always young, it is you who are old.[4]

From the trenchant nature of passages like these it might seem
that the political evolution of the author of *Les grands cimetières
sous la lune* would be comparatively easy to analyse, and yet the
truth is that Bernanos is a much more difficult figure to understand than either Barbusse or Drieu la Rochelle. In part this
difficulty is due to the fact that his work reflects the many
ambiguities that were inherent in the Catholic revival that took
place in France towards the end of the nineteenth century. On
the one hand this movement called on Frenchmen to return to the

orthodox Catholic faith. On the other hand this revival was characterised not merely by an extraordinary emotionalism and a marked propensity for the melodramatic – qualities that are particularly to be found in the work of writers like Barbey d'Aurevilly and Léon Bloy, both of whom Bernanos profoundly admired, but also by a peculiar kind of romanticism that had anarchic and heretical as well as authoritarian implications. Bernanos himself might see no contradiction between the intensely individualistic nature of his religious position and his constant claim that he was one of the Church's most loyal sons. This, however, only increases the difficulty that any reader must experience when he first attempts to come to terms with Bernanos's message.

But Bernanos's capacity for self-contradiction represents only one part of the problem that is raised by his work, for, while it is true to say that the Catholic revival as a whole tended to react violently against nineteenth-century liberalism and its cult of Progress, Bernanos's pessimism is of a rather special kind. The reader of Bernanos's political writings and novels soon becomes aware that he is entering, not into any rational universe, but into a realm that at first sight seems to be one of fantasy, a nightmarish world in which, for every character that is possessed of hope, many more seem to be doomed to panic and despair. Even if he is fascinated by the hypnotic power of Bernanos's writings the reader must repeatedly ask himself whether the man who produced them was not in some ways psychologically disturbed.

These problems have led a number of commentators to lose patience with Bernanos, dismissing him as a manic-depressive and accusing him of chronic confusion and incoherence, and yet the key to an understanding of his work *can* be found if the reader is prepared to take the trouble to acquaint himself with the basic facts of the latter's experience. The main events in Bernanos's life were his childhood and his experiences during the First World War. The answer to many of the paradoxes that exist in his work may be found in an examination of his early career.

Georges Bernanos was born in Paris on 20 February 1888. His father, who owned a business specialising in soft furnishings, came from Lorraine: his mother came from a family of peasant origins in the Indre department. Henri Massis, his most intimate friend for a time in the 1920s, is probably right in attributing many of the contradictory elements in Bernanos's character to the fact that his parents differed widely in temperament for, while Bernanos's father was a pugnacious and somewhat vulgar extrovert, his mother was a sensitive and devoutly religious woman.

It was his mother who was to exercise the dominant influence on him during his childhood, and yet Bernanos was always grateful to *both* his parents for the tenacity and independence with which they held their views. In a short autobiographical sketch, composed only a few years before his death he wrote:

> If I was to sum up in a few words for my friends the basic facts
> of my religious and moral formation, I would say that I was
> brought up to respect and love, and also to interpret as freely
> as possible, not only my country's past but also my religion.
> To understand in order to love, to love in order to understand –
> that is probably the most profound tradition of my country.
> It is this which explains our horror of any kind of pharisaism.
> In the Catholic and Royalist family in which I was brought up
> I always heard people speak very freely, and often very
> severely, of the Royalists and the Catholics. I still believe that
> one cannot really 'serve' – in the traditional sense of that
> magnificent word – except by retaining a complete independ-
> ence of judgment about what one is serving.[5]

Certainly as a child Bernanos was allowed a considerable degree of freedom. At the family home at Fressin in Artois he was permitted to wander round the countryside alone and, in later years, after he had become famous, the villagers who had known him in his youth were fond of recalling the fact that he liked climbing to the top of a tree to read, or, more often, to recite the mass and address unending sermons to an imaginary flock of parishioners.[6]

These anecdotes are not without some significance for an understanding of Bernanos's subsequent career, for the novels that he was to write later on in his life were not to be exercised in Naturalism but studies of the interpenetration of the natural and the supernatural, and even the political views that he was to hold in later years cannot possibly be understood unless they are seen as an extension of his early dreams of a revival of medieval Christendom. Throughout his career, in fact, the vision that he formed of the world was the vision of a child:

I do not know for whom I write. But I know why I write.
I write to justify myself. In the eyes of whom?. . .In the eyes of
the child I once was. What does it matter if he has ceased to
talk to me or not? I will never accept his silence, I will always
reply to him.[7]

To those who objected that the dream-like intensity of his novels
made them fantastic and unreal, therefore, Bernanos replied that
it is adults and not the young who waste their time in the pursuit
of the ephemeral and the insubstantial. Only children and the
saints, he was convinced, are capable of that immediate and
spontaneous relationship with God that the rest of mankind
continually seek: on his death bed he confided to the priest who
was in attendance on him that at the worst moments of his life
the only way in which he had been able to protect himself from
despair had been by his being able to recall the grace that he had
received at his first communion.

Nevertheless, if Bernanos was always to remember the intensity
of his childhood joys, he was never to forget the misery caused
by his early fears, and already as a young boy he was a prey to
those feelings of panic and terror that were to recur at intervals
throughout the rest of his life:

Who first taught me that Faith is a gift of God? I do not know.
My mother, no doubt. But then I realised that it was a gift that
could be withdrawn. . .From this moment I knew the anguish
of death, for after so many years I cannot separate the one
anguish from the other. This double terror entered by the
same breach in my young heart.[8]

In contrast to a writer like Mauriac, then, the problem that
troubled Bernanos was not his lack of faith, nor the conflict
between the demands of the spirit and the desires of the flesh,
but his lack of assurance that he was worthy of being saved. The
fact that he was a sickly child only served to exacerbate his terror
of death and judgement, and in later years he would freely admit
that it was in reaction against these fears that he made such a
nuisance of himself at school.

By the time that he had reached adolescence, however, it
seemed that he was well on the way towards overcoming his
early difficulties. In a letter that he wrote at the age of 17 to one

of his teachers, the Abbé Lagrange, he explained that now more
than ever he had come to realise that it was only by totally dedi-
cating himself to God that he could conquer his fear of death,[9]
and in the Royalist movement that had been created by Maurras
in the aftermath of the Dreyfus Affair he believed that he had at
last found the idealism and the discipline that he needed:

> As for me, I admire with all my heart these valiant men of the
> Action Française, these true sons of Gaul, with their good sense
> and their faith, who do not recoil in front of any idea but
> prevail over others because of their boldness and their ability
> to defend their position without recourse to phraseology. How
> clear they are! How trenchant their style! You may believe in
> them or you may not, but you always have to listen to what
> they say.[10]

In view of the fact that Bernanos's family were supporters of
the extreme Right in French politics, and given the ferocity with
which many sections of the Right reacted to the triumph of the
Dreyfusards and to the harsh treatment that was meted out to the
Church in the aftermath of the Affair, it is hardly surprising that
Bernanos should have felt as he did. It was in a spirit of gay
abandon, then, that some years later, as a young law student in
Paris, he enrolled in the ranks of the Camelots du Roi, the young
militants of the Action Française. And it was not long before his
devotion to the cause was put to the test, for in 1909 he was
condemned to serve a short term of imprisonment in the Santé for
the part that he had played in a demonstration organised by the
Camelots du Roi in the Latin Quarter. This demonstration had
been mounted in protest against a series of lectures that were
being given at the Sorbonne by Professor Thalamas, lectures that
were extremely critical of the reputation of Joan of Arc, the
heroine of the French Right. Throughout his life Bernanos took
pride in the fact that he had suffered imprisonment for so worthy
a cause.[11]

The years between 1905 and the outbreak of the First World
War, the years that saw the ranks of the middle-class youth of
France swept with enthusiasm for the Nationalist and Catholic
revivals, were, in fact, to be the happiest years in Bernanos's life.
But whether he had really emancipated himself from the com-
bination of despair and indiscipline that had plagued his child-

hood is another matter. Admittedly, in the article entitled 'The Effects of the Democratic Prejudice in Literature' that he wrote during his imprisonment in the Santé, he roundly condemned the pessimism and the anarchism that he believed to be inherent in liberalism, and it was with a call to action and political commitment that he attacked those writers who were caught in the impasse of aestheticism:

> War on this race of weaklings! These sensualists do not know how to feel at all. For it is not a question of needlessly multiplying a series of different or contradictory sensations, but of exalting the powers of our sensibility by attaching these sensations to a great passion. Unlucky are they who have never known the primitive pleasure of experiencing in the depths of their being the shock of an insult, of feeling all their nerves respond to the rhythm of an unparalleled hatred![12]

But the violence of this onslaught was indicative of the degree to which he himself was a prey to the temptation of despair, and his own literary efforts during this period, the short stories on great deeds of heroism and sacrifice in the Middle Ages that he published in the magazine *Le Panache*, are notable more for their bombast and artificiality than for their conformity to the Maurrassian canons of order and clarity.

Indeed, it is quite obvious that, in the years immediately before the outbreak of the First World War, the leaders of the Action Française themselves were somewhat embarrassed by the anarchic behaviour of this new recruit to their cause, for, although the Action Française contained many disparate elements within its ranks, and although a certain element of anarchism and romanticism was inherent in the very nature of the French Royalist movement, Bernanos's extremism was quite out of the ordinary, an extremism that was demonstrated, not only by the violence of his language, not only by the enthusiasm with which he supported the radical social and economic policies put forward by the Sorelian element within the Cercle Proudhon, but also by the determined way in which he was prepared to oppose the official policy of the movement when he felt that the situation demanded it.

This was shown very clearly in the period after the Second Moroccan crisis when Maurras introduced an element of caution

into his demands for an immediate overthrow of the Third
Republic once he realised that a war between France and Germany was becoming increasingly likely. To Bernanos, Maurras's
action was so great a betrayal of the movement's principles that
he seriously thought of emigrating with a group of friends to
South America. Nothing came of this idea, but Bernanos was so
determined that the royalist principles of the Action Française
should be maintained that he and a number of his friends became
involved in a plot to restore the Portuguese pretender to his
throne with the help of dissident elements within the Portuguese
fleet. Perhaps it was fortunate that the details of the plot became
known to Maurras and his lieutenants who strictly forbade their
young rebels to proceed any further with their plans.

Already in the years before 1914, therefore, the relationship
between Bernanos and the hierarchy of the Action Française was
far from harmonious, and the controversy that raged between
them over the Portuguese affair was only a portent of further
quarrels that were to arise in the future. After this particular
crisis, however, there was a reconciliation. Maurras, having come
to the conclusion that his young rebel would benefit from a period
of exile in the provinces, offered him the directorship of L'Avant
Garde de Normandie, a royalist weekly that was published in
Rouen, while Bernanos, for his part, was so anxious to secure
some kind of permanent employment that he was prepared to
accept.

In the course of the next few months, however, he was to show
that he had in no way surrendered his independence of mind. He
scandalised the supporters of the moderate Right by attacking
the faint-hearted nature of their convictions:

> Conservatives, opportunists, liberals, I do not set any value on
> you, vegetarians! Although one can criticise the doctrine of
> Leibnitz for its extreme elegance I will not deny that you also
> have a part to play in the agreeable comedy of the universe.
> What part? That of being devoured.[13]

He also became involved in a lively, if somewhat unedifying,
controversy with the philosopher Alain – the most eminent of the
intellectuals who were sympathetic to the Radical Party – over
the latter's opposition to the proposal that was then being debated
by the French Chamber that in view of the German menace the

period of compulsory military service should be extended from two to three years. Almost immediately Bernanos turned the issue into one of personalities:

> You say that you would rather die than live as a slave?. . .If one day we are conquered because of the folly of you and people like you what will remain of the liberty for which you want to die? It is not your idea that I despise it is you yourself. . .[14]

The climax of Bernanos's activity at *L'Avant Garde de Normandie* came in the last moments before the outbreak of the First World War when he produced an editorial in which, while expressing his regret at the death of the Socialist leader Jaurès, he went on to say that this was a death from which France could only gain. In view of the fact that the murderer of Jaurès was reputed to be an admirer of the Action Française the tone of this editorial was, to say the least, inappropriate, and the leaders of the royalist movement themselves were so anxious to secure the unity of France in the face of the German menace that they intervened to prevent it being published.[15]

At the time that this incident occurred, however, Bernanos was completely unrepentant. With the outbreak of the First World War his hopes were high, not only that France would be victorious, but also that within French politics the royalist and Catholic cause would at last prevail. Although it seemed for a time that he would not be accepted for military service on the grounds of ill-health, therefore, he persevered in his efforts to enlist. By the autumn of 1914 he was in the army.

With the outbreak of the First World War, Bernanos found himself transported into a very different world from the one to which he was accustomed, a world in which the very last thing he could do was to continue playing the rôle of an enfant terrible. Never by any stretch of the imagination an individual who relished discipline he found the restrictions and boredom of military life peculiarly difficult to bear, and this, no doubt, was the reason why he was never promoted beyond the rank of corporal. On the other hand it is important to note that he was courageous – he was wounded several times and received a number of citations for bravery – and the fact that his view of the war was that of the common soldier at the front was to have a profound effect in reinforcing the lessons that he had learned from the Cercle Proudhon. Many years later he was to write:

> The part that I played in the war of 1914 was one in which I was in a position of daily familiarity and brotherhood with my peasant and worker friends. They succeeded in alienating me for ever from the bourgeois mentality. It is not the ignorance or the misery of the people that attracts me, it is their nobility. The French worker élite is the only aristocracy that is left to us, the only one which the bourgeoisie of the nineteenth and twentieth centuries has not succeeded in destroying.[16]

With tutors such as these amongst his comrades, therefore it was not long before Bernanos realised that the hopes that had sustained him at the beginning of the war were completely illusory. He was appalled by the contrast between the realities of life at the front and the atmosphere that prevailed in Paris, and within the space of a few months he felt completely alienated from the politicians and propagandists of *all* parties. In a letter of 1915 he confided his views to a friend:

> They talk of relieving us at the end of the month because of the great victorious and decisive attack that will give us the dominion of the world. As for me you know I have no objection to that. Since the newspapers inform me that the Seine has flooded its banks I hope that the waters will reach Ali Baba's cave and drown the parliamentarians.[17]

Whichever way the war ended, he was convinced, the future for mankind was a bleak one. The only principle in which Imperial Germany believed was the power of naked force, while all that the Western powers were defending were the insipid doctrines of nineteenth-century liberalism. As for that vision of heroic and Christian France that had inspired him in the years before 1914 this was nowhere to be seen.

For a time it seemed that the only attitude that he could adopt towards the events that were now taking place in Europe was one of stoical despair, and for a time he found this attitude to be attractive. He wrote in a letter to a friend, dated September 1915:

> This century deceives us, old man, and the glory of old has played us false. I do not know what I am defending nor for

what I can give my life. Extraordinary stupidity! Above the head of the poor trooper who has nothing but his cape and sabre, the diplomatic gentlemen twitter away with their honeyed words. We must stick it out, if only for the sake of honour and because we must not lose the fruits of our efforts. I have decided that my epitaph will consist of these two lines only:

'Here lies the man who fought and died
to satisfy himself and to enrage those who did not fight and die.'[18]

But this was not a position that he could maintain for very long and by the beginning of 1916 he found himself in the throes of a profound psychological crisis. He made an attempt to write, but found it impossible to continue. Writing to his fiancée in January 1916, he complained:

Alas I have become dried up and hard like a miser. I no longer hear my music. I am on my last legs, if I have any left at all. I am working in the darkest night. I am fighting an extraordinary battle with images and words. Every page that I get written costs me a world. I hope it is only an ordeal to which the Good Lord is subjecting me. I hope that He has only blindfolded me and that I will not produce a monster of black melancholy but something beautiful and luminous, like the things that I loved so much.[19]

His hopes that he would soon emerge from his depression were not to be fulfilled, however, and in the course of the next few months the façade that he had presented to the world in the years before the outbreak of the war was completely shattered. Once again Bernanos was to experience the fear that had dominated his childhood. Once again he was to be overwhelmed by a sense that the world had been abandoned by God. In 1917 he wrote:

There is a thicket with a rustic look about it where we have left a hundred and forty horses. I have buried mine in a shell-hole. Animals and men sleep together under several spadefuls of earth, and the living inhale the mud. Ah! it is not only one's sense of reason and one's feelings of sentiment that suffer

violence here! The earth is not so much turned over as
irreparably defiled. The demon in mankind must triumph in
this monstrous, this sickening satiety, a satiety that seems to
make the Devil as powerful as God.[20]

For a few months in the course of 1917 it seemed that Bernanos
was lost in despair. Then two events occurred which helped him
to come to terms with his situation: he rediscovered the work of
Léon Bloy, and he secured the services of a Benedictine monk,
Dom Besse, as his spiritual director. The relentless nature of
Bloy's search for the Absolute, his burning desire to be vouch-
safed some kind of divine revelation, the violent (and often cruelly
hilarious) onslaught that he directed against the vanities and
hypocrisies of the world – all these had a tonic effect on
Bernanos's morale. But it can hardly be doubted that it was the
influence of Dom Besse that was of greater importance in
helping him to face up to the crisis that confronted him. For not
only was Dom Besse a supporter of the extreme Right in French
politics – in the years before 1914 he had welcomed the prospect
of war as a 'purifying' force within French society – he was also
a personality of considerable spiritual depth. Although the letters
that he wrote to Bernanos have not survived it is clear from
Bernanos's replies that the burden of the monk's advice was that
he should not rebel against the fact of human suffering, but accept
it; only by means of a process of total self-surrender, his confessor
reminded him, could man hope to achieve communion with God.
'At last I have found a teacher and a superior', Bernanos
reported to his fiancée, soon afterwards, 'the terrible and tranquil
monk has forced his way into my heart.'[21] Nevertheless, he did
not find the precepts of his spiritual director easy to follow. There
always seemed to be a part of him that resisted his struggles to
devote himself to God, and he quickly became aware that all the
earlier efforts that he had made in this direction had been extraordinarily superficial. What he was now experiencing, he realised,
was a travail of the spirit that was infinitely more exhausting than
anything that he had experienced in the past, and the most
daunting aspect of the situation was that what Dom Besse was
recommending him to do was not something that had a foresee-
able end but something on which he would be engaged for the
rest of his life. And yet, despite all this, in the course of 1917 and

1918 Bernanos gradually came to accept that it was only by trusting God completely that he could hope to come to terms with his despair and be of some help to his comrades. 'After four years of solitude, rumination and pointless argument with myself I no longer have the means to be mediocre', he told Dom Besse in September 1918. 'I must recover my will-power, something which, I know, will lead me far. All or nothing, that is the word of command.'[22]

Just how far-reaching the implications of this decision were to be he could not himself foresee in 1918, but to the present-day observer it is quite obvious that the spiritual drama that Bernanos had experienced in the course of his service at the front, and the acute sense of shock that he was to experience when he again encountered the selfishness and materialism of civilian life were to provide the central theme of all the novels that he was to produce in the years that followed the First World War.

Certainly it is the theme that dominates his first major novel, *Sous le Soleil de Satan*, which was published in 1926. A work of extraordinary intensity and hallucinatory power, this novel (which owed a great deal to the story of that remarkable nineteenth-century parish priest, the curé d'Ars, who was canonised in 1924) is concerned with the struggle of a young parish priest, the abbé Donissan, to devote himself to the service of God and his fellow-men. First of all he tries to save the soul of a girl who has murdered the lover who was preparing to abandon her, but, although he encounters the Devil in the course of his labours, and although he is successful in making the girl aware of the evil nature of her crime, she eventually decides to commit suicide. Nevertheless Donissan continues with his work and, after enduring a series of further disappointments and after submitting himself to the most stringent forms of asceticism and self-sacrifice, he finally dies, respected and loved by his parishioners who venerate him as a saint. Donissan's task has not been an easy one, however, and nothing more strikingly conveys the harshness of the combat to which he has been called than the terms in which, in the closing pages of the novel, God is praised for the 'efficacious suffering', the 'cleansing pain' that Donissan has had to endure:

'You have cast us like leaven into this darkness. Inch by inch we must reconquer the universe of which sin has deprived us;

we shall give it back to you as you gave it to us in all its order
and its holiness on the first morning of our days. We are not
those rosy-cheeked saints with golden beards whom pious folk
behold in pictures, whose eloquence and perfect health even
philosophers would envy. Our task is not as the world imagines
it. Compared with it, even the urge of genius is a frivolous
game. Lord, every life finely lived bears witness to you. But the
witness which is borne by the saints must be torn with iron out
of their bodies.'[23]

'I believe that my book is one of the books that has been born
of the war', Bernanos said on one occasion; 'besides, I started it
only a few months after the Armistice. The aspect of the world
had been ferocious. It now became hideous...The most reassuring words were used to deceive men. The most imposing words
were emptied of their meaning...Even Death had lost its sacred
significance.'[24] *Sous le Soleil de Satan*, then, was conceived as a
gesture of defiance at the atmosphere of escapism that prevailed
in Europe at the end of the First World War. In a world given
over to evil and despair, Bernanos argues, men cannot commit
themselves partially to the service of God: they must strive for
sanctity or perish. However different in intention and spirit this
novel may have been from another work that had been prompted
by the First World War, Karl Barth's famous *Commentary on
The Epistle to the Romans*, therefore, it was with an almost
Barthian sense of the fallen nature of man that Bernanos
regarded the condition of the world in the years that followed
1918.

Despite the hostility with which it was received by some
Catholics who objected to the melodramatic nature of its plot,
Sous le Soleil de Satan made a tremendous impact when it first
appeared in France in 1926. Léon Daudet reviewing it in the
columns of the newspaper, *Action Française*, announced the
arrival of 'a great intellectual and imaginative force' on the
French literary scene, and compared the magnitude of Bernanos's
achievement (somewhat inappropriately) with that of Proust.[25]
Paul Claudel, writing to the author from the French embassy in
Tokyo, praised the way in which he had displayed a 'royal quality
of power', a 'masterly handling of the events and characters', and

that 'special gift of the novelist which is what I would call the gift of dealing with the unity of the whole'.[26] And other critics, too, were quick to point out the merits of Bernanos's work. Now at last, they declared, the Catholic revival had produced a novel that was the equal of the poetry and the drama that it had inspired in the years before 1914, a novel that was worthy of being compared with the finest work of Dostoievski.

Bernanos was so encouraged by all this that he resigned from the post that he had taken with an insurance company on his return from the war, and decided to become a full-time writer. From this moment onwards, he was to encounter many difficulties, however, and not the least of these difficulties were the financial problems that he now had to face. The work that he had done as the representative of his insurance company in the Eastern provinces of France may have been somewhat drab and mono- tonous in character, and many of his friends were quick to point out the contrast between the nature of his employment and the calls that he repeatedly made in his novels for men to ignore the demands of security and live a life of risk and adventure, but at least his work had provided him with a reasonable income and during the early 1920s he possessed a degree of financial pros- perity that he was never to enjoy again. It was ten years before he published another novel that had a success comparable with that of Sous le Soleil de Satan, and by the early 1930s, by which time he had a wife and a brood of extremely unruly children to support,[27] his plight was so desperate that, after an unsuccessful attempt to earn money by writing detective novels, he was forced to leave France and settle in Majorca where the cost of living was considerably cheaper.[28] Admittedly after the publication of the Journal d'un curé de campagne in 1936 the worst of his financial worries were over, but the fact that he emigrated to Brazil in 1938 meant that he was cut off from his royalties in France during the years of the Second World War, and it was typical of the utter impracticality that Bernanos displayed in all worldly matters that the successive attempts that he made to engage in agriculture in Brazil were uniformly unsuccessful. The emphasis that he was to place in all his writings on the virtues of poverty was not merely a piece of conventional piety, therefore; it was something that he had learnt from his own experience of life.

Perhaps he would not have experienced the problems that he

did had he found it easy to get on with his writing, but at times he found the physical and emotional demands of his literary work almost too much to bear. Repeatedly he denied the fact that he was a writer at all, and in the introduction to *Les grands cimetières sous la lune* he admitted that one glance at a sheet of white paper was sufficient to throw him into consternation:

> The kind of physical concentration which such work imposes on me I find so hateful that I avoid it as much as I can. I write in cafés. . .because I could not do without a human face and a human voice for very long. . .[29]

In one degree or another, of course, *all* writers have experienced the kind of revulsion that Bernanos is here describing, but in his case the problem was made even worse by his intense hatred of the Parisian literary world, and his acute sensitivity to the element of dishonesty that can so easily intrude into any kind of creative activity. No doubt this was the reason why the theme of deceit was to be such a common one in his novels. In *L'Imposture* (1927) and *La Joie* (1928), for example, Bernanos describes the life of deception that is led by the abbé Cénabre, a priest who has lost his faith and yet continues to discharge the duties of his priestly office. And in *Monsieur Ouine* (1943) the principal character of the novel, a retired language-teacher (commonly supposed to be a portrayal of André Gide) is a person whose whole being is dedicated to the task of deceiving the villagers amongst whom he has come to live.

Indeed, it would not be an exaggeration to say that the one vice that Bernanos hated above all others was that of facility, the ability of a writer to produce work that has made only minimal demands on his conscience and imagination, and it is a revealing comment on his own inability to engage in this kind of activity that the few pieces of writing on which he embarked for purely financial gain were extremely unsuccessful; in *Un Crime* and *Un mauvais Rêve*, the two attempts he made in the early 1930s to write a detective story, for example, Bernanos completely ignored the conventions that must be observed in this genre, and showed only too clearly that he was far more interested in the spiritual problems of his criminals than in the process by which they might be apprehended by the police. 'It does not take long for the least of professional writers, once he has found a subject, to

dominate it, to reduce it to his own scale, the scale of his readers',
he once wrote; 'please God I may never be completely the master
of the subject I have chosen. It is rather the subject that masters
me.'[30]

The constant sense of dissatisfaction that Bernanos experienced
in connection with his literary work was, in fact, only one
symptom of a much deeper sense of inadequacy and despair that
he was to experience in the years that followed the First World
War. The fact that he had to endure a number of illnesses and
disabilities in these years is no doubt one of the reasons why
he felt himself to be unequal to the task that confronted him: he
continually complained that he was growing old and sick; he
lived in dread of dying from cancer like his father; and his sense
of physical decline was greatly increased by the after effects of an
accident that he sustained whilst roaring round the countryside
on his beloved motor-cycle in 1933, an accident that was to leave
one of his legs permanently disabled. But the main reason why
he was consumed with despair was because he believed that his
vocation to be a writer was a vocation in the most literal sense of
the word: God had placed certain obligations on him, obligations
that he was not worthy to fulfil. The theme of hypocrisy and
deceit is such a common one in Bernanos's novels, therefore,
because he felt that this was a temptation by which he himself
was constantly beset. 'If it is presented to me on the Day of
Judgement', he once remarked of *L'Imposture*, 'I will not dare to
say to it "I know you not", for I know very well that it contains a
part of my secret.'[31]

What the full extent of his suffering was during the years of life
that were left to him after he came back from the First World War,
however, even those who were close to him did not know. 'He
lived a secret life', one of his friends has commented, 'even though
he talked incessantly. It was a life that he reserved and even
preserved from those he loved.'[32] His family and friends were
acutely aware that the sense of anguish and desolation that
Bernanos experienced at intervals throughout the rest of his life
brought him dangerously close to the point of a total breakdown.
They were also aware that these crises were related to a major
crisis that had occurred during his service in the war. But they
found it difficult to be of any comfort to him since they had not
been through the same experience themselves, and he in turn

found it almost impossible to convey to others what it was that tormented him. 'It is scarcely easy for me to express today the frightful solitude of a man of my age who was in the last war',[33] Bernanos admitted in the autumn of 1939. Nevertheless, it did not take the outbreak of another world war to make him realise that his destiny was one of loneliness. This was something that he had known ever since he had been demobilised in 1919.

Perhaps, indeed, it was only in his writing, the task that otherwise he so hated, that he could find some release from the terrors that haunted him, and perhaps it was only in *Monsieur Ouine*, the novel that he started in 1931 but did not finish until 1940, that he was able most clearly to reveal the nature of the problem with which he was obsessed. Already in *Sous le Soleil de Satan*, it is true, Bernanos had given some indication of the extent to which he was concerned with the power of evil in the world, and already in *L'Imposture* and *La Joie* he had created in the abbé Cénabre a character who was a prey to the temptation of despair. But in all these novels the final note is one of triumph: Donissan ends his life having achieved that communion with God for which he had long striven, and Cénabre is finally saved by means of the suffering of others. In the strange and nightmarish world of *Monsieur Ouine*, by contrast, there is no redemption. Monsieur Ouine, having corrupted the entire village in which he is living and having provoked his neighbours into committing the most terrible crimes, finally dies in the belief that human existence is meaningless: 'I see myself now right into the depths, nothing interrupts my view, no obstacle. There is nothing. Remember this word: nothing.'[34] The atmosphere of *Monsieur Ouine* is one of incoherence and madness. God has withdrawn His grace from the world. Humanity is falling into perdition.

It would, of course, be wrong to conclude from this that Bernanos himself believed that human existence is without meaning or significance for the whole emphasis of his other novels is directed towards the quest for salvation. Furthermore he was possessed of a rich and humorous enjoyment of life that was only rarely reflected in his fictional work, and his friends remembered him as much for his laughter as for his anger and despair. Nevertheless the fact remains that the terror that he had experienced in his childhood and had encountered again in the course of the

First World War was to remain with him throughout the rest of his life. In 1925 he confessed in a letter to feeling that:

Age brings no security, but only a ferocious lucidity which is a reflection of Hell. Whoever has delivered himself over once is never free again and will have to defend his soul to the end.
I do not know by how many devils I am tested but they do not allow me any rest, and I shall still be in a rage when Death tears me from their arms. . .[35]

'What can you do for me?' he asked a friend in 1926; 'I am situated between the Angel of Light and the Angel of Darkness and I look at them in turn with the same desperate hunger for the Absolute.'[36]

This, then, was the background against which Bernanos's flirtation with totalitarianism in the course of the next decade must be seen. The driving force that led him near to the point of accepting Fascism in the early 1930s was that of spiritual despair.

8

THE FAILURE OF THE RIGHT

It is hardly surprising that the first political disillusionment that Bernanos experienced in the aftermath of the war should have been caused by the policies that were being pursued by the Action Française, for it has already been seen that he was extremely critical of Maurras's caution in the period before 1914, and, at the outbreak of the war, he was amazed by the ease with which the movement suspended its anti-republican activities for the duration of the Union Sacrée. Matters came to a head at the end of the war when the Action Française took the unprecedented step of participating in the parliamentary elections in 1919, an action that demonstrated quite clearly that the movement was retreating from its policy of total opposition to the republican régime and was now more interested in rallying the middle classes against the challenge of the Left. Maurras might argue that this electoral activity was only on a very limited scale and that the exercise could be justified by the fact that the elections resulted in the return of the Chamber 'Bleu Horizon', the first right-wing chamber that France had elected for forty years. To Bernanos, however, this manoeuvre was unpardonable. He resigned from the movement immediately. He told Dom Besse:

> I gave myself to the Action Française at an age when abstract ideas and the demands of sentiment make an explosive mixture. It became part of my bones. I was much more profoundly influenced by it than these gentlemen probably think. . .But if I am loyal to my masters it is very upsetting to find the thing that one loves turning into a means of employment. It is quite evident that, after having been an instrument of conquest, the League is now obeying a law of History in administering what it has conquered. You can see it becoming a state which, in order to secure its future, is installing a hierarchy of officials in place of the group that used to make up its little army. It is quite proper for it to do this. But I have neither the inclination nor the ability to become a bureaucrat.[1]

The terms in which this letter was written were those of a studied moderation, and yet even in this letter it is clear how concerned Bernanos was by the failure of the Maurras to grasp the real significance of the crisis that now confronted Europe as a result of the First World War. Satanic forces had been released by the war, he believed, forces that would plunge the peoples of Europe into an orgy of barbarism and cruelty even greater than that which they had experienced between 1914 and 1918. Many years later Bernanos was to compare the hysterical and escapist atmosphere of Paris in 1920 with that of some kind of macabre world fair:

> ...where the international rabble of the Palaces and the wagon-lits came to get rid of their money in Montmartre in the same way that a drunkard sleeps off his wine. Even under the February rain the prevailing atmosphere was that of a brothel ...Whoever has not lived through such a time does not know the meaning of disgust. Merely by inhaling the air of the boulevards you could have smelt the odour of the charnel-houses, even though they were not to open their doors for another nineteen years.[2]

Seen against this background Maurras's decision to take part in the game of party politics was bound to appear grotesque.

Already in 1919, in fact, Bernanos was convinced that the only way in which the Right could meet the challenge of Communism was for it to offer the people some great ideal of human brother-hood that would enable them to overcome their despair. And the only ideal that could do *that*, he believed, was the ideal of a Christian monarchy that had inspired St Louis and Joan of Arc in the Middle Ages, the ideal that had inspired so many members of the Action Française in the years before 1914. As he explained on one occasion:

> I am in no sense an archivist or an archaeologist. If there was no chance that the past might be reborn I would scarcely be interested in it. One cannot devote the whole of one's time to venerating the dead. It is the living we must try to save. If I thought that the tradition of the Christian monarchy survived in the memory of a small number of privileged people I would not insist on it: the atmosphere of museums makes me ill and

that of little sects depresses me. But I believe that this tradition
is still alive in the heart of the people. Even though it cannot
be detected in the people as we know them in the field or in the
factory it is there as we knew them in the war when they were
fighting or were under fire.[3]

The whole tragedy of the situation, as he saw it, was that the
Action Française was in the process of abandoning its original
principles just at the moment when the ordinary people of France
might be prepared to listen to its message.

Nevertheless, in spite of the fact that Bernanos was convinced
that Maurras was committing a serious mistake in following the
course of action on which he was now set, his break with the
latter was not a final one. Bernanos still believed that the Action
Française was the only organisation that existed in France that
was capable of translating his ideals into reality, and for some
years he was hopeful that Maurras might see the error of his
ways. In any case an incident occurred in 1926 that seemed to
make it imperative that he should return to the Maurrassian fold.
This incident was the papal condemnation of the French Royalist
movement.

The possibility that the Pope might take action against Maurras
had already been raised in the years before the outbreak of the
First World War when a commission of theologians appointed
by Pius X reported to the Holy See that the principles on which
the Action Française was based were not compatible with the
teachings of the Church. What the commission found repugnant
was not merely Maurras's own lack of religious belief, but also
the fact that, despite the large number of Catholics within its
ranks, the Action Française had as its primary aim the political
and not the religious regeneration of France. Despite the un-
stinting support which Maurras's movement had given to the
Church in its fight against the anti-clerical policies of successive
French governments, and despite the zeal that had been displayed
by the Action Française in attacking the Modernist tendencies
that were apparent in the Catholic Church at the turn of the
century, therefore, the commission recommended that the movement should be condemned.

It was this recommendation that the Vatican finally implemented in 1926. The delay of twelve years between the compila-

tion of the report and the decision of the Papacy to put it into effect had been due to a number of factors: Pius X had been more interested in pursuing the heresies of the ecclesiastical Left than in denouncing those of the Right; and, with the outbreak of the First World War, it had been deemed inexpedient for the Papacy to take any action that might lead the French people to suppose that it was taking sides in the conflict that was now raging throughout Europe. But with the end of the war and with the election of a Pope who was anxious to clarify the relationship between the Church and the republican régime in France these considerations no longer applied and the original condemnation was put into effect. The works of Maurras and the publications of the Action Française were put on the Index. All those who disregarded the condemnation were threatened with the penalties of excommunication.

Immediately the Catholic members of the Action Française were plunged into an agonising crisis of conscience. They could argue with a certain amount of justification that, by condemning the Action Française, the Pope was attacking a movement that had been one of the most loyal supporters of the Papacy in the past. They could also protest that, by framing the condemnation in the way that he did, Pius XI was using theological arguments to justify a decision that had been dictated by political expediency. But for the Catholic supporters of Maurras merely to register their sense of shock and dismay in this way was clearly no answer to the dilemma that now confronted them. Ought they to remain faithful to Maurras and, by doing so, to disobey their spiritual father in Rome? Or should they follow the dictates of the Vatican, and come to terms with the republic?

Naturally enough Bernanos found the answer to this problem to be a simple one. The Catholics should stand by their principles. 'My friend', he wrote to Henri Massis (at that time director of the *Revue Universelle* and throughout Maurras's lifetime one of the latter's most devoted Catholic supporters):

'a new Modernist invasion is beginning and you see here the forerunners. A hundred years of concessions and equivocations have resulted in the clergy being deeply contaminated with anarchy...I believe that our sons will see the majority of the Church's troops on the side of Death. I will be shot by

Bolshevik priests who will have the 'Social Contract' in their pocket and a cross on their breast.[4]

When it was suggested by Jacques Maritain, therefore, that a possible compromise that might enable Catholics to remain within the Action Française would be for them to group themselves into study circles with chaplains appointed by the Church, Bernanos dismissed this proposal as a move that would lead to the destruction of the movement just as surely as if it were to submit without a struggle. Always intensely suspicious of the subtleties of theologians and the ultramontane tendencies of converts, he announced that he hoped the Catholics would demonstrate to the Pope that they were men and not a flock of sheep.

In asserting his willingness to defy the authorities of the Church over this issue, Bernanos did not, of course, claim that the Action Française was beyond criticism. His opposition to Maurras's growing conservatism in matters of political and social policy has already been noted, and he was deeply concerned, too, by the flippant and cynical aestheticism that was current amongst many of the young intellectuals who were close to the movement. As he constantly reminded his friends, he had prayed for many years that Maurras himself might be granted the gift of faith, and he was convinced that the spiritual quality of the Catholic element within the Action Française had suffered a serious decline in the years that had followed the outbreak of the First World War. On the other hand he was confident that, if the believers within the movement could assert their independence of Maurras, and if the latter could in turn be persuaded to leave to the Catholics to fight the matter out with Rome, then it was possible that some agreement could be found that both Maurras and the Papacy could accept. Indeed, he argued, if matters turned out in this way, the Action Française would emerge from its ordeal stronger than before.[5]

These hopes were not to be fulfilled, however. Pius XI was so determined that the condemnation should be put into effect that he was reluctant even to listen to any pleas that might be made in the movement's favour, while Maurras not only refused to retire into the background but refused even more stubbornly to delete the passages from his writings that had prompted the condemnation in the first place. As a result of the intransigence that was displayed by both parties in the dispute a large number of the Catholic supporters of the movement (including Maritain) felt that they had no alternative except to submit to Rome and withdraw from the Action Française completely.

Bernanos was appalled by the act of treachery that he believed the Church had committed. When, on 28 March 1927, the Action Française was finally and formally condemned in Rome, it was in despairing terms that he wrote to Massis:

> You must be wretched today like me. It is the moment when
> we forget that Our Father is in heaven. What worse event can
> befall us? What greater effort has been made to tear up and
> uproot men's souls? I am dying of shame and disgust.[6]

And it was no accident that it was during the months that he witnessed the repercussions of the condemnation of the Action Française on the Catholic world within France that he wrote an essay on the subject of Joan of Arc, for in this essay he was concerned to point out, not only the contrast between the heroic behaviour of the simple peasant girl who followed the promptings of her conscience and the pusillanimity of the doctors of the Church who followed the dictates of the English and the Burgundians by condemning her to be burnt at the stake, but also the contrast between what had recently happened in France and the experience of the soldiers of the First World War:

> We respect the offices of the commisariat, the provost-marshal,
> the majors and the cartographers, but our heart is with the men
> at the front, our heart is with those who are being killed. None
> of us who carry the burden of our country, our employment,
> our family – with our poor faces lined with anxiety, our hands
> calloused with work, with the enormous boredom of daily life,
> with the daily duty of earning our living and protecting the
> honour of our home – none of us will ever have sufficient
> theology to become a canon. But we know enough to become
> a saint.[7]

With the Papal condemnation of the Action Française Bernanos's hopes were once again shattered. Whatever the faults of Maurras's movement may have been, he argued, it had shown itself to be a

fierce opponent of the same tendencies that he himself hated
within modern civilisation and – at least in theory – it believed as
he did that the only salvation for France lay in a reassertion of
the values of the ancien régime. What possible hope could there
be for mankind if the Church rejected the only political force that
could help it ensure that its message would prevail? Already in
the pessimism that Bernanos felt in the aftermath of the events
that had taken place in 1926 there was more than a hint of the
kind of despair that was to make itself manifest in *Monsieur
Ouine.*

Indeed, so intense were Bernanos's forebodings over the future
that, although for a number of years after 1926 his quixotic sense
of chivalry demanded that he should continue to give public
support to Maurras, support that involved him and many others
in a constant quest for priests who would defy the Vatican and
administer the sacraments to them, the long-term effects of the
condemnation were to leave him more than ever convinced that
drastic action was necessary if the world was to be spared from
the catastrophe that awaited it, and more than ever convinced
that something much more dynamic than the Action Française
was needed if the Right were ever to win over the mass of the
French people to their cause. Both these preoccupations are
clearly stated in the biography of Édouard Drumont that he
published in 1931 under the title of *La Grande Peur des Bien-
pensants.*

In one sense a study of the most notorious French anti-semite
of the nineteenth century may appear to be a somewhat strange
vehicle for Bernanos to choose to express his views on the future
of the Right in the early 1930s for, apart from his one great
moment of triumph in revealing the extent of parliamentary
corruption at the time of the Panama Affair, Drumont was essentially an isolated figure on the French political scene: by many of
his contemporaries he was regarded as an eccentric because of
the obsessive nature of his hatred of the Jews; to others, such as
Maurras, it was evident that Drumont's view of the world was
archaic and that he lacked the organisational ability and ideological flair that was necessary to create a lasting and effective
political movement.

Why, then, was Bernanos so fascinated by Drumont? It must
be made clear at the outset that it was not primarily because of

the latter's anti-semitism. It would be foolish to deny the fact that, like so many supporters of the French Right, Bernanos had an intense dislike for Jews: this went back to his childhood when his father had been an avid reader of Drumont's newspaper *La Libre Parole*, and although Bernanos was at pains to point out during the Second World War that his hostility towards the Jews had never been racialist in character, certain of his admirers have done no service to his reputation by attempting to minimise the anti-semitic views that he held throughout most of his life. On the other hand, it is quite evident from an examination of his writings that to Bernanos the Jew was a symbol of capitalism as a whole, and even in *La Grande Peur des Bien-pensants* it is quite obvious that what attracted him towards Drumont was more the uncompromising nature of the latter's onslaught on the bourgeoisie in general than the particular attack that he levelled against the economic activities of the Jews. As the title of the book implies, in fact, *La Grande Peur des Bien-pensants* is not so much a biography of the author of *La France Juive* as a polemic against that section of the French middle class that had been Voltairian and free-thinking in the years before 1848 but had then rallied to Catholicism as the best means by which they could defend the rights of property, a polemic which utilises the views of Drumont, not so much in order to attack the Left, but in order to illuminate the process by which the Right had failed the French people in the second half of the nineteenth century.

At the very beginning of the book Bernanos made his intentions clear:

I write this book for me and you – yes, you who are reading me: not for anyone else but for you yourself. I swore to myself that I would provoke you, into anger or sympathy, what does it matter? I am giving you a book that is alive.[8]

And it could hardly be disputed that he lived up to this claim. As an indictment of the 'respectable' classes in France the book is unequalled. Bernanos points out that, in the 1870s, when the Royalists had had a majority in the Chamber and there was a real opportunity of restoring the monarchy in France, the bien-pensants had applauded the methods by which the 'little bespectacled megalomaniac',[9] Thiers, had crushed the Commune and had in this way alienated the workers from the cause of the Right for ever. Then, in the period after the Commune, the middle class and their clerical allies had inaugurated the era of the Ordre Moral in order to purge the French people of their sins, and had in this way discredited Christianity as well. Their crowning folly had been their choice of the hapless MacMahon as president of the Republic in 1873, for the man they had chosen to prepare the way for a restoration of the monarchy had presented to the world the extraordinary spectacle of an honest man who, in order to gain the support of all other honest men, ended up by lying to everybody.[10] In view of all this it was no wonder that the Right had forfeited the respect of the masses. It was no wonder that, despite all the crises and scandals that the country had had to endure, the Third Republic had taken root and survived. The Left might produce fanatical opponents of the Church like Gambetta and Ferry. It might produce creatures consumed with a cynical lust for power like Clemenceau.[11] But at least the men it brought forth were men who had the courage of their convictions. All that the Right had to offer was impotence and hypocrisy.

The significance of Drumont, according to Bernanos, was that he had been one of the few men on the Right who had realised all this. Bernanos admitted that the author of La France Juive could never have been a successful politician: he had been so obsessed by the Jewish problem that he did not sufficiently appreciate the fact that the power exercised by the Jews was a symptom and not a cause of French decadence; and the issues raised by the Dreyfus Affair had shown that Drumont's approach to politics was far too simple and far too naïve. But at least he had been aware that the Right must abandon its alliance with the bourgeoisie if it was to make any appeal to the common people, and at least he had fought a relentless battle to preserve the traditions of an older France against the dehumanising power of money. In any case, Bernanos argued, did not the very hopelessness of the struggle that he had waged give his career a tragic grandeur? Drumont must surely have known that the Church would shrink from any open confrontation with the republican régime. In his heart of hearts he must have realised that the intriguers and the compromisers would always succeed. But still he had fought on to the end:

Everything that he wrote had this tragic sign, this fatal signal. In almost every line of his book. . .there appears a kind of heroic resignation, a deliberate acceptance of death. . .All in all his aim was not to conquer but to hold on as long as possible. After which, it was necessary, it was necessary for the beauty of the thing, that he should lose his footing and that, alone in a world of enemies, he should be immediately trampled down and lost.[12]

The greatness of Drumont, then, was that he was impelled by a sense of urgency that was born of despair. It was this quality, Bernanos maintained, that made his message so relevant to the needs of the modern world, for, since Drumont's death in 1917, the forces of materialism had become immeasurably stronger and the nihilism inherent in modern civilisation was becoming daily more oppressive. In the quite remarkable conclusion that Bernanos wrote to *La Grande Peur des Bien-pensants* he carries the story beyond the point at which Drumont's career came to an end. He relates his own experiences during the First World War. He describes the disillusionment that he feels with the nature of the post-war world. And at the end of the book he calls on the youth of France to follow Drumont's example and to fight to the limit of their resources against the kind of Europe in which they were being asked to live:

The society which is being created little by little in front of our eyes will realise as completely as possible, with a kind of mathematical rigour, the ideal of a society without God. The only thing is that we will not be living in it. Our lungs are short of air. We are short of air. The world, which is looking at us with a growing distrust, is startled to see the same hidden anguish in our eyes. Already some of us have stopped smiling . . .They will not have us. . .They will not have us alive.[13]

La grande peur des bien-pensants is certainly open to some criticism: its anti-semitic overtones are repellent; the account it gives of the origins and development of the Third Republic degenerates at times into grotesque caricature; and it would be difficult to deny that in reality Drumont was a more cruel and a more hypocritical personality than the author of this biography was prepared to admit. And yet as a record of Bernanos's position at the beginning of the 1930s the value of the book is considerable. From the evidence of this work alone it could be conjectured that Bernanos was moving to a position that was very close to Fascism, and that this was indeed the case seemed to be confirmed in November 1931 when he accepted the literary editorship of *Le Figaro*, for the proprietor of that newspaper, the perfume millionaire and press magnate, François Coty, was a virulent anti-semite and one of the most influential proponents of a Fascist solution to the problems of France in the early 1930s.

The collaboration between Bernanos and Coty did not last for very long, however. For a time, it is true, Bernanos was hopeful that their joint venture would be successful. 'We must make *Le Figaro* into the sole intellectual centre of Paris', he told his friends; 'the youth, the intellectuals, the public, and ultimately the Pretender himself will rally to us.'[14] And with the onset of the Depression and the growth of Fascist and quasi-Fascist movements elsewhere in Europe the circumstances of the time seemed to indicate that this initiative might succeed. But, like Maurras, Drumont, and so many other of Bernanos's heroes, the proprietor of *Le Figaro* was a somewhat strange figure for anyone to choose as the saviour of France: despite his enormous wealth Coty, in fact, was an extremely lonely and unhappy man who attracted Bernanos more because he seemed doomed to misery and failure than because he seemed likely to fulfil his ambitions. Furthermore, despite the fact that the many disparate groups on the French Right were prepared to accept Coty's subsidies, they were not prepared to agree to his exercising any control over their policies, especially since he behaved towards them in a tactless and unscrupulous manner. Although Bernanos supported Coty in the inevitable quarrel that broke out between the latter and the Action Française, therefore, and although as a result of this quarrel Bernanos was eventually forced to make a final break with Maurras after a bitter public controversy that took place in 1932, his own relationship with the proprietor of *Le Figaro* was never as harmonious as he might have wished, and by the beginning of 1933 his association with Coty had come to an end.

This did not mean that Bernanos was no longer attracted towards Fascism, however. On the contrary, it must be remembered that in 1933 and 1934 he was in the throes of one of his most serious psychological depressions, and the despair that he experienced during these years, the years in which he was engaged in writing *Monsieur Ouine*, rendered him particularly vulnerable to the Fascist temptation. Admittedly, after his break with both Maurras and Coty he was determined to avoid too close an identification with any political party or group: in 1934, for example, he refused to become involved in the anti-republican agitation at the time of the February riots; and in 1936 he repulsed the overtures of Drieu la Rochelle and Bertrand de Jouvenel who made a special journey to Majorca in an attempt to enlist his support for Doriot. But by doing this he did not intend to imply that he had now renounced the ideals that he had proclaimed in his biography of Drumont. He simply wanted to show that he no longer had any confidence in the men who led the Right in France.

Indeed, when Bernanos moved to Spain in 1934 his first reaction was to feel a great sense of liberation. The Spanish political system might be collapsing into anarchy and the Spanish bourgeoisie might be even more greedy and short-sighted than that of France, but in José Antonio's Falange party Bernanos believed that he had at last discovered the kind of Fascist movement that he could support, a movement that was nationalist and socialist, but also Catholic, a movement that was free of the weaknesses of French Fascism, but was equally uncontaminated by the paganism of Hitler and Mussolini.

Whether the Falange was really quite as admirable as Bernanos claimed is, of course, open to some argument. Despite the fact that José Antonio was possessed of a highly developed sense of chivalry and a genuine compassion for the poor he himself spoke of engaging the Left in 'a dialectic of fists and pistols', whilst many of his followers embarked on a campaign of violence well in advance of the outbreak of the civil war. This campaign was not simply a reprisal against the violence of the Left, and, once the civil war had started, many of the original Falangists were to take part in the purges without any noticeable crises of conscience. To this extent, therefore, it was perhaps fortunate for José Antonio that, once having earned Bernanos's admiration, he did not live long enough to incur Bernanos's wrath; several months before the outbreak of the civil war he was put in prison, and in November 1936 he was shot by the Republicans.

In the summer of 1936, however, all this lay in the future.

When the civil war finally broke out it seemed natural that Bernanos's sympathies should be on the side of the Nationalists. The burning down of churches and the executions of priests in Republican Spain could not but convince him that the rebellion of the generals was justified, and in August, when the first Italian aeroplanes arrived in Majorca to give their support to the Nationalist cause and repel a Republican invasion, Bernanos's initial reaction was one of whole-hearted approval. Although there is no evidence to support his repeated claim that his father's family was ultimately of Spanish origin, there seems no doubt that the quality of extremism in Spanish civilisation was something to which he instinctively responded. In the letters and the articles he sent to France he expressed his pleasure at the fact that a substantial proportion of the Spanish people were now prepared to repudiate the disorder that had been endemic under the republican régime, and he was delighted by the way in which, by rallying to the support of the generals, the Spanish nation was once again demonstrating its contempt for the materialistic values of the modern world. 'This great people', he wrote, 'remain faithful today to their deepest instinct, they remain faithful to their age-old tradition to defend their moral and religious unity above anything else, to defend it by means of iron and fire if necessary. You can deplore these fratricidal struggles. But after all it is better to fight and die for one's altars and one's gods than for one's national trade.'[15] 'I am grateful to the Lord for allowing me to observe a kind of general rehearsal of the universal revolution,' he commented in one letter. 'What a chapter I could now append to my *Grande Peur*', he proclaimed in another.[16]

For a time he believed that the war would be over quickly and would end in a victory for Franco. By the end of 1936 he was not so sure. But by this time in any case his attention was moving away from the prospects of victory on the mainland to the purges that were taking place in Majorca. In December he reported to a friend that now the hyenas were appearing on the scene and that what was happening now was 'not for people like you or me'.[17] Early in the following year he wrote that he was now witnessing at close quarters the 'disgusting spectacle' of a military and clerical revolution, 'disgusting' because 'it is difficult to imagine so paradoxical and explosive a mixture of cynicism and hypocrisy'.[18] For some weeks he was so hypnotised by this spectacle that he could hardly tear himself away. Nevertheless in the spring of 1937 he *did* manage to escape, and he returned to France determined to reveal to the world the truth about the events that he had witnessed in the last few months.

Les grands cimetières sous la lune did not appear until 1938, but already in his novel, the *Nouvelle Histoire de Mouchette* which had been published in the previous year, Bernanos had given some indication of the impact that his recent experiences in Majorca had made on him. At first sight this novel – the story of a girl who believes she has been raped by a murderer and is so terrified by her inability to find anyone in whom she can confide her secret that she wanders into a lake and is drowned – seems very remote from the events that he had witnessed in Spain. And yet Bernanos was insistent that there was a close connection between the two: not only had he been inspired to write the novel by the spectacle of the lorry loads of men being taken away to be shot in Majorca, but the fate of Mouchette was identical with that of those who had suffered in the purges. 'Poor Mouchette!' he exclaimed in the course of an interview with André Rousseaux in 1937; 'what are people to make of her story if they take her to be a creature of despair? It is quite the opposite for me. Mouchette is a little heroine...Mouchette does not really kill herself. She falls and goes to sleep after waiting for help that does not come to her.'[19]

Although Bernanos tended to exaggerate the extent to which the Spanish Church was the uncritical ally of the Nationalists in *Les grands cimetières sous la lune*,[20] most of the hierarchy of the Church and the great bulk of ordinary Catholic opinion both inside and outside Spain took the view that, whatever reservations they might entertain over the methods that were being employed by Franco's followers, the basic aims of the anti-republican forces were worthy of their most ardent support. Despite the fact that there were a number of other prominent French Catholics (like Maritain and Mauriac) who were openly hostile to the Spanish 'crusade', therefore, Bernanos was subjected to a series of bitter attacks after the publication of his book. A number of priests rushed to defend the reputation of the Archbishop of Palma and claimed that, by writing *Les grands cimetières sous la lune* Bernanos had abused the hospitality of the Spanish people. So great was the hostility that was felt towards Bernanos in the Vatican that it was rumoured that it was only the personal intervention of Pius XI that had prevented the book from being officially censured. And behind all the attacks that were made on him at this time there was the constant charge that, by adopting the attitude that he did on the Spanish civil war, he was betraying the principles that had governed his conduct up to 1936.

Many of the charges that were made against him at this time were so scurrilous that they may be immediately discounted, but *were* the opinions that he had expressed in *Les grands cimetières sous la lune* in flat contradiction to the views that he had held in earlier years?

In one sense it can hardly be denied that a major change had taken place in his attitudes. Admittedly this change was not merely the result of his experiences during the Spanish civil war: already in 1935 he had been appalled by the barbarities committed by Italian troops in Abyssinia; in any case it will be seen in the next chapter that by 1936 the whole basis of Bernanos's spiritual life had been altered by the discoveries that he had made whilst writing *Monsieur Ouine* and the *Journal d'un curé de campagne*. Nevertheless, once all these qualifications are made, it is still true to say that a new spirit is discernible in Bernanos's work in the years after 1936. From now on he was completely alienated from Fascism and in the course of the next few years he was to manifest a degree of hostility to the policies of the extreme Right that he had never exhibited before.

And yet he himself saw no inconsistency in all this. Throughout his whole life, he insisted, he had attacked the same evils – the avarice of the bourgeoisie and the hypocrisies of conventional Christianity, and what he had witnessed and had then promptly denounced in Spain was only a further manifestation of these evils, only a further example of that unholy alliance between the Church and the middle classes against which Drumont had inveighed in the course of the nineteenth century. Whatever the Left might make of *Les grands cimetières sous la lune*, therefore, Bernanos himself was at pains to point out that he had not been converted to the cause of liberalism and democracy and that he was and remained a royalist and a man of the Right.

Perhaps it is relevant at this point to mention one of the most interesting letters that he received after the publication of his book. This came from the young Simone Weil, who had gone to Spain to give her support to the Anarchists, but had been rapidly disillusioned by the cruelties that had taken place behind the Republican lines. In the letter that she wrote to Bernanos she explained that while she had been in Spain she had heard of many atrocities that had been perpetrated by supporters of the Republic, but never once, either amongst the Spaniards themselves or amongst the French who were in Spain as combatants or as visitors, had she heard anyone confess even in private to any feelings of repulsion, disgust, or even disapproval, at the bloodshed that had taken place:

> Having been in Spain, I now continually listen to and read all
> sorts of observations about Spain, but I could not point to a
> single person, except you alone, who has been exposed to the
> atmosphere of civil war and has resisted it. What do I care that
> you are a royalist, a disciple of Drumont? You are incomparably
> nearer to me than my comrades of the Aragon militias. . .[21]

To Bernanos this was the highest praise that he could be offered. This young Jewish girl accepted him for what he was. What he had tried to show by his reaction to the events that had taken place in Spain was that he refused to remain silent when atrocities were being committed in the name of Christianity. What he had been determined to demonstrate was that he was a free man. It was not he who had abandoned his principles. The real treachery had been committed by those who professed their allegiance to a higher power than that of brute force.

Indeed, it was precisely because Bernanos believed that by writing his book on Spain he was upholding the most honourable traditions of the Right that the policies that were pursued by the French Right were to cause him so much anguish in the years that followed the outbreak of the Spanish civil war. On his return to France in 1937 he was appalled by what he found. The atmosphere in his own country bore an uncanny resemblance to that which he had recently experienced in Spain. Just as on the other side of the Pyrenees the political situation was polarised between the supporters of a Popular Front government on the one hand, and the parties of the Right on the other. And just as in Spain the two sides regarded each other with hatred and with fear:

The spring of 1937, was without doubt one of the most tragic that France has ever seen, a spring of civil war. Political rivalries were giving way to social hatreds in an intolerable atmosphere of mutual terror. Fear! Fear! Fear! It was the spring of fear. The life force must have been very powerful for the chestnut trees to have come into flower in this oppressive climate.[22]

And the worst part of it all was that in their hatred of the Popular Front in Spain and in France the French nationalists were prepared, not only to condone the brutalities that were committed by Franco, but also to look with increasing favour on Mussolini and Hitler. Here indeed was the beginning of a gigantic miscalculation on the part of the men of the Right:

For these fools Hitler, Stalin or Mussolini are men of cunning, nothing more, 'Doriots who have been successful'. This great upheaval that is taking place within the Western conscience, an upheaval in which men are demonstrating that they will no longer assimilate a degenerate Christianity but want to eliminate it as if it were poison, provokes only frivolous comments from the Right, comments that reflect the monotonous and unchanging nature of their concerns...They believe that they will be able to 'use' Hitler against Stalin, without thinking for a moment that the rivalry between the two reformers is justified by the fact that their methods are identical.[23]

Even this, however, did not convey the full horror of the situation, for the reason why Hitler subscribed to the mystique of race and Stalin to that of class was that by doing this they would more effectively influence men to forget that they were created in the image of God. The satanic quality of the dictators lay in the fact that they were clever enough to utilise the most generous instincts of mankind to pursue their perverted ends:

There was something in the purely utilitarian materialism of the last century that repelled men of noble temperament. Our modern reformers supplement it with ideas of sacrifice, grandeur and heroism. Influenced in this way by passions that resemble those of the saints and the martyrs, the people break with God painlessly and almost without their knowing it. There seems to be no way in which they can be warned that universal hatred lies at the end of their experience.[24]

But the enemies of the Popular Front in France were incapable of understanding this. At least the dictators had the courage to commit their own evil deeds. At least when Franco 'purified' Spain by using the methods of the Bolsheviks he could claim that he was assuming responsibility for the blood that was being shed. In contrast to this all that the French Right could exhibit to the world was a mixture of cynicism and pusillanimity. It applauded the 'realism' of the dictators while deploring their dynamism. It proclaimed its belief in the greatness of France while hating the great mass of Frenchmen. Nothing gave it the right to impose on France the insolent ultimatum 'Communism or us'. The clerical party of the nineteenth century was now happily defunct, but the Right had retained its vocabulary, its methods, and even its tone of insupportable condescension. Fifty years of experience had shown that it was utterly incapable of speaking to the mass of the French people in terms that were worthy of them.[25]

Symptomatic of the spiritual decline that had taken place within the French Right, Bernanos maintained, was the deterioration that had taken place with the Action Française, a theme that obsessed him more and more in the period between his return from Spain and the outbreak of the Second World War. At one time, he pointed out, Maurras had believed that it was possible to rally the support of the common people to the royalist cause: now he was not so much concerned with the restoration of the monarchy as with his passion for authority and the defence of bourgeois interests. At one time Maurras had been one of the most ardent believers in French grandeur: now all that he could talk about was the weakness and decadence of France, the necessity for France to withdraw into herself, the need for her to abandon the rest of Europe to the dictators and cultivate the friendship of Franco and Mussolini against Hitler. Bernanos denied the charge that he was motivated by a personal hatred of the leader of the Action Française. On the contrary, he explained, far from regarding Maurras with anything like hatred the only emotion that he felt when he contemplated the latter's mysterious and exceptional destiny was that of holy terror.[26] The reason why he was obsessed with Maurras was because he had once believed that Maurras might be the saviour of France. Now he realised that he had been wrong. All his life Maurras had been condemned to live in a world of abstractions, but the real decline of the leader of the Action Française had come during the First World War when, cut off from the spirit of the soldiers in the 'Avant', he had succumbed to the senile hatreds of the civilians in the 'Derrière'. The position into which he had now manoeuvred himself was perhaps one of the most cruel forms of damnation in the world.[27]

Clearly the criminal folly of the Right was something that Bernanos could not tolerate for very long. In the spring of 1938, therefore, one year after his return from Spain and six months before the Munich conference he left France again – this time for South America. He did this partly in order to fulfil the dreams that he had had as a young man of abandoning Europe and attempting to help recreate the Christian civilisation of the Middle Ages in the New World, but mainly because he realised that this was the only step that he could take to avoid the psychological breakdown which he knew awaited him if he was to stay in France. In 1939 he wrote:

> To those who ask why I left my country for Brazil, I can say that I came here to recover from my sense of shame. Shame depresses some people and reduces others to despair. I am one of the latter. I do not want to stop writing about and bearing witness for the things that I love. I am well aware that shame and disgust would have reduced me to impotence or to hatred, which is impotence in its pure state, the demonic form of impotence.[28]

If Bernanos's decision to go into exile was to spare him from the worst consequences of his own inner torments, however, the events that were to take place in Europe between 1938 and 1945 were to confirm his most pessimistic prophecies concerning the future. Already at the beginning of the Second World War the conduct of the Western democracies inspired him with little confidence. In 1914, he lamented, they had sent out their youth to be killed in their millions, but there had been no revolutionary transformation of society to give meaning to their sacrifice, and now England and France were entering another major conflict, a conflict in which they were completely incapable of countering the perverted idealism of Nazi Germany. Chamberlain and Daladier might think that Hitler was made in the same mould as Mussolini, but Mussolini was only a successful demagogue, a dictator whose vanity had been satisfied, whereas Hitler was a demonic personality, a creature of despair, a man whose ambitions could never be appeased:

> The modern world has had no other thought except to confront him with politicians, diplomats, businessmen, men who think they are astute because they do not take anything seriously, but men who in reality are characterised only by triviality. Whenever Hitler took a step forward these fools asked themselves: 'What does he want? What does he need now?' But M. Hitler never did stop – precisely because he wanted everything.[29]

With the defeat of France and the German occupation, therefore, Bernanos was in despair. It is significant, however, that it was not so much the activities of the Fascists and the collaborators that appalled him as the behaviour of the traditional Right. Needless to say he denounced all the inhumanities that were committed by the Germans and their allies during the occupation, and the former disciple of Drumont did not hesitate to castigate in the most violent terms the racialist and anti-semitic policies that were implemented in France during the years of the Second World War. And yet it seemed to him that, evil though the actions of the Fascists and the collaborators undoubtedly were, the latter were at least responding in a positive way to the spiritual crisis that now faced mankind, whereas all that he could see in the supporters of Vichy was the timorousness of the bien-pensants. The men around Pétain talked in terms of a renewal of the Christian virtues, and yet sanctioned the persecution of the Jews. They talked of the restoration of French greatness, and yet acceded, however reluctantly, to the demands that were made on them by the Germans. If Vichy was not such a tragedy it would be a farce, 'a kind of grotesque entertainment like something out of Molière, a ballet performed by academicians, society women, admirals and archbishops, against a backcloth of blood, a ballet in a cemetery'.[30]

There was only one way in which France could emerge from

her ordeal with any hope left for the future, Bernanos was convinced, and that was for her to support de Gaulle and the Resistance. It was no good for England and the United States to attempt to come to terms with personalities associated with the Vichy régime such as General Giraud and Admiral Darlan.[31] The French people knew that they had been dishonoured in 1940, he asserted: they knew that they must repudiate Vichy in order to wipe out the memory of their decadence and defeat.[32] France herself must decide her destiny. All the efforts that had been made by the Resistance would be in vain if a compromise was reached between the Western allies and Pétain. It was only through the efforts of the Resistance the French nation could recover those reserves of youthful energy that had saved her in the time of Joan of Arc. It was only through the victory of de Gaulle that France could regain her self respect.

Events did not quite turn out in the way that Bernanos hoped, however. Despite the courage that was exhibited by the Resistance, France owed her freedom more to the efforts of others than to the heroism that had been displayed by her own citizens. And in matters of internal policy, too, the Liberation was not quite what it seemed. Apart from the savage 'épuration' of the collaborators in 1944 and 1945 the revolution that was to sweep away the old order – the revolution for which Bernanos had prayed ever since 1918 – did not in fact take place, and, once the euphoria induced by the departure of the Germans had been dissipated, the political and social immobilisme from which France had suffered under the Third Republic asserted itself yet again.

When Bernanos, at the invitation of de Gaulle, finally returned to France in July 1945, therefore, he was overwhelmed by the signs of demoralisation that he saw around him. Everywhere the forces that had been responsible for the defeat in 1940 seemed to be in the process of reviving. The same people who had welcomed the Munich agreement and the Armistice at Rethondes were busily engaged in convincing themselves that they had been in the Resistance from the start, and the same sections of public opinion that had supported Daladier in 1938 and Pétain in 1940 were now rallying behind de Gaulle. How long could the leader of the Resistance hold out against them? Bernanos was sceptical that de Gaulle could last for any length of time. Sooner or later the mediocrities would assert themselves and de Gaulle would be forced to resign.[33]

Bernanos's public activities after his return to France reflected the pessimism with which he now regarded the future. He angrily rejected de Gaulle's amazing proposal that he should take political office as Minister of Education. He made a number of bitter attacks on the left-wing Catholics, associated with Emmanuel Mounier and the magazine *Esprit*, who hoped that it might be possible for the Church to come to some kind of agreement with the Communists.[34] In addition to all this he repeatedly refused to associate himself with the M.R.P., the new Christian Democratic Party that had been founded in France at the end of the war.

Indeed, although Bernanos's final position was one of support for the R.P.F., the authoritarian and anti-Communist movement with which de Gaulle hoped to return to power in the late 1940s, the shrill tones in which he denounced the deficiencies of the French people and their institutions in the last years of his life seemed to indicate that he believed that it was too late for his country to be saved from disaster. To Gaëton Picon he confessed that he could not reconcile himself to the fact that he had lost the image that he had formed of his country during his childhood: if he knew where it was buried he would die by its grave just like a dog lying on the tomb of its master.[35] In a newspaper article he claimed that if he had his life to live over again he would become a Communist,[36] and, if this was nothing more than a piece of polemical exaggeration, he certainly told a monarchist who came to see him that he had no hope left – either for the monarchy or for France.[37] He even thought of returning to Brazil, and, although nothing came of this idea, he found it impossible to stay in France for any length of time.

By 1947, therefore, his home was in Tunisia. But even here Bernanos found no peace. In a seemingly endless series of books, pamphlets and lectures he continued to denounce the dehumanising and totalitarian tendencies implicit in modern civilisation. He was terrified by the invention of the atomic bomb, and he was appalled by the fact that, whatever way the contest between the United States and the Soviet Union was decided, the world was moving with ever-increasing rapidity into an era in which the human race would be dominated by the forces of science and technology. It seemed as if the Word had never become flesh. It seemed as if mankind was taking the opposite road to that of the Incarnation.[38] But the most frightening aspect of the situation was the seeming impotence of Christianity to halt this process. The Church had not publicly condemned the terrible acts that had been committed by the Nationalists and their allies during the Spanish civil war, and during the Second World War Pius XII had failed to make a public protest against the worst excesses of Hitler and the Nazis.[39] What hope could there be for the future if Christians remained silent in situations like these?

'It is a great disgrace for the Church that it has suffered a persecution without martyrs. The assault that has been made against institutions and doctrines has not had its supernatural compensation in the spilling of blood.'[40] Bernanos wrote these words soon after the outbreak of the Second World War, and this was still the problem with which he was obsessed when he suffered the onset of his final illness. For several weeks he refused to take to his bed until he had finished the script that he had promised to write for a film that was to be based on the martyrdom of a group of Carmelite nuns during the French Revolution. By the time that he was taken to the American hospital at Neuilly, therefore, his cancer was found to be inoperable. During the last days of his life Bernanos vowed that, if the time left to him was sufficient, he would abandon his polemical writings altogether and devote himself to writing a *Vie de Jésus*. To the very end, however, there were flashes of his old self. 'Why does the Pope not speak out?' he exclaimed on his death-bed. 'You have only to make men stand up straight and they will march.'[41] He died on 5 July 1948.

9

THE COMMUNION OF SAINTS

In some ways it seems unnecessary to defend Bernanos against the charge that he was guilty of excessive pessimism, for the temptation of despair has been an experience common to most writers in the twentieth century. 'Our universe is not merely bankrupt, there remains no dividend at all; it has not simply liquidated, it is going out of existence, leaving not a wrack behind.'[1] H. G. Wells wrote this in 1945 after many years in which he had hoped that the progress of science would enable men to construct a just and civilised society. Clearly Bernanos cannot be accused of eccentricity in fearing that mankind might be entering into the era of its final destruction in the years that followed the First World War.

And yet it would be impossible to deny that certain aspects of his work are deeply disturbing:

> I have dreamed of saints and heroes, neglecting the inter-
> mediate forms of species, and I realise that the intermediate
> forms scarcely exist, that only the saints and heroes count. The
> intermediate forms are a kind of pulp, a magma which takes
> hold of them at random. If you know a handful of them you
> know the rest, and this jelly would not deserve a name if the
> saints and heroes did not give it one, if they did not give their
> name of honour.[2]

From the evidence of passages such as this is it not clear that there is a terrible kind of dialectic at work within Bernanos's universe, a remorseless and implacable dialectic according to which it is only the saints and heroes who finally achieve salvation while the rest of humanity are doomed to perdition? Is it not clear that in Bernanos's view the vast majority of mankind are not merely spiritually mediocre but irrevocably damned?

Certainly this has been the reaction of a number of those who have read his novels. Writing to Bernanos in 1928 following the publication of *L'Imposture* the theatrical director Antonin Artaud (later to be celebrated as a pioneer of the 'Theatre of Cruelty') confessed that the experience of reading the pages in which the abbé Chevance dies in physical and spiritual agony had been one of the most distressing experiences of his life:

> Am I destined then to perish in this way in a death that for me would be without hope? Rarely has an event or a human being made me feel the extent to which we are dominated by misery, rarely have I seen the impasse of a destiny full of gall and tears, made worse by dark and useless sorrows.[3]

And, while defending Bernanos against the charge of Manichaeism and Jansenism, the Italian critic Guido Piovene has openly wondered whether the hallucinatory quality of Bernanos's work is not a quality that repels many of those who might otherwise be attracted by his message:

> Admittedly in speaking of people who are repelled in this way I am not thinking of those who would want to substitute in place of Christianity an ethic based on pride and honour. But I am thinking of those for whom, like me, the guiding principle of any religious life must be 'to know what one is doing'. This principle is opposed to any pre-eminence of the unconscious in whatever way it shows itself. The key to what happens in the novels of Bernanos is always *elsewhere* – it is one of the reasons for the power of his art. But for people like me the transformation of the psychological unconscious into the metaphysical unconscious is necessarily bad. Charity demands above all that we make of ourselves a centre of clarity and innocence, that we free ourselves from the temptation of deceit. We must submit to forces that are mysterious but not accept them, for the mysterious is our enemy, our principal sin, the source of our duplicity and lack of sincerity.[4]

The points that are raised by Artaud and Piovene are important ones, and, even if the reader is sceptical of some of the more extreme claims that have been made on behalf of the psychological approach to literature, it can hardly be pretended that there was not *some* neurotic element present in Bernanos's writings. On the one hand, he was consumed with the fear that God had withdrawn His grace from mankind: on the other, he was obsessed with the need for the Kingdom of God to be established on earth. Is it not obvious that these two preoccupations were closely related and that each tended to intensify the other? Was it not because Bernanos was so terrified by the fallen nature of the world that he was so concerned to emphasise the qualities of heroism and sanctity? And was it not because he made such superhuman demands on himself and the rest of mankind, that he was so vulnerable to the temptation of despair? 'It would seem to me', Claudel commented in his memoirs, 'that there was a great deal in Bernanos of the sufferings of a man who, let us be frank, is a failure, a man who in fact believes that he deserves a place that has not been granted to him and bears a grudge against the world because of this.'[5] Claudel had suffered greatly at the hands of Bernanos ever since he had supported the cause of the Nationalists during the Spanish civil war, and his view of the latter was coloured by his own obsessive preoccupation with worldly success and recognition. And yet, however unfair the implications contained in Claudel's remarks, it would be impossible to deny that they contain an element of truth. Bernanos attacked the rest of mankind with such violence because he never really came to terms with the sense of *his own* inadequacy and failure. The shortcomings of his fellow men threw him into despair because that was his reaction to *his own* torments.

Bernanos's hopes for a rebirth of the spirit of the Middle Ages were doomed to failure, then, not only because his vision of a regenerated Christendom was hopelessly archaic – it is interesting to speculate what his reaction would have been to some of the decisions of the Second Vatican Council – but also because no political system could have satisfied him for very long: he was in revolt against the human condition as such, not merely against the crimes and follies of contemporary man. Nevertheless, it would be foolish to conclude from this that his work is in any way irrelevant. No one who has observed the terrible events that have taken place in the twentieth century could honestly claim that Bernanos's preoccupation with evil was simply the result of his own imagination. Furthermore, it would be a complete misrepresentation of Bernanos's achievement to ignore the extent to which he attempted to triumph over his despair, to recover the spirit of his childhood, to make of himself, in Piovene's words, 'a centre of clarity and innocence'.

This can clearly be seen in the shift that took place in his political sympathies in the course of the 1930s, but it can also be seen in the profound change that took place in his spiritual attitudes at the time that he was writing *Monsieur Ouine* and the *Journal d'un curé de campagne*. This was a change that antedated the outbreak of the Spanish civil war, and a change without which his subsequent political evolution would have been unthinkable. Perhaps it would be useful at this point to examine this period in Bernanos's life in greater detail.

It has already been seen that *Monsieur Ouine* reflects the despair that afflicted Bernanos in the early 1930s, but when this novel was first published in France in 1946 (several years after it had first appeared in Brazil during the war) it seemed to many people that it reflected something even more disturbing, for, in addition to its nightmarish obsession with the problem of evil, this work seemed to be so disordered and lacking in shape, the events taking place within it so arbitrary and unexplained, that it seemed as if the author's grasp on reality had been becoming increasingly tenuous.

This is not the way in which *Monsieur Ouine* is regarded by many critics today, however. What the public did not realise in the 1940s was that it had taken Bernanos nine years to complete this novel, that he regarded it as his most ambitious work, and that the incoherence of which they complained was due, not to any carelessness on his part, not to any decline that had taken place in his abilities as a writer, but to his growing awareness that evil is by its very nature incoherent and unstable. The nightmarish quality of this novel is in fact deliberate.[6] Bernanos started work on *Monsieur Ouine* in order to give expression to the spiritual crisis that he encountered in the early 1930s, but in the course of this work he came to realise that if nihilism and despair lead to evil, then evil itself is only an expression of nothingness. Interpreted in this way, therefore, *Monsieur Ouine* provides a remarkably lucid analysis of the via negativa by which Bernanos emerged from complete despair. Since nature abhors a vaccum, he argues, the nothingness of evil cannot possibly endure for very long. Sooner or later the world must turn again to God.

This represented a major breakthrough in Bernanos's thinking, and from now on a new spirit was to inform his work. But, although the significance of *Monsieur Ouine* cannot be underestimated in any examination of Bernanos's career, the extent to which his attitudes had changed in the course of writing this work can only properly be gauged from an examination of his next major novel, the *Journal d'un curé de campagne*. This does not mean that *Monsieur Ouine* is not of fundamental importance in any analysis of Bernanos's subsequent evolution: indeed, it is a striking indication of the catharsis that Bernanos experienced in the course of writing this work that one of the reasons why he found it difficult to complete it was that he found himself increasingly unable to prevent the character of the curé, the one personality who tries to combat the despair and immorality of Monsieur Ouine's village, from dominating the book; as a matter of fact, it was because of this very problem that Bernanos found it necessary to abandon *Monsieur Ouine* for a time and turn instead to the creation of another novel in which a parish priest would play a leading rôle. But although in this sense the *Journal d'un curé de campagne* is a derivative work in comparison with *Monsieur Ouine*, it gives a more positive expression of the change that had taken place in Bernanos's view of the world in the course of the early 1930s, and for this reason a comparison between it and a work of the previous decade like *Sous le Soleil de Satan* is particularly illuminating.

There are, it is true, certain similarities between these two novels. Both are concerned with the activities of parish priests who are convinced that they must be prepared to sacrifice everything, even their lives, in order to bear witness to God. Both priests become engaged in a dramatic encounter with the person whose soul they are trying to save: in *Sous le Soleil de Satan* Donissan confronts the girl who has murdered her lover; in the *Journal d'une curé de campagne* the priest confronts a countess who is consumed with hatred and bitterness as the result of the death of her son. But, in spite of these similarities, there are also important differences. In his famous letter of congratulation to Bernanos at the time of the publication of his earlier novel Claudel remarked of Donissan that 'the problem is to know whether he is impelled by the love of God or by pride in his own strength and it seems that in your book the second feeling is stronger: love of God and men appears only in a few pages'.[7] The same remark could not be made of the *Journal d'un curé de campagne*. In this work there is no confrontation with the Devil, comparatively little of that recourse to the miraculous and the extraordinary that Bernanos had taken from the Catholic novel of the late nineteenth century and that had laid his early writings open to the charge of theatricality. On the contrary, the priest in the *Journal d'un curé campagne* performs his duties in a world of drab monotony, he is acutely aware of his spiritual mediocrity, and he is fully aware of the element of pride that can hide behind the kind of self-torture in which Donissan had indulged. During his encounter with the countess, for example, at the moment when the latter throws into the fire her most treasured possession, a locket containing a strand of her dead son's hair, in order to demonstrate that she is now prepared to submit herself totally to God, the priest cannot contain his anger:

> Do you take God for an executioner? God wants us to be merciful with ourselves. And besides our sorrows are not our own. He takes them on Himself into His heart. We have no right to see them there, mock them, outrage them. Do you understand?[8]

And when the priest discovers that he is dying of cancer he comes to realise that the advice he had given to the countess applies with even greater force to himself. 'How easy it is to hate one-self', he observes towards the end of his life. 'True grace is to forget. Yet if pride could die in us the supreme Grace would be to love oneself in all simplicity as one would love any of those who have loved and suffered in Christ.'[9]

'I believe that I can now write properly because I am really without anger. At least without hatred', Bernanos wrote to a friend in 1935 at the time that he was engaged on writing the *Journal d'un curé de campagne*:

> Everyone is an unfortunate. God chooses His friends amongst the mediocrities in order to raise them up to Him. They were no less mediocre before this happened. He gives them every-thing, riches, prerogatives, titles, new places of residence – even their name. We love them because He loves them. We venerate them and pray to them for the same reason. In this situation I find it useless to batter the others with invectives. The others, alas, are us.[10]

Already before the outbreak of the Spanish civil war, therefore, a profound change had taken place in Bernanos's attitudes, and when, in the course of that war, he was to publish the *Nouvelle Histoire de Mouchette* and *Les Grands Cimetières sous la Lune*, these books were important, not because they seemed to show that Bernanos was now repudiating the loyalties that had inspired him in the past, not even because they demonstrated the fact that he was now declaring his independence of all the political ideologies that competed for the soul of Europe in the 1930s, but because they revealed the extent to which he was now entering into a new dimension, the dimension of hope. In the years before he had embarked on *Monsieur Ouine* Bernanos had experienced such a degree of despair that the only position that he thought he could adopt was that of a defiant stoicism, the position that he had taken up in 1915 and again in his biography of Drumont. Now, with his discovery that the mediocrity he hated in others was a reflection of everything he hated in himself, he could begin to hope that, if he began to fight against the pride that had prevented him from putting his trust in God, he, too, could be worthy of grace.

Bernanos's awareness of the need for charity is not, of course, confined to his novels: it is clearly discernible in *all* his writings after 1936. While Barbusse and Drieu remained trapped in the ideologics they had adopted in the middle of their careers, Bernanos's thought was in a perpetual process of change and development to the very end of his life. During the years of the Second World War, for example, a period in which he read a great deal of Péguy, he was quick to admit that in the past he had misunderstood many of the passions that had inspired the supporters of the Left: demagogic politicians may have been able to exploit the naïve enthusiasm of the republican masses for slogans like 'Liberty', 'Justice', 'Progress' and 'Science' at the time of the Dreyfus Affair, he conceded, but the Right had committed a grave error in not recognising the idealism of the masses for what it was – a secularised but sincere version of Christianity.[11] And again looking back to the period before the outbreak of the First World War Bernanos was forced to admit that many of those who had been inspired by the Catholic revival in France had been too narrow in their sympathies. The Catholics, he confessed, had never reached, nor had they ever really tried to reach, the hearts of the French people: they had argued too much, debated too much, proved too much; they had not loved enough.[12] Even in the violent polemics that he wrote in the last years of his life Bernanos was perpetually on his guard to avoid expressing any views that might seem to be inspired by hatred, and he was always ready to apologise for any injustices that he might have committed.

'There are millions of saints in the world, known to God alone, not deserving in any way to have altars raised to them. Saints of a very inferior and rustic kind, of very humble origins, with nothing but a drop of sanctity in their veins.'[13] Bernanos wrote this passage whilst meditating on the fate of the victims of Hitler's policies in Occupied Europe, and a passage such as this provides further confirmation of the fact that, under the shattering impact of the events that were taking place in the world during the Second World War, he was constantly modifying his earlier attitudes, and was continually engaged in an attempt to escape from the siege mentality that had been characteristic of many French Catholics in the early years of this century. But whether he was ever really capable of extending to himself the kind of charity that he was increasingly able to display towards others is a question to which it is doubtful that one can give an affirmative answer. In one sense he had a tendency to take the whole burden of the world's sufferings on his own shoulders, and in this he resembled Simone Weil: when the latter confessed in the middle of the Second World War that she was suffering from 'an ever-increasing agony' in her mind and in the depth of her heart from her 'incapacity to think at the same time and in truth of the misery of man, the perfection of God and the relationship between the two',[14] this was a problem with which Bernanos had long been obsessed. But at least Simone Weil was able to make a heroic response to the sufferings of those living in Hitler's Europe by the fact and manner of her death, whereas Bernanos was condemned to fret in impotence in Brazil. In view of all this he must often have asked himself whether he was really entitled to talk of the failure of the Church to provide martyrs in the face of Nazi persecution, when what he was saying amounted to a condemnation of others for failing to do what he himself had been unable to accomplish.

Although Bernanos never openly raised this issue in such crude and direct terms, it can hardly be doubted that the anguish caused by this problem contributed greatly to the renewed attacks of despair and depression from which he suffered in the years after 1938. The despair that haunted him was not due to his lack of *physical* courage: he had shown his bravery during the First World War, and it would be quite absurd to uphold the charges of those of his enemies who have claimed that he was guilty of a base form of cowardice in leaving France for South America. And yet in a very real sense Bernanos *had* deserted his country in her hour of need. In spite of the attempts made by his admirers to avoid the issue, the fact remains that it was not the bien-pensants, but Bernanos himself, the advocate of heroism and sanctity, who had fled from the supreme moral and psychological challenge of his life. It was he, and not Maurras or Claudel, who had abandoned France at the end of the 1930s.

And yet, if it would be foolish to minimise the extent to which the closing years of Bernanos's life were rendered bitter by his acute sense of failure, it would be equally foolish to ignore the fact that it was during these years that he made his most ambitious attempt to come to terms with the anguish that tormented him. He did this by writing what many people regard as his masterpiece, the *Dialogues des Carmélites*.

Based on Gertrud von Le Fort's novel *Die letzte am Schafott* (which was based in turn on an actual historical event, the martyrdom of a group of Carmelite nuns from Compiègne who were guillotined on 17 July 1794) this play has its central character a young girl, Blanche de la Force, who, finding it impossible to escape from her constant sense of fear and personal inadequacy, decides to enter a convent. When the Terror approaches she flees from the convent and hides in Paris. Eventually however she is given the strength to come out of her hiding because, without their knowing it, three of the other nuns have prepared the way for her salvation: on her behalf the Prioress, Madame de Croissy, has endured intense spiritual agonies on her death-bed; on her behalf the proud and aristocratic Mother Marie of the Incarnation has renounced her dearest wish – that she herself should be one of those chosen for martyrdom; and Sister Constance of Saint-Denis, by her own trust in God and happy acceptance of death, has given Blanche the confidence to follow her example. As a result of all this Blanche de la Force takes her place with the other nuns and is executed.

'We do not die for ourselves, but for one another, and even, who knows, in place of one another.'[15] These words are spoken by Sister Constance to Blanche de la Force at the point in the play when the two nuns are in the garden making a cross of flowers for the tomb of the Prioress, and the doctrine behind these words, the doctrine of the communion of saints, had been a constant point of reference in Bernanos's writings ever since he had experienced the comradeship of the trenches during the First World War. Already in *Sous le Soleil de Satan*, for example, it was evident that there was a mysterious affinity between the destiny of Donissan and that of the murderess whose soul he was trying to save, and in the *Journal d'un curé de campagne* the fact that the fate of the curé is closely linked to that of the countess is made abundantly clear. And yet nowhere in Bernanos's work is his belief that all men are united with each other in a common fellowship and a common destiny so explicitly stated in this play.

The significance of the *Dialogues des Carmélites*, then, is that it demonstrates that the final stage in the evolution of Bernanos's thought was concerned with the themes of reconciliation and hope. In some respects the self-hatred that tormented Blanche de la Force may be likened to that which Bernanos himself had endured throughout most of his life. Her situation may also, quite legitimately, be seen as symbolic of the humiliated and demoralised France of the 1940s. But the implications of the play are much wider than this. Shortly after the riots that took place in Paris in February 1934 Bernanos had written that the thing that distressed him was not the Stavisky scandal, but the great and unique scandal that men could believe that the one and a half million Frenchmen who had been killed in the war had died in vain.[16] And in the years after 1934 he was forced to witness another world war in which an even greater number of men were to die. But, if Blanche de la Force had been saved by the sacrifices of others, was it not possible that all those who had laid down their lives for others had died to some purpose? And, if someone like Blanche de la Force could be granted the courage to overcome despair, was it not possible that all those who lived in isolation and fear could be given reason to hope? These were the questions that Bernanos raised in his last work. These were questions that all three writers studied in these essays had tried in their different ways to answer.

More than twenty years have now elapsed since the suicide of Drieu and the death of Bernanos and in some respects it might seem that the situation that confronted them during their lifetime has undergone a profound change. Communism and Fascism originally developed in a Europe that had just been through the experience of one world war and was hastening towards another, whereas since 1945 the idea of total war in the nuclear epoch has been unthinkable. A further factor responsible for the development of extremist ideologies in the inter-war years was the mass unemployment that resulted from the Depression. In contrast to this the situation of Western Europe for many years after the end of the Second World War was one of unparalleled growth.

Is one obliged to conclude from this that the problems that preoccupied Barbusse, Drieu and Bernanos are now irrelevant, that their political careers, like the campaigns and battles of the First World War, are only of historical significance? The answer to this question must surely be, No. The particular combination of circumstances that faced them may not yet have recurred, but the peace and prosperity that Western Europe enjoyed in the years after 1945 have clearly been based on extremely precarious foundations. Furthermore, the spiritual crisis that all three writers diagnosed at the heart of Western Civilisation has in no way been resolved. On the contrary, this crisis has intensified and is now world-wide in its dimensions: the forces of science and technology become daily more potent; the decay of traditional structures and values continues at an accelerated rate; themes of violence and despair abound in contemporary culture and society. Against this kind of background no one could claim that the three writers dealt with in this study are outdated figures whose work is only of academic interest. 'Every twenty years the youth of the world pose a question to which our society cannot make an answer. For lack of an answer, it mobilises.'[17] Although it is now over thirty years since Bernanos wrote these words; they could still turn out to be prophetic.

NOTES AND REFERENCES

Unless otherwise stated all the translations into English are my own.

Introduction

1 *Selected Literary and Political Papers and Addresses of Woodrow Wilson*, Vol. II, New York, 1927, pp. 55–6.
2 P. Valéry, *History and Politics*, translated by D. Folliot and J. Matthews, London, 1963, p. 23.
3 C. Péguy, *Par ce demi-clair matin*, Paris, 1952, p. 24.
4 For an examination of Bergson's influence on the French intellectual scene in the years before 1914, see: R. Arbour, *Henri Bergson et les lettres françaises*, Paris, 1955.
5 Quoted in: F. Grover, *Drieu la Rochelle*, Paris, 1962, p. 78.
6 J. Ramsay MacDonald, *Socialism and Society*, London, 1905, p. 190.
7 For Bernanos's attack on the superficiality of *Le Feu*, see his *Le Crépuscule des Vieux*, Paris, 1956, p. 194. For Drieu's hostility to Barbusse's Amsterdam–Pleyel movement, see p. 101 of the present study.
8 Quoted in Grover, *op. cit.*, p. 141.
9 G. Bernanos, 'Nour retournerons dans la guerre', *Nouvelle Revue Française*, May 1940, p. 582.
10 *Ibid.*, pp. 579–80.
11 'Though the comparison might have been rather displeasing to Orwell, his nearest parallels probably exist amongst French Catholic radicals like Bernanos and Péguy': G. Woodcock, *The Crystal Spirit, A Study of George Orwell*, London, 1967, p. 185.

Barbusse – Chapter 1: Under Fire

1 Quoted in: V. Cowles, *The Kaiser*, London, 1963, p. 351.
2 Barrès published his *Les diverses familles spirituelles de la France* in 1917.
3 H. Barbusse, *Under Fire*, translated by Fitzwater Wray, London 1926, p. 5. This translation of *Le Feu* published in the Everyman series has been used as a source of reference since it is the most easily accessible edition of the novel available in English. However, a number of minor modifications have been made to the translation in order to make the meaning of certain passages more clear.
4 *Ibid.*, p. 5.
5 *Ibid.*, p. 30.
6 *Ibid.*, p. 31.
7 *Ibid.*, pp. 34–5.

8   *Ibid.*, p. 157.
9   *Ibid.*, p. 218.
10 *Ibid.*, pp. 280–1.
11 *Ibid.*, p. 329.
12 *Ibid.*, p. 256.
13 *Ibid.*, p. 336.
14 This interview, printed in the 'Berliner Tageblatt', is quoted in:
    A. Vidal, *Henri Barbusse, Soldat de la Paix*, Paris, 1953, p. 129.
15 This poem entitled 'Les choses' was first published in *L'Écho de Paris
    Littéraire Illustré*', 1 January 1893. A revised version may be found in:
    H. Barbusse, *Pleureuses*, Paris, 1895, pp. 99–100. An English translation
    of these three verses for the poem would run as follows:

    You consider them to be inanimate,
    But they see our torment,
    They come mysteriously to life
    When our hands animate them.

    They are gentle with us,
    Caressing our timid souls.
    Down there the branches are sad
    We have wept under them so much.

    All our most fleeting dreams
    Love them a little in turn,
    And that is why their vague love,
    Follows us with its placid eyes.

16 *Pleureuses*, p. 52.
17 H. Barbusse, *L'Enfer*, Paris, 1908, p. 122.
18 *Ibid.*, pp. 182–7.
19 H. Barbusse, *Paroles d'un combattant*, Paris, 1920, pp. 7–8.
20 *Lettres d'Henri Barbusse à sa femme, 1914–1917*, Paris, 1937, p. 16,
    letter of 4 August 1914.
21 Quoted in Vidal, *op. cit.*, p. 58.
22 *Lettres d'Henri Barbusse à sa femme, 1914–1917*, p. 148, letter of
    June 1915.
23 *Ibid.*, p. 202.

Barbusse – Chapter 2: Towards Communism

1   Quoted in: B. Bergonzi, *Heroes' Twilight. A study of the literature of
    the Great War*, London, 1965, p. 104.
2   Quoted in: V. Brett, *Henri Barbusse, sa marche vers la clarté, son
    mouvement Clarté*, Prague, 1963, p. 330.
3   Vidal, *op. cit.*, p. 65.
4   *Ibid.*, p. 64.
5   *Ibid.*, p. 67.
6   H. Barbusse, 'La polémique du Feu', *Le Populaire de Paris*, 20 July
    1918. The German Government banned *Le Feu* after the periodical
    Die Weissen Blätter (then being published in Switzerland) had printed
    excerpts from the novel in May 1917. For details of this incident:

I. Deak, *Weimar Germany's Left-wing Intellectuals*, Berkeley and Los Angeles, 1968, p. 69.

7   H. Barbusse, 'Un telégramme de Barbusse à Wilson', *Le Populaire de Paris*, 16 October 1918.

8   H. Barbusse, 'Le citoyen du Monde', *Le Populaire de Paris*, 15 December 1918.

9   Vidal, *op. cit.*, p. 82.

10 Quoted in: A. Kriegel, 'Naissance du mouvement Clarté', *Le Mouvement Social*, Jan.–March 1963, p. 123.

11 D. Caute, *Communism and the French intellectuals*, London, 1964, p. 43.

12 Quoted in: D. Shub, *Lenin*, New York, 1951, p. 129.

13 *Ibid.*, p. 136, quoting an article of Lenin's in the Swiss-published journal *Sotsial Demokrat*, 1 November 1914.

14 *Paroles d'un combattant*, p. 49.

15 Brett, *op. cit.*, p. 248. See also: N. Racine, 'The Clarté Movement in France, 1919–1921', *Journal of Contemporary History*, Vol. 2, No. 2, 1967, pp. 195–208.

16 *Paroles d'un combattant*, p. 17.

17 Caute, *op. cit.*, pp. 77–8.

18 H. Barbusse, *La lueur dans l'abîme: ce que veut le groupe Clarté*, Paris, 1920, p. 1.

19 *Le couteau entre les dents*, Paris, 1921, pp. 41–2.

20 Because of his disputes with the young radicals on the editorial staff who wanted an immediate affiliation of Clarté to the Comintern Barbusse disassociated himself from Clarté and finally severed his connections with the magazine in May 1924. In 1928 the editors of *Clarté* allied themselves with the Surrealists and changed the title of the magazine to *La lutte des classes*. This publication supported Trotsky against Stalin, and attacked Barbusse in violent terms. For details of this: N. Racine, 'Une revue d'intellectuels communistes dans les années vingt: Clarté (1921–1928)', *Revue Française de Sciences Politiques*, Vol. xvii, No. 3, June 1967, pp. 484–520.

21 H. Barbusse, 'Clarté et les pacifistes', *Clarté*, 10 July 1920.

22 Quoted in: J. Robichez, *Romain Rolland*, Paris, 1961, p. 70.

23 Barbusse's contributions to this debate may be found in *Clarté* (3 December 1921, 1 February 1922, 1 April 1922). Rolland's contributions may most conveniently be studied in his *Quinze Ans de Combat*, Paris, 1935, pp. 38–58.

24 Quoted in: J. Duclos and J. Fréville, *Henri Barbusse*, Paris, 1946, p. 15.

Barbusse – Chapter 3: The Fight against War

1   Rolland, *op. cit.*, p. xxvii.

2   Quoted in: E. Vandervelde, *Souvenirs d'un militant socialiste*, Paris, 1939, p. 52.

3   Details of Barbusse's attitude towards the problem of proletarian literature may be found in: J-P. Bernard, 'Le parti Communiste Française et les problèmes littéraires, 1920–1939', *Revue Française de Science Politique*, Vol. xvii, No. 3, June 1967, p. 526.

4   Barbusse's delaying tactics over this issue were not entirely un-

successful. In 1932 the Russian Association of Proletarian Writers
(R.A.P.P.) which had been the principal agent behind the Kharkov
congress was dissolved, and in 1934 Zhdanov introduced a somewhat
watered-down version of these proposals when he announced the new
policy of 'socialist realism'. For details of this, see the chapters by
Edward J. Brown and Ernest J. Simmons in: M. Hayward and
L. Labedz (eds), *Literature and Revolution in the Soviet Union
1917–1962*, London, 1962.

5   Quoted in: R. H. S. Crossman (ed.), *The God that failed. Six studies in
Communism*, London, 1950, p. 71. For further information about
Münzenberg, see: B. Gross, *Willi Münzenberg*, Stuttgart, 1967.

6   For details of Barbusse's conduct of *Monde*, see: Caute, *op. cit.*,
pp. 102–3.

7   H. Barbusse, *Staline*, Paris, 1935, p. 7.

8   Quoted in: Caute, *op. cit.*, p. 125.

9   Rolland, *op. cit.*, p. xxviii.

10   L. Fischer, *Men and Politics*, London, 1941, p. 193.

11   E. Sinkó, *Roman eines Romans, Moskauer Tagebuch*, Cologne, 1962,
p. 185.

12   M. Buber-Neumann, *Von Potsdam nach Moskau. Stationen eines
Irrweges*, Stuttgart, 1957, p. 326.

13   V. Serge, *Memoirs of a Revolutionary*, London, 1963, p. 238.

14   H. Barbusse, *Clarté*, Paris, 1919, p. 282.

15   Quoted in: Vidal, *op. cit.*, p. 210.

16   I. Ehrenburg, *Eve of War, 1933–41*, London, 1963, p. 88.

17   *Staline*, p. 282.

18   In spite of Barbusse's opposition to Fascism, however, it was typical
of the confusion that prevailed in the Communist Party early in 1934,
when the 'class against class' policy of the Sixth Congress of the
Comintern was still in operation, that, at a time when Barbusse was
denouncing the Right for its participation in the Stavisky riots, a
detachment of the A.R.A.C. was present at a demonstration very near
to the Place de la Concorde on the 6 February. Although this demonstration against the decadence of the parliamentary régime was
supposed to be separate from that of the Right, its purpose could easily
be misconstrued. For the complicated story of the French Communist
Party's move from the 'class against class' policy to that of the
Popular Front in the course of 1934, see: N. Racine and L. Bodin,
Le Parti Communiste Français pendant l'entre-deux-guerres, Paris,
1972, pp. 205–8.

19   Barbusse intended to make this film because he had been greatly
struck by the use which Goebbels had made of the cinema for
propaganda purposes and he was determined that the Communists
should make an effective reply. For details: Vidal, *op. cit.*, pp. 357–9.

20   Quoted in: M. Nadeau 'Romain Rolland', *Journal of Contemporary
History*, Vol. 2, 1967, p. 217. It is only fair to add that Rolland did not
join the Communist Party and was never a slavish supporter of the
party line. It was his intercession with Stalin that was largely responsible
for the release of Victor Serge from imprisonment; and, despite his
public pronouncements he had many private reservations about the
nature of the Soviet régime. In 1939 Rolland ignored the Nazi–Soviet

pact and assured the French government of his support for the war
against Nazi Germany.
21   Quoted in: Duclos and Fréville, *op. cit.*, p. 22.

Drieu la Rochelle – Chapter 4: The Decadent

1   Drieu la Rochelle, *Écrits de jeunesse*, Paris, 1941, p. 264.
2   Drieu la Rochelle, *La Comédie de Charleroi*, Paris, 1934, p. 30.
3   *Ibid.*, p. 54.
4   *Ibid.*, pp. 57–8.
5   As the summer blazed throughout Europe in the
         fields of corn and the dark bowels of factories
         A strength was reborn
         The strength of the soldier
         Our dull life was roused by it and set in motion,
         The excitement created by the sunny glint of trumpets
         Took possession of us suddenly
         We felt ourselves to be numbered in thousands and
         thousands and felt adored by our people
         The women with red mouths said: "We
         are your women
         Oh men, go and kill."

     Drieu la Rochelle, *Écrits de jeunesse*, Paris, 1941, p. 10.
6   This cry that left me, this cry that I uttered
         to the world in the pain of being born.
         This cry born in a fold of my innermost flesh.
         I would not eliminate it from the order of accomplished
         things by any denial.
         There will be no need to confess it until the end of my life.
         This cry of revolt
         That day at Verdun, I was the one who cried No
         to pain.
         I was one of those who cry No to pain.

     Ibid., p. 32.
7   M. Martin du Gard, *Les Mémorables*, Vol. i, Paris, 1957, p. 127.
8   Quoted in: H. Tint, *The Decline of French Patriotism*, London, 1964,
     p. 96.
9   M. Barrès, *Pour la haute intelligence française*, Paris, 1925, p. 80.
10 Drieu la Rochelle, *Mesure de la France*, Paris, 1964 edition, pp. 38–9.
11 Maurras once commented on Drieu, 'I saw Drieu la Rochelle only
     once. . .But we got nowhere. I read his book *Mesure de la France* and I
     found in it a taste for paradox more than talent': C. Maurras,
     Lettres de Prison, Paris, 1958, p. 370.
12 *Mesure de la France*, p. 76.
13 *Ibid.*, p. 111.
14 Drieu's admiration for Bismarck and Disraeli is expressed in his *Genève
     ou Moscou*, Paris, 1928, p. 7.
15 *Mesure de la France*, pp. 99–101.
16 *Ibid.*, pp. 113–14.

Drieu la Rochelle – Chapter 5: The Fascist

1 Quoted in: Andreu, *op. cit.*, p. 166.
2 Drieu la Rochelle, *Gilles*, Paris, 1939, p. 417.
3 For the importance that Drieu attached to his visit to the Argentine, see: Drieu la Rochelle, *Récit Secret*, Paris, 1951, p. 60.
4 'Réponse de Drieu la Rochelle à l'enquête de Gilbert Comte', *La Grande Revue*, No. 3, March 1934.
5 Quoted in: F. Grover, *Drieu la Rochelle*, Paris, 1962, p. 42.
6 Drieu la Rochelle, 'Nietzsche contra Marx', *Socialisme Fasciste*, Paris, 1934, p. 66. Drieu's views on the Nietzschean element in Bolshevism may also be studied in 'L'Actualité du 20ᵉ siècle', *Chronique Politique 1934–42*, Paris, 1943, pp. 197–203.
7 *Socialisme Fasciste*, p. 96.
8 *Ibid.*, p. 153.
9 *Ibid.*, p. 229.
10 This résumé of Drieu's apologia for the P.P.F. is based on the articles in his *Avec Doriot*, Paris, 1937 and *Chronique Politique 1934–42*, Paris, 1943.
11   To you Germans – with my voice that has been stilled for so long on military orders – I speak.
      I have never hated you.
      I have fought with an unconcealed desire
      to kill you. My joy has poured forth with your blood.
      But you are strong. I could never hate
      your strength, the mother of all things.
      I have rejoiced in your strength.
      Men all over the world, let us rejoice
      in the strength of the Germans.

      Écrits de jeunesse, p. 43.
12 Drieu la Rochelle, 'Le mouvement politique', *Revue de l'Amérique Latine*, November 1923.
13 Quoted in Grover, *op. cit.*, p. 42. 'Listening to the Germans talking of their dynamism makes one writhe, or, rather, give a bitter laugh. It's like listening to the French talking about their clarity or the English about their fair play. When you are dynamic you do not have time to notice it, even less to talk about it': Drieu la Rochelle, 'Mesure de l'Allemagne', *Nouvelle Revue Française*, March 1934, p. 458.
14 Drieu's views on the importance of the Nordic element in France may be found in his preface to *L'Ode aux voiles du Nord* by J-L. Le Marois, Paris, 1928.
15 Not merely was Drieu's first wife Jewish, it was his intervention that led to her being released by the Gestapo during the occupation: Grover, *op. cit.*, p. 54.
16 Drieu's views on racialism may be studied in the following articles: 'Souvenirs du mouvement ouvrier', *Émancipation Nationale*, 11 February 1938; 'À propos du racisme', *Émancipation Nationale*, 29 July 1938.
17 Drieu la Rochelle, 'La fonds philosophique de notre doctrine', *Émancipation Nationale*, 19 August 1938.
18 Drieu la Rochelle, *Avec Doriot*, Paris, 1937, p. 109.
19 *Ibid.*, p. 8.

20 Drieu la Rochelle, 'Il faut d'abord liquider le communisme' *Émancipation Nationale*, 26 November 1937. The German author of the most scholarly account of Doriot's career maintains that, in raising the possibility that Hitler might be allowed by France to make annexations at the expense of Russia, Drieu was expressing his personal views and not the policy of the P.P.F.: D. Wolf, *Doriot*, Paris, 1969, p. 273.

21 Drieu la Rochelle, 'L'Europe s'engage sur le chemin des derniers jours', *Émancipation Nationale*, 26 November 1937.

22 Drieu la Rochelle, 'À propos d'un certain A.V.', *Nouvelle Revue Française*, January 1938, p. 122.

23 Drieu la Rochelle, 'Lettre à Édouard Daladier', *Émancipation Nationale*, 14 October 1938.

24 For an analysis of the many different Fascist and quasi-Fascist groupings in France in the 1930s, see: J. Plumyène and R. Lasierra, *Les Fascimes français 1923–1963*, Paris, 1963.

25 Wolf, *op. cit.*, p. 311. At this point in his work Wolf repeats his warnings that Drieu's views on Fascism were not necessarily typical of the membership of the P.P.F. He also emphasises that Doriot could not be described as an anti-semite in the 1930s (*Ibid.*, p. 312).

26 Drieu la Rochelle, 'Entre l'hiver et le printemps', *Nouvelle Revue Française*, April 1942.

27 Drieu la Rochelle, 'La prochaine guerre', *Socialisme Fasciste*, pp. 162–172.

28 Quoted in: Grover, *op. cit.*, p. 45.

29 Like Montherlant, Saint-Exupéry, and so many other French writers who were distressed by the senile and arthritic condition of French civilisation in the period between the wars, Drieu was clearly obsessed with images of youth and athleticism. In an article written in 1937 he admitted that Doriot wore spectacles but then went on to praise the leader of the P.P.F. for not being 'a fat intellectual of the last century . . .but an athlete. . .Doriot is our champion against death': 'Le P.P.F., parti du corps vivant', *Émancipation Nationale*, 27 August 1937. Soon afterwards Doriot began to drink heavily: Wolf, *op. cit.*, p. 251.

30 *Ibid.*, p. 46.

31 This is a summary of Drieu's views expressed in his article entitled: 'Ne plus attendre', *La Gerbe*, 10 October 1940.

Drieu la Rochelle – Chapter 6: The Collaborator

1 C. Péguy, *Oeuvres en Prose*, Vol. ii, Paris, 1957, p. 516.

2 This quotation is taken from the official record of the Nuremberg War Trials: *Nazi Conspiracy and Aggression*, Vol. vii, Washington, 1948, p. 733.

3 E. Jünger, *Strahlungen*, Tübingen, 1949, p. 336.

4 Quoted in: Grover, *op. cit.*, p. 96.

5 Drieu la Rochelle, 'Souvenir d'hier', *Le Figaro*, 21 December 1939.

6 J. Grenier, 'Une conversation avec Drieu la Rochelle', *Nouvelle Revue Française*, September 1953, p. 390.

7 Quoted in: Grover, *op. cit.*, p. 105.

8 *Ibid.*, p. 78.

9   *Ibid.*, p. 52.
10 *Le Fait*, 10 October 1940. *Le Fait* was a weekly newspaper (founded by Drieu la Rochelle, Bertrand de Jouvenel and others) which was published between October 1940 and April 1941.
11 Drieu la Rochelle, 'L'Allemagne européenne', *Nouvelle Revue Française*, January 1942.
12 Drieu la Rochelle, *Notes pour comprendre le siècle*, Paris, 1941, p. 161.
13 O. Abetz, *Histoire d'une politique franco-allemande*, Paris, 1953, p. 267.
14 A useful summary of Hitler's lack of interest in a policy of collaboration with France may be found in: E. Jäckel, *Frankreich in Hitler's Europa*, Stuttgart, 1966.
15 According to Abetz (*op. cit.*, p. 217) this congress took place in spite of the Germans. Goebbels was so fearful of the reaction of the other Nazis to any encouragement of the 'European Idea' that he attempted to prevent it from opening.
16 Article in *La Révolution Nationale*, 14 August 1943.
17 Quoted in Andreu, *op. cit.*, p. 199.
18 Article in *La Révolution Nationale*, 20 November 1943.
19 Article in *La Révolution Nationale*, 27 December 1943.
20 Article in *La Révolution Nationale*, 11 December 1943.
21 This summary of Drieu's views on the events likely to take place at the Liberation is based on information contained in: Andreu, *op. cit.*, p. 81.
22 Quoted in: Grover, *op. cit.*, p. 104.
23 Quoted in: P. de Boisdeffre, *Barrès*, Paris, 1962, p. 106.
24 Quoted in: Andreu, *op. cit.*, p. 200.
25 This article, entitled 'Bilan Fasciste', was written for *La Révolution Nationale* in July 1944, but it was not until December 1950 that it was eventually published in the review *84*. It was later published, together with other material written by Drieu in 1944, under the title 'Notes sur l'Allemagne' in *Défense de l'Occident*, February/March 1958.
26 Quoted in: Grover, *op. cit.*, p. 57.
27 Brasillach's attack on Drieu may be found in his book: *Portraits*, Paris, 1935, pp. 227–38.
28 *Récit Secret*, pp. 30–1.
29 F. Mauriac, *Journal*, Vol. IV, Paris, 1950, p. 24.

Bernanos – Chapter 7: 'This century deceives us'

1   This phrase comes from the closing lines of Orwell's study of Charles Dickens, reprinted in: *The Collected Essays, Journalism and Letters of George Orwell*, Vol. I, *An Age Like This, 1920–1940*, London, 1968, p. 460.
2   G. Bernanos, *Les grands cimetières sous la lune*, Paris, 1938, pp. 124–5.
3   *Ibid.*, pp. 72–3.
4   *Ibid.*, pp. 272–3.
5   G. Bernanos, 'Autobiographie', *La Nef*, August 1948, p. 3.
6   Quoted in: A. Béguin, *Bernanos par lui-même*, Paris, 1954, p. 28.
7   G. Bernanos, *Les Enfants Humiliés*, Paris, 1949, p. 195.
8   *Les grands cimetières sous la lune*, p. 239.
9   Quoted in: A. Béguin (ed.), *Georges Bernanos. Essais et témoignages*, Paris, 1949, pp. 18–19.

10 *Ibid.*, p. 253.
11 It was typical of Bernanos that, whilst he was in the Santé, he made friends with some Anarchists who were fellow-prisoners. Together they sang royalist songs and the 'Internationale'. *Les grands cimetières sous la lune*, p. 49.
12 Quoted in: *Bulletin de la société des amis de Georges Bernanos*, Vol. xiv, p. 6.
13 Quoted in: *Georges Bernanos. Essais et témoignages*, p. 271.
14 *Ibid.*, p. 269.
15 H. Massis, *Maurras et notre temps*, Vol. i, Paris, 1961, p. 134.
16 'Autobiographie', *La Nef*, p. 4.
17 G. Bernanos, 'Lettres de Guerre', *Études*, May 1949, p. 172.
18 Quoted in: *Georges Bernanos. Essais et témoignages*, p. 31.
19 Quoted in: *Bernanos par lui-même*, p. 101.
20 *Ibid.*, p. 106.
21 Quoted in: H. Aaraas, *Georges Bernanos*, Vol. i, Oslo, 1959, p. 77.
22 Quoted in: J. de Fabrègues, *Bernanos, tel qu'il était*, Paris, 1963, p. 72.
23 G. Bernanos, *Star of Satan*, translated by Pamela Morris, London, 1940, pp. 335–6. There has been some discussion in recent years over the question of Dostoievsky's influence on Bernanos. It used to be thought that Bernanos did not read any of Dostoievsky's work until after the publication of *Sous le Soleil de Satan*, but this now seems to be an error: M. Milner, *Georges Bernanos*, Paris, 1967, pp. 97–8, Note 3.
24 Quoted in: *Bernanos par lui-même*, p. 70.
25 Daudet's review may be found in: *L'Action Française*, 7 April 1926.
26 Quoted in: G. Bernanos, *Oeuvres Romanesques*, Paris, 1961, p. 1763.
27 In May 1917 Bernanos had married Jeanne Talbert d'Arc, a descendant of one of the brothers of Joan of Arc. They had six children.
28 Back in France his angry landlord sold off his furniture in order to pay off his arrears in rent.
29 *Les grands cimetières sous la lune*, p. ii.
30 G. Bernanos, *Le crépuscule des vieux*, Paris, 1956, p. 51.
31 Quoted in: *Bernanos par lui-même*, p. 173.
32 Quoted in: G. Gaucher, *Georges Bernanos, ou l'invincible espérance*, Paris, 1962, p. 15.
33 Quoted in: *Bernanos par lui-même*, p. 131.
34 *Oeuvres Romanesques*, p. 1550.
35 Quoted in: *Bernanos par lui-même*, p. 112.
36 *Ibid.*

Bernanos – Chapter 8: The Failure of the Right

1 Quoted in: *Bulletin de la Société des amis de Georges Bernanos*, No. xi, p. 9.
2 G. Bernanos, *La France contre les robots*, Paris, 1947, pp. 94–5.
3 G. Bernanos, *Nous autres Français*, Paris, 1939, pp. 268–9.
4 Quoted in: Massis, *op. cit.*, Vol. i, p. 174.
5 Details of Bernanos's views on the issue of the papal condemnation of the Action Française may be found in: *Ibid.*, pp. 184–220; Fabrègues, *op. cit.*, pp. 85–99.
6 Quoted in: Fabrègues, *op. cit.*, p. 92. The papal ban on the Action

Française was lifted in 1939 when Maurras at last agreed to make concessions to Rome. The death of Pius XI and the accession of Pius XII was another factor that facilitated this reconciliation, a reconciliation that was generally taken to indicate a further shift to the Right in the politics of the Vatican.

7   G. Bernanos, *Jeanne, relapse et sainte*, Paris, 1934, pp. 66–8.
8   G. Bernanos, *La grande peur des bien-pensants*, Paris, 1931, p. 7.
9   *Ibid.*, p. 73.
10 *Ibid.*, p. 98.
11 *Ibid.*, pp. 332–3.
12 *Ibid.*, pp. 7–8.
13 *Ibid.*, pp. 457–8.
14 Quoted in: T. Molnar, *Bernanos. His political thought and prophecy*, New York, 1960, p. 68.
15 Quoted in: *Bulletin de la société des amis de Georges Bernanos*, No. 28–9, p. 8.
16 *Ibid.*, pp. 8–9.
17 *Ibid.*, p. 23.
18 *Ibid.*, p. 24.
19 *Candide*, 17 June 1937, quoted in: M. Estève, *Bernanos*, Paris, 1965, pp. 244–5.
20 See, for example, the evidence of friction between the Church and the Nationalists quoted in: G. Hills, *Franco*, London, 1967, pp. 299–305.
21 S. Weil, *Seventy Letters*, translated and arranged by Richard Rees, London, 1965, p. 109.
22 *Les grands cimetières sous la lune*, pp. 116–17.
23 *Ibid.*, p. 341.
24 *Ibid.*, p. 343.
25 *Ibid.*, p. 336.
26 G. Bernanos, *Scandale de la Vérité*, Paris, 1939, pp. 27–8.
27 *Ibid.*, pp. 28–9.
28 *Ibid.*, p. 73.
29 G. Bernanos, *Le chemin de la croix-des-âmes*, Paris, 1948, p. 27.
30 *Ibid.*, 445. On hearing that Georges Mandel, a faithful follower of Clemenceau and a former Minister of the Interior, had been arrested by the authorities and that his life was in danger because he was Jewish, Bernanos warned the Right that 'every drop of Jewish blood spilled in hatred of our former victory is more precious to us than the purple of a Fascist cardinal's cloak': *Ibid.*, p. 316. Mandel was eventually shot by agents of Darnand's Milice in 1944.
31 An Englishwoman who came to visit Bernanos in an attempt to persuade him to moderate his attacks on the Anglo-Americans over their leniency towards Vichy had to make a hasty retreat after provoking him into one of his volcanic rages: D. Gordan, *Freundschaft mit Bernanos*, Cologne, 1959, p. 13.
32 Bernanos repeatedly insisted that the French people knew that they had been dishonoured by Vichy: *Le chemin de la croix-des-âmes*, p. 200, p. 221, p. 307.
33 For Bernanos's disillusionment with the state of France at the end of the war, see: G. Bernanos, *Français, si vous saviez*, Paris, 1961, pp. 285–6 and pp. 291–304.

34 *Ibid.*, pp. 161–2.
35 *Oeuvres Romanesques*, p. xi.
36 G. Bernanos, *Français, si vous saviez*, Paris, 1961, p. 93.
37 A. Travers, 'Bernanos n'était pas un politique', *L'Herne*, No. 2, 1962, p. 64.
38 G. Bernanos, *La France contre les robots*, Paris, 1947, p. 67.
39 Bernanos's attack on the failure of the papacy to denounce the Nationalists during the Spanish civil war may be found in: *Les enfants humiliés*, p. 152. For his attack on Pius XII for remaining silent over Hitler's extermination of the Jews: *Nous autres Français*, pp. 240–4.
40 *Les enfants humiliés*, p. 148.
41 Quoted in: *Georges Bernanos. Essais et témoignages*, p. 351.

Bernanos – Chapter 9: The Communion of Saints

1 Quoted in: N. Nicholson, *H. G. Wells*, London, 1950, p. 95.
2 *Les enfants humiliés*, pp. 199–200.
3 Quoted in: *Oeuvres Romanesques*, p. 1771.
4 Quoted in: *Georges Bernanos. Essais et témoignages*, p. 224.
5 P. Claudel, *Mémoires improvisés*, Paris, 1954, p. 297.
6 Bernanos himself insisted that although *M. Ouine* was dream-like in character, it should not be regarded as the disordered product of his private imagination: 'Nothing is more real or more objective than dreams. But there are many limited individuals who can only accept the realities of Zola...Do they not understand how logical things can become dream-like in novels, logically by a process of hypnosis? The fact is that there is nothing that is so lucid as a dream. And is there anything more deliberate than the frenzy of Art?' Quoted in *Bernanos par lui-même*, p. 167. Albert Béguin has also pointed out that during the Second World War Bernanos, as if to school himself in the virtues of lucidity and clarity, read a great deal of Racine: A. Béguin, 'Bernanos et la raison', *L'esprit des Lettres*, No. 1, 1 January 1955.
7 Quoted in: *Oeuvres Romanesques*, p. 1764.
8 G. Bernanos: *Diary of a Country Priest*, translated by Pamela Morris, London, 1956, p. 148.
9 *Ibid.*, p. 251.
10 Quoted in: *Bernanos par lui-même*, p. 174.
11 *Le chemin de la croix-des-âmes*, p. 100.
12 *Ibid.*, p. 103.
13 *Ibid.*, pp. 203–4.
14 Weil, *op. cit.*, p. 178.
15 *Oeuvres Romanesques*, p. 1613. As Father Hebblethwaite has pointed out in his study of Bernanos, this passage, which is crucial to an understanding of the whole play, has been omitted from the English translation of this work published under the title of *The Carmelites* in 1961: P. Hebblethwaite, *Bernanos, An introduction*, London, 1965, p. 38.
16 *Oeuvres Romanesque*, p. xlvi.
17 *Les enfants humiliés*, p. 71.

BIBLIOGRAPHY

The following list of works by and on these three authors is by no means complete. Reference is made only to those works which have particular relevance to the theme of this study. Details of the most important articles written by these authors may be found in the Notes and References. The place of publication is Paris unless otherwise stated.

WORKS BY HENRI BARBUSSE

Pleureuses (1895)
Les suppliants (1903)
L'Enfer (1908)
Nous autres (1914)
Le Feu (1917)
Clarté (1919)
Paroles d'un combattant (1920)
La lueur dans l'abîme: ce que veut le groupe Clarté (1920)
Le couteau entre les dents (1922)
Les enchaînements (1924)
Les bourreaux (1926)
Force (1926)
Jésus (1927)
Les Judas de Jésus (1927)
Voici ce qu'on a fait de la Géorgie (1929)
Russie (1930)
J'accuse (1932)
Zola (1932)
Connais-tu Thaelmann? (1934)
Staline (1935)
Lettres d'Henri Barbusse à sa femme 1914–1917 (1937)

Works Relating Directly to Henri Barbusse

Brett, V., *Henri Barbusse. Sa marche vers la Clarté, Son mouvement Clarté*, Prague, 1963.
Caute, D., *Communism and the French intellectuals*, London, 1964.
Cru, J.-N., *Témoins*, 1929.
Duclos, J., and Fréville, J., *Henri Barbusse*, 1946.
Éditions Sociales Internationales, *Henri Barbusse, écrivain et révolutionnaire*, 1935.
Special number on Barbusse and Whitman, *Europe*, November–December 1955.

Fréville, J., 'Le réaliste du XXᵉ siècle', *Les Lettres Françaises* No. 328, 1958.

Kriegel, A., 'Naissance du mouvement Clarté', *Le Mouvement Social*, January–March 1963.

Küchler, W., *Romain Rolland, Henri Barbusse, Fritz von Uhruh, Vier Vorträge*, Frankfurt am Main, 1949.

Lacouture, J., 'Barbusse, cent ans après', *Le Monde*, 27–8 May 1973.

Paraf, P., 'Henri Barbusse – le poète', *Les Lettres Françaises*, No. 328, 1950.

'Les carnets de guerre d'Henri Barbusse', *Les Lettres Françaises*, Nos. 636 and 637, 1956.

'Avant le Feu...l'Aurore – Henri Barbusse, l'enfant, l'adolescent, le jeune homme, d'après des documents inédits', *Les Lettres Françaises*, No. 685, 1957.

'Barbusse et ses amis', *Les Lettres Françaises*, No. 636, 1956.

Racine, N., 'Les écrivains Communistes en France 1920–36'; unpublished thesis, Paris, Fondation Nationale des Science Politiques, 1963.

'The Clarté movement in France 1919–21', *Journal of Contemporary History* Vol. 2, No. 2, 1967.

'Une revue d'intellectuels communistes dans les années vingt: Clarté (1921–1928)', *Revue Française de Science Politique* Vol. xvii, No. 3, June 1967.

Tison-Braun, M., *La Crise de l'Humanisme*, Vol. ii, 1967.

Vidal, A., *Henri Barbusse. Soldat de la Paix*, 1953.

WORKS BY DRIEU LA ROCHELLE

Interrogation (1917)
Fond de cantine (1920)
État civil (1921)
Mesure de la France (1922)
Plainte contre inconnu (1924)
L'homme couvert de femmes (1925)
La suite dans les idées (1927)
Le jeune Européen (1927)
Blèche (1928)
Genève ou Moscou (1928)
Une femme à sa fenêtre (1930)
L'Europe contre les patries (1931)
Le feu follet (1931)
Drôle de voyage (1933)
Journal d'un homme trompé (1934)
La comédie de Charleroi (1934)
Socialisme Fasciste (1934)
Béloukia (1936)
Doriot ou la vie d'un ouvrier français (1936)
Rêveuse bourgeoisie (1937)
Avec Doriot (1937)
Gilles (1939)
Écrits de jeunesse (1941)
Notes pour comprendre le siècle (1941)

Chronique politique 1934–1942 (1943)
L'homme à cheval (1943)
Charlotte Corday and *Le Chef* (2 plays) (1944)
Le français d'Europe (1944)
Récit Secret (1961)
Sur les écrivains (1964)
Mémoires de Dirk Raspe (1966)

Works Relating Directly to Drieu la Rochelle

Andreu, P., *Drieu, témoin et visionnaire*, 1952.
Bonneville, G., *Prophètes et témoins de l'Europe*, Leyden, 1961.
Brasillach, R., *Les quatres jeudis*, 1951.
Special number of *Défense de l'Occident*, February–March 1958.
Frank, B., *La panoplie littéraire*, 1958.
Grenier, J., 'Une conversation avec Drieu la Rochelle', *Nouvelle Revue Française*, September 1953.
Grover, F., *Drieu la Rochelle and the fiction of testimony*, Berkeley, 1958. *Drieu la Rochelle*, Paris, 1962.
Special number of *La Parisienne*, October 1955.
Mabire, J., *Drieu parmi nous*, 1963.
Martin du Gard, M., *Les Mémorables*, Vol. i, 1957, Vol. ii, 1960.
Sartre, J-P., *Situations*, Vol. iii, 1949.
Sérant, P., *Le romantisme fasciste*, 1959.
Simon, P-H., *Procès du héros*, 1950.
Tucker, William R., 'Fascism and Individualism: The political thought of Pierre Drieu la Rochelle', *Journal of Politics*, Vol. 27, 1965.
Vandromme, P., *Drieu la Rochelle*, 1958.

WORKS BY GEORGES BERNANOS

Sous le soleil de Satan (1926)
L'Imposture (1927)
Saint Dominique (1927)
La Joie (1928)
La grande peur des bien-pensants (1931)
Un crime (1935)
Journal d'un curé de campagne (1936)
Nouvelle histoire de Mouchette (1937)
Les grands cimetières sous la lune (1938)
Nous autres Français (1938)
Scandale de la verité (1939)
Lettre aux Anglais (1942)
Monsieur Ouine (Rio de Janeiro 1943, Paris 1946)
Écrits de Combat (Beirut, 1943)
Le chemin de la croix-des-âmes (Rio de Janeiro 1943–45, Paris 1948)
La France contre les robots (Rio de Janeiro 1944, Paris 1947)
Les enfants humiliés (1949)
Dialogues des Carmélites (1949)
Un mauvais rêve (1950)
La liberté pour quoi faire? (1953)

Dialogue d'ombres (1955)
Oeuvres Romanesques (1961)
Français si vous saviez (1961)
Le lendemain c'est vous! (1969)
Correspondance inédite Vol. ɪ *Combat pour la vérité* (1971)
Correspondance inédite Vol. ɪɪ *Combat pour la liberté* (1971)
A number of hitherto unpublished texts by Bernanos may be found in the
Bulletin de la Société des amis de Georges Bernanos. The publication of this
periodical began in 1949 and its current sequel is the *Courrier Georges
Bernanos.*

Works Relating Directly to Georges Bernanos

Aaraas, H., *Georges Bernanos*, Vol. ɪ, Oslo, 1952.
Balthasar, H. Urs von., *Le chrétien Bernanos*, 1956.
Béguin, A., *Bernanos par lui-même*, 1954.
—— ed. *Georges Bernanos. Éssais et témoignages*, 1949.
Chaigne, L., *Georges Bernanos*, 1954.
Chabot, J., 'Georges Bernanos au tribunal de l'inquisition maurrassienne'
     Études, No. 7, 1969.
Estève, M., *Bernanos*, 1965.
Études Bernanosiennes, published at intervals by *La Revue des Lettres
     Modernes*, 1960 to date.
Fabrègues, J. de., *Bernanos tel qu'il était*, 1963.
Gaucher, G., *Georges Bernanos ou l'invincible espérance*, 1962.
Germain, A., *Les croisés modernes. De Bloy à Bernanos*, 1959.
Gordan, P., *Freundschaft mit Bernanos*, Cologne, 1959.
Halda, B., *Bernanos. Le scandale de croire*, 1965.
Hebblethwaite, P., *Bernanos. An introduction*, London, 1965.
Special number of *L'Herne*, 1961.
Hughes, H. Stuart, *The Obstructed Path. French Social Thought in the
     years of desperation 1930–1960*, New York, 1966.
Jamet, H., *Un autre Bernanos*, Lyons, 1959.
Jurt, J., *Les attitudes politiques de Georges Bernanos jusqu'en 1931*,
     Fribourg, 1968.
Special number of *Livres de France*, January 1962.
Massis, H., *Maurras et notre temps*, 1961.
Milner, M., *Georges Bernanos*, 1967.
Molnar, T., *Bernanos. His political thought and prophecy*, New York, 1960.
Mounier, E., *L'espoir des désespérés*, 1953.
Picon, G., *Georges Bernanos*, 1948.
Simon, P-H., *Témoins de l'homme*, 1951.
Speaight, R., *Georges Bernanos*, London, 1973.

INDEX

DATE DUE
